DATE DUE

D0397559

Also by Raymond Sokolov

Raymond Sokolov

WHY WE EAT WHAT WE EAT

How the Encounter Between the New World and the Old Changed the Way Everyone on the Planet Eats

 SUMMIT BOOKS

New York   London   Toronto   Sydney   Tokyo   Singapore

SUMMIT BOOKS

Simon & Schuster Building
Rockefeller Center
1230 Avenue of the Americas
New York, New York 10020

Designed by Laurie Jewell
Manufactured in the United States of America

1   3   5   7   9   10   8   6   4   2

Library of Congress Cataloging in Publication Data

Sokolov, Raymond A.
Why we eat what we eat : how the encounter between the New World and the
Old changed the way everyone on the planet eats / Raymond Sokolov.
p.   cm.
1. Gastronomy—History.   2. Food habits—History.   3. Cookery—
History.   I.Title.
TX631.S65   1991   91-16586
641'.01'3—dc20   CIP

ISBN 0-671-66796-3

ACKNOWLEDGMENTS

CAROL BRESLIN, my editor at *Natural History* magazine since 1974, guided me in the preparation of the columns that formed the kernel of this book. Florence Edelstein scrutinized the diction. Carole Lalli brought me to Simon & Schuster and gave me much wise advice over no-cal beer, and when she left to become editor-in-chief of *Food & Wine* magazine, she saw to it that I fetched up happily with Robert Asahina. When Bob moved down the hall at S & S to Summit, he clutched my manuscript under his arm and continued to improve it, with much strenuous help from Laura Yorke and assistance from Sarah Bayliss. Although Summit was, in a technical sense, a second home for this project, it was actually a continuation, for me, of old and fond connections, with Wendy Nicholson and James Silberman, friends for more years than I can count anymore.

My agent, Kathy Robbins, was tireless in her support from the start. Colleagues at the *Wall Street Journal* offered expertise, hospitality and enthusiasm. My son, Joseph, helped with research early on. Marjorie Reas and Carmelita Parker got me started on Spanish long ago in Detroit, where my parents set everything in motion with a bowl of chili.

Far and away the most useful aid I received was from my wife, Johanna Hecht. Through some suspiciously propitious coincidences of fate, we found ourselves working on colonial Spanish America at the same time. Johanna was in charge of the so-called viceregal section of the mammoth Mexico show that opened at the Metropolitan Museum in October 1990. This meant that she and I both were preoccupied with the encounter of Old and New Worlds after 1492. You could say it was a conjugal conjunction. Without those domestic conversations, I doubt I would have dug into the food heritage of the Spanish Empire as deeply as I did or known enough to see the way we eat now as a direct legacy of galleons and the lateen-rigged caravels connecting the rest of the world with Seville.

For Alan Ternes,
who told me to rediscover Columbus

CONTENTS

INTRODUCTION

M Y W O R K on this book began in 1944 when my father was sent to El Paso, Texas, to stamp out VD among servicemen and their "contacts" with a new wonder drug called penicillin. A slightly bewildered family from Detroit, we spent our first few days in town in a hotel whose nightclub featured an orchestra of serape-swathed Mexican musicians playing "Guantanamera" and "Cielito Lindo." Soon I had my own serape to wear at these occasions, and a small guitar so that I could sit in with the musicians. I was three years old and seemingly born to strum. Actually, most of what I know about my career as an honorary Mexican and our life in wartime Texas I owe to family legend, repeated when I was old enough to understand what happened to me back then. As a toddler I am sure I did not anticipate the most amazing and long-lasting result of the Jewish family Sokolov's sojourn in El Paso. Our cuisine changed.

My mother, the assimilated American-born daughter of immigrants, began to cook Tex-Mex. To her repertory of East European and Midwestern dishes she added a very hot *chili con carne.* My father, who had spent part of his early youth on a Yiddish-speaking Zionist commune near Gunnison, Utah, acquired a taste for jalapeño peppers. Back home in Michigan after the war we kept on eating chili, and there was always a bottle of hot peppers in the refrigerator. As I grew up I learned to like the chili and eventually began to eat those peppers too.

When we took these foods into our diet, it was as if we had incorporated some Spanish into our speech. I make this comparison to casual bilingualism because it is such a familiar phenomenon, something that happens to those on both sides of the United States–Mexican border. These individual speech patterns are what linguists call idiolects. Everybody speaks an idiolect—his own personal language that functions within the larger speech community. A full-blown dialect is a set of idiolects so similar they form a recognizable minilanguage: the Spanglish of United States Chicanos, the nasal twang of the Great Lakes, Valley Girl talk in California.

The same thing happens in the kitchen. Every family has its own set of recipes and eating habits, its idiocuisine formed by foods being passed down from the previous generation and through contacts with new foods, flavors, and tastes. And if the similar experiences of many neighboring families evolve into a new "dialect" of eating and cooking—because these families have all changed their idiocuisines after galvanizing contact with new conditions, ingredients, and food ideas—then the world has a new regional cuisine.

In the United States this happened over and over again as European colonists and their descendants moved westward and met indigenous peoples, learned to eat indigenous plants and animals, and mixed their Old World heritage with what they found in the New World. Indian pudding is the result of mixing New World corn and Old World sugar (in the New World form of molasses). The Creole food of New Orleans mixes French and Italian notions with local ingredients (sassafras root or filé) and the African vegetable okra.

These new foods and new cuisines sprang up almost overnight in the freedom of the frontier—before the comforts of the home culture had time to arrive and eliminate the need for improvisation. And when those comforts did arrive, innovation ceased and most of the new recipes became mere regional oddities in an increasingly homogeneous North America. This was what I discovered in doing research for *Fading Feast: A Compendium of Disappearing Regional American Foods* (1981).

In almost every part of the country there had been a brief moment of precarious originality, a time when that place had been a frontier, where settlers made do in the wilderness, absorbed and mastered new foods and ideas, and remade their idiocuisines. And in each of those minifrontiers, in the log cabin Indiana that learned to exploit the wild persimmon in dozens of dishes or in the roadless days of early cheesemaking on the Oregon coast, the diversity of human gastronomy increased. Later, that diversity seemed threatened. Just as modern life threatens to reduce the diversity of animal and plant species, so too the triumph of modern American supermarket-based agribusiness seemed to threaten the diversity of American "dialectal" cuisine. Regionalisms were surviving only as relics or stunts for special occasions, like my mother's chili and the jalapeños in our icebox.

That was how it seemed to me before 1981. Then came the

commercial triumph of nouvelle cuisine. Suddenly every trendy restaurant in the country was flaunting its regional American dishes and ingredients. People I had interviewed in the ultimate boondocks of the country in order to record the death of the regionalism they still were preserving turned up in food-page articles as purveyors of luxury specialties to Manhattan and Los Angeles restaurants.

Menus at these fashionable eateries flaunt the geographic origins of their dishes' ingredients. Reading them is a bit like flipping through an atlas: Michigan morels in *vol-au-vent,* California goat cheese soufflé, New Mexico blue corn tortillas. Some people have started calling this kind of fare "roadmap cuisine."

Of course this vogue for regional ingredients and recipes is not a straightforward revival of regionalisms. It only dabbles in these vestiges of early American rural life and merges them into other, more cosmopolitan culinary systems—French, Italian, and so on. Just as postmodern architects have recently taken to plucking decorative motifs from the history of design and using these cornices, pediments, and columns as ornaments in an eclectic reordering of new and old, and of foreign and vernacular styles, so too nouvelle cuisine chefs here and everywhere from Lyons to Manila have been mixing and matching ingredients and methods from hither and yon.

The chefs who are stirring this global melting pot are deliberately creating new things, hatching idiocuisines in a notional frontier made possible by jet planes and advanced techniques for food preservation. These chefs can also count on a sophisticated clientele ready to experiment with a cuisine that knows no boundaries, a global cuisine that rests nervously on the earthiest, deepest local traditions.

This contrast between novelty and tradition is at the heart of nouvelle cuisine. After all, there cannot be novelty unless there is tradition for it to play off with wit and irony (a vegetable terrine is a play on words, a little joke, as well as something new to eat). But the greatest irony in all of this is that culinary tradition in almost all countries and cultures is itself the result of radical change, of wholesale additions of exotic ingredients and importations of ideas from halfway around the planet.

Make no mistake about it: The great preponderance of the evidence argues against permanence in anybody's food heritage. We have all grown up believing in the principle of culinary authenticity and tradition as an axiom of human civilization, but the norm around the world has been change, innovation. Mexican cuisine bears only a faint resemblance to the verminous, milkless, almost meatless food of the

Aztecs. China has absorbed foreign foods for most of its long recorded history, starting with rice eons ago. To the chefs who pioneered the nouvelle cuisine in France, the *ancienne* cuisine they were rebelling against looked timeless, primordial, old as the hills. But the cookbook record proves that the haute cuisine codified early in this century by Escoffier barely goes back to Napoleon's time. Before that, French food is not recognizable as French to modern eyes. Europe's menu before 1700 was completely different from its menu after 1800, when national cuisines arose along with modern nations and national cultures.

This process of constant evolution in the world's kitchens went into high gear five hundred years ago when Columbus landed in the West Indies. Even from that first voyage he brought back new foods to Spain. This is not surprising perhaps since one of his principal motives in seeking a new westward route to Asia was to seize an advantage in the spice trade, but what is truly surprising about the transoceanic interchange of food and food ideas after 1492 is how fast it happened. Within fifty years the Spanish had established full-scale European agriculture in the West Indies, Mexico, Peru, and the Caribbean coast of South America (the so-called Spanish Main, which is now divided between Colombia and Venezuela). The Spanish had also opened up a regular trade with China from their base in the Philippines. Food and food ideas flowed freely between Seville and Asia on the same ships that carried goods from China and the Americas to Europe, and on the return trip brought European necessities for the colonists. The so-called Manila galleons took five months to make the passage across the Pacific to Acapulco. Their cargoes were then transported overland to Veracruz on Mexico's Gulf coast, reloaded on shipboard, and sent on to the mother country.

Along with the gold and silver an unofficial cargo of tomatoes, potatoes, and green beans also made the voyage to Europe, while pigs, cattle, radishes, and pomegranates sailed westward. Before the century was out, African foods and dishes had also crossed the Atlantic with slaves brought in to work the new plantations. And the Portuguese had colonized Brazil. By 1600, Europe and the Americas (and to a lesser but not inconsequential extent Africa and Asia) had exchanged the fundamental ingredients and ideas of their cuisines.

The exchange of foodstuffs began as a deliberate policy of the Spanish crown. Old World crops and livestock were introduced to Mexico and Peru to support a civilized (that is, Spanish) way of life for the colonists, and New World exotica were sent to Spain as novelties and for agricultural exploitation. But once tomatoes had taken root in Italy, once cattle provided beef and gave milk in Mexico, then local cooks put these wonderful new foods to new uses. And the world changed.

In order to understand how overwhelming all this was, it is crucial to have a clear picture of the immensely different gastronomic status quo before 1492. From one end of Europe to the other people ate much the same food. This medieval menu bore almost no resemblance to the national cuisines that evolved in the various nation states of the continent in the eighteenth century. The French, Italian, and Spanish food "traditions" we now think of as primeval all sprang up relatively recently and would be unrecognizable without the American foods sent across the water, mostly in Spanish boats.

Today the world feeds itself on a post-Columbian cuisine. Italians eat post-Columbian pizza; Irish have post-Columbian shepherd's pie; the French wax chauvinistic about post-Columbian *haricots verts* (originally American green beans, which the British call French beans, much as they call that other American import, syphilis, the French disease). Meanwhile, West Africa survives in no small part on American manioc naturalized long ago. Sichuan food would not be Sichuanese without the hot chilies that arrived before 1700 from South America.

These once-revolutionary changes are now part of the orthodoxy of kitchens from Nome to Pietermaritzburg. Dishes that were novelties as recently as the nineteenth century—most tomato dishes in most northern countries, for example—are now part of what passes for an authentic tradition stretching back to Noah. Food purists fight to preserve each quarter teaspoon of this heritage while the second great wave of global culinary revolution—the nouvelle cuisine—washes over them.

The nouvelle cuisine, as I will show, plays games, clever games, with everybody's sense of tradition. The guardians of authenticity rail against the artful innovations of the nouvelle cuisine chefs, even as these adventurers pay tribute to the cuisines they inherited by using them as the theme in an elaborate conceit of learned variations incorporating new ingredients and ideas from other "traditions." A Filipino cook with French experience uses a Japanese system of food decoration learned in Paris to decorate a traditional Filipino recipe in Manila. In California a restaurateur steeped in the traditions of the American Southwest extends the logic of mayonnaise by flavoring it with smoked chipotle chilies. Most food writers dismiss this kind of cross-cultural hybridization as decadent, but they miss the point, just as the whole world missed the point the first time around during the original Columbian food revolution.

Historians did not notice this major upheaval in world civilization. There are no books about it written by those who lived through it, but another kind of evidence for it survives in abundance on tables all over the world. The ostensibly traditional foods of billions of living people are the mute documents of a process set in motion by Columbus.

When I first began thinking about the effect of 1492 on world eating patterns, I did not suspect how profound the changes started by Columbus were, nor did I anticipate how crucial to all that followed were those first one hundred years of colonization. The more I looked into the matter, the more convinced I became that the Spanish empire was the crucial instrument of change and that it did its work with amazing rapidity.

All over the world the Spanish empire (and to a much lesser extent the Portuguese) established culinary "frontiers" where cultural collisions gave rise to complex and original cuisines. The most important centers of gastronomic change outside Europe were Mexico, Peru, Caribbean Colombia, the Philippines, and especially Puerto Rico, that hub of imperial traffic. These places and many others like them were laboratories of cross-cultural culinary innovation without rival in history until the jet plane and refrigeration ushered in the era of postmodern superheated food exchange we call nouvelle cuisine.

To write the history of this post-Columbian revolution in gastronomy it is necessary to read the cuisines of the world as if they were a palimpsest with one text written on top of another. Shining through the "traditional" text of today is the earlier culinary tradition that absorbed the new items that came in after 1492.

In this book I have tried to read this palimpsest and deduce from it how we came to eat the way we do. I trace the odysseys of influential ingredients (livestock and dairy to Mexico; corn to Lombardy and Romania; olives to Peru; tomatoes to southern Europe) as they were adopted in new places in the sixteenth and seventeenth centuries. Next I show how the process has continued in this country whose regional foods (Indian pudding, Utah scones, corn fritters) came about when European and African cuisines already changed by American importations on their home grounds were introduced to this hemisphere in the seventeenth century and were Americanized all over again. Finally, all these layers of accreted tradition are now being creatively reshuffled with still newer and more exotic arrivals as part of that global impulse, nouvelle cuisine, which is really just the latest epicycle of Columbus's influence making itself felt on the eve of his quincentennial.

As I argue in the final section, the modern world has known two periods of rapid change in eating habits. The first came in the sixteenth century when the Spanish empire brought two hemispheres together at, so to speak, the same table. The second is occurring now in our global village. Both of these revolutions have followed on revolutions in transportation that merged far-flung cultures and carried new foods to new consumers.

In the first instance, beginning around 1500, the result was the national cuisines of the major gastronomic countries of Europe, the Americas, Asia, and Africa. In the second, our current period of radical food change, I suspect that the results will be every bit as profound, spreading exotic ways of eating from place to place—tofu to my corner grocery, chocolate to China—with results impossible to foresee.

Two ideas seem beyond doubt: Cuisines evolve almost instantly when two cultures and their ingredients meet in the kitchen, and old cuisines never die, they add new dishes and ingredients to old recipes and slough off the losers, the evolutionary dead ends (remember creamed chipped beef on toast). The net quantity of culinary diversity probably remains the same, and of course we now take cooking seriously enough to write down recipes for the dishes that are in danger of disappearing.

From a biological point of view, the history of human gastronomy since 1492 exhibits a rich proliferation of new genera branching from common ancestors. Their evolution has proceeded in two spurts (the two periods of rapid change: after Columbus and today), bringing with them some extinction of species (individual dishes), but even these, in great part, can be resuscitated because their raw materials still survive and their genetic information has been preserved in recipes from the past. If culinary evolution follows the punctuational rhythm espoused for all living organisms by my "Natural History" colleague Stephen Jay Gould and other biologists, it is a gentler process than biological evolution, for it generates diversity of species every day and feeds billions of *H. sapiens* with ever greater variety.

From a social perspective the history of eating over the last five hundred years can be described as an international process in which the products and customs of all the different places and cultures in the world have become increasingly available to all people at all times. In principle the culinary life we owe Columbus is a progressive dinner in which the whole human race takes part but no one need leave home to sample all the courses.

In my own case I did leave home quite often. As a journalist my reflex was to be on the spot where my "story" was happening. For a story as broad as gastronomy since 1492, I had to be selective about picking datelines, but once it became clear that the Spanish empire of the sixteenth century was the mechanism that caused most of the change I was reporting, I decided to visit the great colonial centers of that time (including the great Portuguese/African settlement in the New World, northeast Brazil). I had already traveled widely in Europe and North America as a gastronomic journalist; the Hispanic diaspora was new ground that I needed to cover.

But why? I often asked myself that, especially when buying yet another mysterious food at a third-world market or risking ridicule once again in a ratty workingman's bar by asking my neighbor what that was he was eating. Imagine someone with a foreign accent asking the guy on the next stool in an Irish tavern in Hell's Kitchen to identify that sausage in the bun with yellow sauce on it, and you will get the picture.

France and Spain and England all produced cookbooks by the late middle ages that show how people (mostly aristocrats) ate in those days, and much can be deduced by comparing those recipes with recipes in subsequent books. Indeed, much of what we think of as food history is the result of such deductions. What we do not have in any significant amount for premodern European cuisines is the evidence for a social history of eating. From literature of those days we can once again deduce what Shakespeare or Pope's dinners were like. Much can be learned in this way, and has been, but food historians of Europe would be in a better position to reconstruct the alimentary life of the continent before Napoleon if someone had set out at any time in any European country to report directly on food as a dynamic fact of life. Yet premodern Europe did not have food journalists, and the science of anthropology was not yet born. Nor have we received informal pieces of food ethnography or food reporting that might, for example, help us situate in a more than fragmentary way the rise of regional cuisines or the development of popular cooking styles.

It is true that most of the hard information about food in Mexico and Puerto Rico and certainly Cartagena, Colombia, was already available in reliable books before I ever started thinking about going to those places. I read those books, all of them that seemed to matter and many more, but I still thought it would help to witness things firsthand.

As a gastroethnographic reporter, so to say, I thought I should see what people were actually eating in the places where, four hundred years ago and more, the culinary collisions that comprised my beat first happened. If I were on the spot in Lima and Atlixco, I reasoned, I might get lucky and discover something. At the very least I could taste the foods, haunt markets, and observe how these hybrid New World dishes fitted into daily life.

Sometimes I did get lucky, mostly in Puerto Rico where I went almost by accident and suddenly found myself in the middle of the most complex tangle of culinary influence and geography in the world. And in Cartagena, having gone from *carimañolas* at breakfast in the elegant Hilton to *enyucado* at lunch in a no-name dive in the colonial center of town, I got a new perspective on the homely manioc I never would have attained just by reading two more recipes for this superficially unprepossessing root vegetable.

I couldn't taste everything everywhere, so I made some guesses about what to try and where to go. The result is a selection, but it isn't just a *menu à dégustation*. The idea was to understand a sixteenth-century encounter between New World and Old by capturing the flavor of its profound and lingering effects on the way we, all of us, eat now.

PART I

COLUMBUS
THE UNWITTING

Duelos, espantos, guerras, fiebre constante
en nuestra senda ha puesto la suerte triste:
¡Cristoforo Colombo, pobre Almirante, ruega
a Dios por el mundo que descubriste!*

—RUBÉN DARÍO

C O L U M B U S may be history's foremost example of a man who did great things without knowing what they were, but posterity has honored even his most spectacular blunders. We don't hesitate to memorialize Columbus's confusion about what he had discovered when we continue to speak of the West Indies. We defy logic and adopt his Eurocentric arrogance when we celebrate this "discovery" of a place previously inhabited for centuries. Even the modernist Nicaraguan poet Rubén Darío fell into this error after lamenting the violence and "constant fever" that Columbus brought to the Americas.

It is hard to turn Columbus into an unambiguous villain. Yes, he unleashed European diseases that wiped out millions of indigenous peoples with no immunity to them, and he blazed a trail for invading armies that butchered myriads of Mexicans and Incas, while uprooting their cultures and subjugating their pitiful survivors. But that same ghastly imperialism knitted the world together and spawned great new civilizations.

It may be that Columbus was just a lucky Johnny-on-the-spot

---

*Sad luck has put duels, terror, wars, constant fever in our path. Cristoforo Colombo, poor Admiral, pray to God for the world you discovered!

when Ferdinand and Isabella decided to get ambitious in their rivalry for Asian trade with Portugal. No doubt, the next determined west-ward explorer who made his pitch and got his funding would have succeeded as well as Columbus. But it doesn't matter. Columbus did it.

The celebration of his achievement, as those of us preparing to survive the hoopla of the quincentenary know all too well, has never stopped, and so the temptation to take shots at Columbus is a natural impulse. I am, for example, only too willing to castigate Columbus as the tool of bigots. He set sail on a literal wave of anti-Semitism. The tide that took his fleetlet down the Río Saltes to destiny on August 2, 1492, was the very same one that carried the last ship of Jews expelled from Spain. August 2 was the deadline set by Ferdinand and Isabella for cleansing the country of its once-chosen people. 1492 was also the year those other Semites, the Moors, were finally driven from their last Spanish stronghold at Granada, after many centuries of occupation and incalculable contributions to the culture of Spain and the rest of Europe. It could be said that the expulsion of the Moors and the Jews ended Christendom's medieval crusade to establish itself over threatening infidels and that Columbus's first voyage, catching the same wind on the Saltes as the Jews' ship of defeat and exile, was the perfect symbol of the beginning of modern Christian Europe's crusade to spread its imperium over unconverted peoples everywhere under the sun.

But I come to praise Columbus, not to harry his memory. I come to laud the most unassailably admirable of his achievements—the diversification and betterment of the human diet.

Columbus had no idea, of course, of the almost infinite ramifica-tions of his voyages on the way future people would eat. He made many foolish mistakes in his attempts to identify and describe the edible plants and animals he saw in the Americas, but his innocence adds to the charm of the log* and the exhilaration it gives to the reader with five hundred years of hindsight. There is pleasure, too, in those numerous places in the log of the first voyage where Columbus freely admits to his mystification and amazement at all the new and unknown things he was finding.

In the first week after the first landfall, he tarried at a harbor in the Bahamas waiting for crewmen to fetch water from a nearby village.

---

*The Log of Christopher Columbus translated by Robert H. Fuson (Camden, Maine: International Marine Publishing Co., 1987). The Great Explorers, the European Discovery of America by Samuel Eliot Morison (New York: Oxford University Press, 1978).

"During this time," he wrote, "I walked among the trees, which are the most beautiful I have ever seen. I saw as much greenery, in such density, as I would have seen in Andalusia in May. And all of the trees are as different from ours as day is from night, and so are the fruits, the herbage, the rocks, and everything."

He has put ashore in a new world and he knows it, even if he persists in hunting for Cathay and Japan around the next cove. And by October 19, on another Bahamian outcropping, he muses: "I simply do not know where to go next. I never tire of looking at such luxurious vegetation, which is so different from ours. I believe that there are many plants and trees here that could be worth a lot in Spain for use as dyes, spices, and medicines, but to my great sorrow I do not recognize them."

That Sunday he remarks again on the trees and their fruits, chastises himself for his ignorance of them, and resolves to bring back a "sample of everything I can."

That same day he sights what must have been an iguana, "a serpent" about six feet long, which "we killed with lances" and presumably ate, since he attests that "the meat is white and tastes like chicken."

Later in the month he finds a lot of purslane and amaranth on Cuba, eats "wonderful-tasting fruit . . . some large tasteless snails," probably conchs.

By early November he has begun to pay attention to native agriculture. He tries sweet potatoes, which he compares to carrots and says they taste like chestnuts. He calls them *niames,* from the word for yams, *inhames,* brought by the Portuguese to Europe from West Africa. He encounters unfamiliar beans and, most fatefully for posterity, maize, which he calls *panizo,* a name used previously for millet.

By November 15 he has tasted manioc in the form of cassava bread. ("Some of these islands are covered with roots from which the Indians make their bread.") A month later, on Hispaniola, he tastes what must have been the same bread, which is still typical of the region today. But this time he thinks the root the bread was made from was *niama,* the yam. Columbus, like many of us today, had trouble keeping the various roots, rhizomes, and tubers of the tropics separate in his mind. He saw sweet potatoes and manioc again and again, but he called them *niamas* and *ajes* indiscriminately. Still, he observed manioc cultivation quite accurately:

These fields are planted mostly with *ajes.* The Indians sow little shoots from which small roots grow that look like carrots. They serve this as bread by grating and kneading it, then baking it in the fire. They plant a small shoot from the same root again in another place, and once more it produces four or five of these roots. They are very palatable and taste exactly like chestnuts. The ones grown here are the largest and best I have seen anywhere. I have also seen them in Guinea, but those that grow there are as thick as your leg.

During a later visit he took the time to set down the classic procedure for turning manioc into bread: "They shred those turnips on certain stones that look like cheese graters . . . then they put on the fire a very large stone on top of which they place that grated root, and they shape it in the form of a cake and use it as bread and it keeps for fifteen to twenty days, which bread several times was very handy for us."

The day after Christmas 1492, he was offered a sumptuous meal by the "king" of one region of Hispaniola. The menu will not surprise anyone who has spent time in the islands: two or three kinds of root vegetables (*ajes*) with shrimp and cassava bread (*cazabe* is Columbus's spelling of the Taino word).

Finally, on his last day before sailing home, Columbus "discovers" the chili pepper, referring to it as *ají*, the indigenous name still used in South America. "There is also much *ají*, which is their pepper and is worth more than our pepper; no one eats without it because it is very healthy. Fifty caravels can be loaded each year with it on this Isla Española."

Greedy Columbus, not yet having found the lucrative black pepper he was supposed to bring back from the Indies, hopes to compensate with chilies, so he calls them peppers and starts a worldwide nomenclatural confusion that complicates culinary communication in dozens of languages even today. Of course, chilies did not sweep Europe (except in Hungary); instead, they conquered Asia and Africa and continued to flourish in the warm parts of the Americas.

As usual Columbus had hit on a good thing without quite knowing what it was or why it would be beneficial. In three months of island hopping he had "discovered" four of the five most economically important New World plants: maize, sweet potatoes, manioc, and chili peppers. If potatoes had been growing in the Caribbean, he would doubtless have noticed them too. As a gastronomic explorer, Columbus did extremely well. He was also prophetically alert to the potential exchange of foods between Old World and New that lay just ahead.

After his banquet with the Hispaniolan king on December 16, he wrote expansively:

All the people here are strong and courageous and not feeble like the others I have found before. They converse very easily and have no religion. The trees are so luxuriant that the leaves are not green but very dark in color. It is a wonderful thing to see these valleys and rivers and good water and the lands suitable for bread foods and herds of animals of which they have none, and suitable for orchards and anything on earth a man might wish.

Accounts of subsequent voyages provided an even fuller sense of the brave new world of the American tropics through fifteenth-century Spanish eyes. As you read this description, try to guess the modern vernacular names of the two fruits: "There are trees . . . that give a fruit like the apricot, which is full of small seeds like the seeds of a fig, red as scarlet which the inhabitants eat, but to us it is none too good. . . . There are also some like the artichoke plant but four times as tall, which give a fruit in the shape of a pine cone, twice as big, which fruit is excellent, and it can be cut with a knife like a turnip and it seems to be very wholesome." The first is probably a guava or a papaya; the second a pineapple.

Later in the same letter there is also a report on the results of some horticultural experimentation done with seeds brought from Europe. Spring melon, cucumber, Old World squash, and radishes flourished. Onions, lettuce, other salad plants, and scallions failed, except for parsley. "Wheat, chick-peas, and beans in ten days at the most grow nine inches; then all at once they wilt and dry."

Columbus brought his own livestock from Spain and successfully bred pigs, cattle, horses, sheep, and goats. His men went native, though, and consumed parrots and local wild pigeons with gusto. The Indians ate dogs, snakes, lizards, spiders "as large as chickens," all manner of seafood, including oysters and sea urchins, and maize.

These glowing reports were meant to drum up support for new expeditions. One of them, hyping sweet potatoes as it were, inadvertently describes the real beginning of transatlantic culinary cross-fertilization: "When eaten raw as in salads, they taste like parsnips; when roasted, like chestnuts; when cooked with pork you would think you were eating squash. You will never eat anything more delicious than *asses* (sweet potatoes) soaked in the milk of almonds." There it is: New World meets Old in this typically medieval Spanish use of almond milk. The voyagers must have brought indispensable almonds with them. Soon they would return home and usher in the modern era in the Spanish kitchen. New World spices would supplant the antique, Oriental mixture called *salsa fina*. Similarly, the tomato would join the onion in that most typical of Spanish culinary preparations, the *sofrito*, a prefried flavoring combination added to countless dishes in Spain and Latin America today. In fact, U.S. supermarkets with a Hispanic clientele sell bottled *sofrito*. If only Columbus could see what he started.

PART II

THE COLONIAL
LABORATORY

I N E A C H of the major centers of Iberian settlement in the New World and Asia, the sixteenth-century colonizers brought the food of Spain and Portugal to new lands with new foods and to strange new peoples with exotic cuisines of their own. After a remarkably brief time, a new cuisine arose in each of these places. Each one evolved in its own way, depending on the indigenous cuisine, the agriculture underlying it, and the social mix of each new colonial society.

Where the native population was large, ate a varied diet, and shared its traditions successfully with the Iberian newcomers (Mexico), a truly mixed, integrated cuisine came to be. An informed observer can detect major components of the indigenous and the immigrant cuisines in the modern hybrid. Indeed, the essence of Mexican cuisine, as of Mexican culture, is the palpable mixture, the pervasive equipoise of Spanish and Indian traditions.

On the other hand, where the native population was small and perished almost completely from persecution and imported disease (Puerto Rico), the exotic foodstuffs brought in by the commerce of the Spanish empire produced an original cuisine in a tropical laboratory, with a Spanish gastronomic syntax inspiring new dishes made with ingredients never found all together in one place before.

Where, however, a sparse community of Spaniards—many of them serving only a hitch and not putting down roots—ruled a large and self-sustaining native population (the Philippines), the native cuisine survived largely intact, with Spanish names applied to its best-known dishes and local food ideas imposed on ingredients brought in by the galleons from Mexico.

Where natives and conquerors lived side by side (Peru), indigenous and imported foods both flourished and influenced each other without fundamentally altering the nature of either inherited cuisine.

In societies heavily repopulated with African slaves brought in to run plantations (the Caribbean coast of Colombia, northeast Brazil), tribal West African dishes were either transplanted almost completely or acquired an Iberian flavor.

In other words, history, politics, and demography determined the culinary outcome of colonialism. Here are detailed sketches of what happened in the important centers of early European colonialism, as the documents show and as I encountered the modern-day life of these societies through their food.

CHAPTER I

MEXICO

M E X I C O is the great example of a melting pot society. The United States, with its much greater initial ethnic diversity, has remained a nation of distinct nationalities, languages, and heritages, a union of hyphenated enclaves, but Mexico, while retaining some pure remnants of pre-Hispanic life, is overwhelmingly Mexican, an original civilization blended together from more or less equal parts of Iberian and indigenous roots. True, there are significant groups of Mexicans who speak the old languages—Nahuatl, Zapotec, Mixtec—and even some people who don't know Spanish. But the pitch of life is neither Indian nor Spanish nor even something basically postcolonial that might be called Hispanic. There is no other word for Mexican culture except Mexican.

This may be an elusive proposition to prove for Mexican society as a whole, but it is ostentatiously true in the Mexican kitchen. Yes, there are regional dishes (Oaxacan black *mole*, Veracruzan snapper) and dishes imported from Spain. There are even dishes that have survived from Aztec days basically intact (tacos with living insects in them). But they are curiosities, and even when one finds them in a restaurant, they get mixed up with the real, mixed cuisine of post-Conquest Mexico.

The Fonda Mesón de Alonso is only a short distance from Mexico City's main square, the Zocalo, near the location of the old central market of La Merced. This restaurant militantly devotes itself to foodstuffs that predate the arrival of the colonists from Spain in 1519. On the way in you pass mounds of grasshoppers and wormlike butterfly larvae harvested from cactus. Other, more normal restaurants in town serve some foods like this; it isn't unusual to encounter *huitlacoche* (the fleshy grey-black corn smut) or *nopales* (cactus paddles) in normal markets and even in luxury hotels. But this center of Mexican "roots" food is in a class by itself.

Under a ceiling hung with dozens of pastel-colored "chopped paper" (*papel picado*)—cut-out banners saying *felicidades*—the first-time visitor focuses on the ant eggs in green sauce (*escamoles en salsa verde*) and the toasted grasshoppers in guacamole. There are also crunchy patties of mosquito eggs in mole and iguana consommé. It looks fearsome but turns out to be a bit of a stunt since the weird ingredients do not have weird tastes, only interesting textures. The flavor of these dishes comes from their sauces, which may or may not have been added to these foods before 1519 (or even 1979).

A serious look at the menu confirms one's sense that this raffish bistro is not making any real effort to reproduce Aztec cookery but only means to incorporate some surviving Aztec ingredients into a general offering of macho dishes that includes venison meatballs, quail and, allegedly, mountain lion. The methods of cooking often include some process or ingredient of European origin. The quail is cooked in wine.

The crucial difference between this menu and any selection of food possible before Cortés is also the one that most of us would take as its least dramatic feature: It has red meat on it, red meat from domestic livestock unknown in Mexico before the Spanish imported them. Amid the bugs and worms and indigenous game on the Fonda Mesón de Alonso's menu are many dishes made from calf's foot, bull's testicles, and goat meat, but it is the sheer fact of finding beef, pork, and goat in any form on this menu that brands it irrevocably as post-Hispanic.

The Aztecs had only five domesticated animals, as Sophie Coe reminded us in her survey of their cookery in *Petits Propos Culinaires* (Nos 19–21): the turkey, the Muscovy duck, the dog, the bee, and the cochineal insect. (The situation was not much better in the Andes where the guinea pig was—and is—a basic meat source, and various camelids, notably the llama, substituted for horses, oxen, and other beasts of burden widespread in Europe.)

So before 1492, Mexican cuisine had no dishes with beef, pork, or lamb. There were no dairy products, no milk, no cream, no butter, no cheese. Fried foods were unknown. Then, in 1493, Columbus returned to the New World on his second voyage and brought with him horses, dogs, pigs, cattle, chickens, sheep, and goats. These pioneering animals were intended to supply Spaniards with familiar foods, but their real contribution was much more original and important. Their meat, milk, and cheese made Mexican food possible: cheese-filled *quesadillas*, barbecued beef *carnitas*, pork-stuffed *tamales*, chicken *tacos.* Columbus came with seventeen ships and twelve hundred men, and in the holds of those ships were, literally, the seeds of colonization. Columbus brought what was needed to start plantations, orchards, and kitchen gardens, the wherewithal to grow onions, grapes, fruit, radishes, and sugarcane. The Antilles soon were producing such exotics as lettuce, cauliflower, citrus, figs, and pomegranates. The banana, originally Asian, had been established in the first Spanish colony, the Canary Islands, and was brought from there to the Caribbean in 1516 and flourished.

So did wheat. In *The Columbian Exchange* (1972), Alfred W. Crosby catalogs the spread of the Spanish staple, planted wherever the conquistadors established farms. This was official policy, and by 1535, Mexico was exporting wheat to the Antilles.

Even more spectacular was the swift adaptation of the pig to the New World. Reading Crosby's several pages on the subject, one is tempted to say that the New World was conquered by swine just as much as it was by the Spanish. There were literally thousands of pigs on this side of the Atlantic by 1550.

In many of the places where hog and *hidalgo* settled, they were free to adapt the cuisine of the mother country to local conditions with no, or only trivial, contact with indigenous foodways. Whatever Arawak or Taino cuisine may have been, its practitioners were few, led uncomplicated lives, and soon perished from imported diseases or interbred into the new Spanish master culture. But in Mexico the vigorous indigenous civilization survived and truly mixed with the Spanish. Mexico is the outstanding case of a fair trade-off, where the pre-Columbian Europeans and native Americans benefited more or less equally.

Almost from the beginning of the fateful encounter between native Mexicans and Spanish, then, it is legitimate to speak of mixture, *mestizaje.* The hybrid food vocabulary seems to have arisen first and the rich repertory of *mestizo* recipes soon after, as Spanish settlement took hold on Mexican soil.

The importation of European-style foods began with Cortés, who conquered Mexico in short order after landing in 1519. To celebrate victory in battle, Bernal Díaz tells us he held a banquet at Coyoacán with "much wine from Castilla" and pork from Cuba. In 1538 the first viceroy of Mexico, Antonio de Mendoza, and Cortés held banquets to celebrate a peace treaty between Spain and France. Bernal Díaz del Castillo writes magniloquently of the Mendoza feast (Porrúa, 1977, pp. 314–15):

Although I'm not going to write down everything, I will say
what I remember because I was one of those who dined at
those great celebrations. First, there were some salads made
in various ways, and afterwards, kids and hams roasted in
the Genoese style; after that quail and pigeon pies, and then
wattled cocks and stuffed hens; then blancmange; after that
a stew (pepitoria); then a royal cake (torta real); then local
fowl and partridges and quail en escabeche, and then they
replaced the tablecloths twice and left clean ones with nap-
kins; then they brought pasties [empanadas] filled with every
kind of bird and game; these they did not eat, nor many
other things that had been served to them; then came fish
empanadas; neither did they eat any of them; then they
brought in roast mutton, and beef and pork, and turnips
and cabbage and chick-peas, of which they also ate nothing;
and in the midst of these dishes they put down fruits of
different flavors, and then they brought local fowl boiled
whole, with beaks and feet covered with silver; after that
whole ducklings and goslings with gilded beaks, and then
hogs' heads and whole stags and calves of great size, and
along with these came large bands with singers at either end
of each table and brass players and other kinds of instru-
ments, harps, viols, flutes, treble and alto shawms [chirimías
y dulzainas], especially when the stewards passed cups to the
ladies who were dining there, many more than had attended
Cortés's dinner, and many gilt goblets, some with hydromel,
others with wine, others with water, and others with chocolate and with claret; and afterward they served other, more
important ladies even bigger empanadas, and in some of
them were pairs of live rabbits, and others were full of live
quail and pigeons and other little birds; and they served
them all at the same time; and when the waiters took them
away, the rabbits ran away, the rabbits ran away across the
tables and the quail and birds flew off. And I still haven't
said anything about olives and radishes and cheese and
cardoons. And local fruit. But what more is there to say
except that the table was full for that course. At the same
time there were clowns and jesters who said many funny
things in praise of Cortés and the viceroy. And I still haven't
talked about the fountains of white wine, made by Indians,
and red wine, too, that they put in front of us. . . . Then I

almost forgot to mention the heifers, roasted whole and stuffed with chickens and fowl and quail and pigeons and ham. . . . And all this was served with gold and silver and very luxurious big china plates.

The foremost Mexican gastronomic writer of our day, Salvador Novo, expounds the phenomenon of this mixed cuisine almost ecstatically in his *Cocina Mexicana o Historia Gastronómica de la Ciudad de Mexico* (Porrúa, 1967):

> The encounter was a fortunate one, the marriages were happy, their offspring abundant. Atoles (a category of beverage) and cacao drinks benefit from sugar and milk; tortillas, after being fried or sprinkled with chorizo (a Spanish pork sausage), will transform themselves into *garnachas, chalupas, sopes, tostadas, tacos, enchiladas, chilaquiles, infladas, molotes, bocoles, pellizcadas.* Tamales will be fluffier with lard. . . . Refried beans will be more delicious than plain boiled beans; and beans as well as strips of chili fried with onion will accept the white, tasty caress of cheese and cream.
>
> The union of corn with cheese will give birth to quesadillas; like Spanish empanadas, yes, but accented with little bits of chili, or ennobled with squash blossoms or with epazote.

This is not just a deduction. Mr. Novo has based his remarks on the remarkably detailed documentary information that survives from the earliest days of the evolution of his national cuisine. Mexican food offers us the special opportunity to see in detail what the historical record from other cultures has rarely preserved. We know in detail what native Mexicans ate before the Spanish conquest. We know how they ate their food, how they prepared it, how it fitted into the life of Aztec society. And we know this from native informants as well as from reliable outsiders and evidence in pre-Columbian and colonial Mexican art and from the concrete survivals of ancient foodways still abundantly practiced in Mexico today.

The Aztecs wrote about their own civilization, and some of this material has survived. Other documents of an ethnographic character were produced at the direction of the Spanish soon after the Conquest, complete with illustrations of daily life, including culinary scenes. Cortés himself wrote letters, and Bernal Díaz produced a full history of the Conquest, *Historia Verdadera de la Conquista de la Nueva España (The True History of the Conquest of New Spain)* based on eyewitness accounts.

The most important ethnographic record of indigenous life in Mexico to come down to us from the sixteenth century, however, is *Historia General de las Cosas de Nueva España (General History of the Things of New Spain)* compiled by the Franciscan friar Bernardino de Sahagún. This monumental work is based on Aztec testimony that he faithfully gathered and eventually translated from the Nahuatl language of his informants into Spanish. It is a big book and covers the whole panorama of Aztec life in great detail. Foodways are not slighted. From Sahagún we know that the Aztecs' diet was based on corn, tortillas, tamales, and plenty of chilies in many varieties. In other words, Sahagún provides evidence of a continuity from Aztec food to the demotic Mexican food of today.

In Book VIII, devoted to aristocratic life, Sahagún devotes chapter 13 to enumerating the foods the Aztec noblemen were accustomed to:

1. The tortillas the lords ate every day were called *totonqui tlaxcalli tlacuelpacholli,* meaning white and hot tortillas, folded tortillas piled in a *chiquihuitl* and covered with a white cloth.

2. They also ate other tortillas every day that they called *ueitlaxcalli,* meaning big tortillas; these are very white, very thin, narrow, and very smooth.

Dozens of similar descriptions are set forth in this bilingual mixture, which is, among other things, symbolic of the mixed cuisine we know today as Mexican. Already in the 1570s, just a half century after the arrival of Cortés's ships, the flat cornbread of the Aztecs, *tlaxcalli,* as it was called in Nahuatl, had acquired a Spanish name, *tortilla.* The name must have been in general use because Sahagún felt no need to explain it, even though in peninsular Spain, then and now, *tortilla,* the diminutive of the word for cake (*torta*), refers to a cold omelet and nothing else.

Sahagún had no way of knowing how successful various foods he thought of as Mexican would be when exported. It would be two hundred years before the tomato really came into its own in Europe. Sahagún would also be astounded by the universal acceptance of Mexican standbys such as chocolate, vanilla, and all the multifarious

Capsicum peppers, from hot chilies to the mildest bell peppers. A complete list of foods derived from the New World can never be compiled since the process continues today and may even be accelerating as refugees from oppressive regimes in Central and South America spread their cuisines northward and as adventurous palates in the United States and elsewhere create a secondary "gourmet" market for previously unfamiliar foods. The pickled jalapeño pepper is now a supermarket item in New York, not a specialty food.

When Cortés conquered Mexico, he bit off more than he or the Spanish empire could conveniently chew. Mexico was no Caribbean island with Stone Age Arawaks or Tainos spearing fish for survival. Mexico was a major world civilization with a vigorous culture that continues to challenge imported European culture today. Even after smallpox and other European diseases wiped out vast numbers of people—those hordes that had been baptized and preached to in the outdoor "open" chapels that now grace outlying ghost towns all over Mexico—even after these indigenous innocents had perished, there were still more than enough native Mexicans to carry on local food traditions in tandem with the new ideas and foods from Spain and the Spanish empire.

Tequila is a well-known case in point. It is a distillation of a special cultivar of the agave called *maguey*. Only the distillation (and its commercial systematization in the state of Jalisco) owes anything to Europe. The plant itself, and its numerous related varieties, was at the heart of pre-Hispanic cooking. Its sap was and is tapped from its heart and drunk fresh as *aguamiel,* honey water. When the *aguamiel* is fermented, which it was long before Cortés, the result is *pulque,* a perishable, low-alcohol, milky beverage that still demands the loyalty of local connoisseurs.

Some people cook with *pulque;* others eat the maguey's flowers. But the most dramatic pre-Hispanic culinary contribution of the maguey to modern Mexican gastronomic life is entomological: the worms that infest the plants' thick pointed leaves and its roots. Sahagún mentioned both: "There are some worms they call *meocuili,* which means maguey worms. They are very white and they grow in the magueys; they cut a hole and go inside, eating and sending out their excrement through the hole by which they entered. They are very good to eat." (11.13.81)

These worms (really larvae) are also known as *palomillas de maguey* (maguey squabs), *champolocos, meocuilines, pecahs,* or scientifically, *Aegiale (Acentrocneme) hesperiaris.* The butterfly that produces them flutters about between June and October, laying its eggs under the fleshy leaves of the *maguey pulquero* (*Agave salmiana* and *A. mapisaga*). Modern science ratifies Sahagún's account of the ravenous life of the maguey worm in the heart of the plant.

Worm harvesters (I paraphrase the account in Teresa Castelló Yturbide's magnificent and sometimes terrifying *Presencia de la Comida Prehispánica*, with photographs by Michel Zabé, Banamex, 1986) poke about among the maguey's lower leaves, looking for the telltale worm tunnels at the base of the leaves near the outer edges. Working very carefully with a machete so as not to disembowel the worms unwittingly, they cut open the leaf. To extract the worms whole, they use hooks formed by cutting thin strips from the edge of a maguey leaf. They remove all of its spines except for one at the end of the strip. This they form into the hook they use to catch the worms by the head. To store the worms they make pouches with the skin of a tender new maguey leaf that looks like parchment and is called *mixiote*. (It gives its name, synecdochically, to a dish made of chunks of marinated meat wrapped in *mixiote* pouches and steamed.)

To cook the worms, people sometimes just put a whole *gusano*-filled *mixiote* over coals or hot ashes, or they might just put the worms directly on a bakestone (*comal*) until they swell and stiffen, turning golden brown and crunchy. And this is not some quaint account of a long-forgotten practice. Castelló Yturbide nonchalantly mentions that maguey worms can be obtained in April in the market of San Juan in Mexico City, on Wednesdays in Actopán, on Mondays in Ixmuquilpán (two villages of the state of Hidalgo), or in farm hamlets around Mexico City.

Gusanos de maguey are only one of a long list of surviving pre-Hispanic oddments, mostly what we would call vermin, that Castelló Yturbide catalogues and presents to us with Michel Zabé's eerily elegant photographs. Even more primitive survivals that she mentions are the various algae and pond scum, such as *cuculito del agua* (*Phormidium tenue*, *Chroccus turgidus*), gathered in baskets, mixed with the herb epazote, dried chilies, and salt; the "dough" (*masa*) is then spread over a corn leaf, steamed like a tamal, and eaten by itself or in stews. Castelló Yturbide says she bought these tamales from vendors of fish tamales in the capital district at Xochimilco and Texcoco.

The story of another edible alga—*espirulina, tecuilatl, Athrospira* (*Spirulina*) *platensis*—is even more exotic and inspiring. In 1582, Juan Bautista Pomar described a kind of food called *tecuitlatl* made into cakes from pond slime, dark green in color and called cheese of the earth (*queso de tierra*) by the Spaniards. *Tecuitlatl* flourished in abundance in Lake Texcoco in the Valley of Mexico, but then it seemed to have vanished. However, following the suggestion of a Belgian botanist in 1964 and drawing on research done in the biologically similar waters of Lake Chad in Central Africa, Mexican scientists were able to revive the plant and harvest a ton of *espirulina* a day in 1973, thus returning the alga to the diet of Mexicans.

The list of insects eaten in Mexico then and now is awesomely long. Water bugs (*moscos de pájaro, axayacatl*) whose eggs (*ahuautli*) are still gathered in the same manner described by Sahagún: Bundles of reeds that are stuck upright in the muck in shallow water attract the *moscos*, which lay eggs on them. After a month of this, people "harvest" the bundles, dry them out, and shake the eggs onto cotton sheets. Sahagún says they were then eaten in tamales and tortillas. Today, according to Castelló Yturbide, they are toasted, ground up, and made into little cakes held together with turkey egg. This is a documentable survival of a dish that goes back at least to 1798 when, according to Manuel Orozco y Berra, a scientist of the day, these apparently humble concoctions were a garnish for the festive dish called *revoltijo*, served on Christmas Eve and at the vigil on Thursday night of Holy Week. "The taste," he wrote cryptically, "is like caviar but not so tasty."

Mexicans also continue to eat locusts (*chapulines*), available all year at markets in Oaxaca and Atlixco (Puebla), by toasting them and eating them with tortillas and a sauce of *chile pasilla*; mountain chinch bugs, which are eaten toasted or living; oak-boring beetles, which are popular as snacks among Mixtec peasants; red ant eggs (*escamoles*), actually the pupas and larvae, which are eaten in a special mole with nopal cactus or in turkey egg-bound cakes; and wasps, at Jungapeo, Michoacán.

Some other out-of-the-way vestiges of pre-Hispanic cookery include the primitive salamander called *axolotl* ("good to eat"—Sahagún), which were formerly consumed two at a time wrapped in corn leaves but today, allegedly, are served in broth to frail children; frogs and tadpoles; iguanas, which are sold live in Acapulco and stewed in a tomato-chili broth thickened with corn flour; rattlesnake, which is served with hot sauce in Chihuahua and added to the still (for good luck?) during the preparation of the country rotgut made from the false palm called *sotole*; cayman; monkeys, which are roasted like suckling pigs in Chiapas; opossum; armadillo; and rodents too numerous to mention.

It would be possible to go through dish after dish in this manner, sorting out the Aztec and Spanish contributions to each, but the most impressive part of the *mestizaje* in Mexican cuisine is how rapidly it took hold, both in agriculture and in the kitchen. Already in Cortés's lifetime the process had permeated all sectors of Mexican life, and by the seventeenth century the invention of new, self-consciously Mexican dishes was pursued at the highest levels of the vicerealm.

In particular, well-born or well-connected women in convents created many hybrid recipes, notably a whole repertory of elaborate sweets. The greatest of Mexican sauces, *mole poblano* (Pueblan sauce), was by legend invented by a religious, Sor Andrea de la Asunción, at the convent of Santa Rosa in Puebla. Whether the attribution is correct or not, the notion of Puebla as the origin of this savant sauce is convincing. A great colonial center, Puebla was a cosmopolitan place, open to new things. It was Puebla that welcomed a Chinese girl and made her into a Mexican folk symbol, the China Poblana, whose colorful dress is still recognizable to every Mexican, a charming relic of the seaborne trade with China conducted between Manila and Acapulco.

Puebla in the seventeenth century was a hub of novelty, just the sort of place where a refined nun would mix chocolate, chilies, and imported ingredients such as cinnamon and coriander for a sauce to go with the great Aztec bird, the turkey. If the final taste of the sauce seems Asian, perhaps our taste buds are hinting at a historical truth. Probably not, but the legend of *mole poblano* as an invented sauce concocted by a non-Aztec with non-Spanish and local ingredients is itself worthy of note. Even if the account is only a fable, it is a fable that shows how eagerly Mexicans embrace the idea of a mestizo or hybrid origin for the national cuisine.

What seems clear, in any case, is that out of the extremely fertile period of Mexican sauce development in the eighteenth century, the *mole* that combines chocolate and chilies emerged firmly identified with Puebla.

I emphasize this because the acme of refinement in classical Mexican cookery is another dish that, beyond any doubt, had to be invented at some point after the Conquest because it combines chilies and milk. The chili is the big green *chile poblano*, the chili of Puebla. The dish is called *chile en nogada*. It is an elaborate member of a family of dishes that involve stuffing poblano chilies with one thing or another. *Chile en nogada* is stuffed with chopped pork and served in a sauce of ground nuts and cream. In some versions peaches, pears, acitron (the candied flesh of the *biznaga* cactus), and other fruits are added to the stuffing. Perhaps this is a relic of a pre-Columbian, and therefore pre-pork, stuffed poblano dish in which the stuffing was all fruit.

Chile en nogada is still a seasonal dish of late August, but now the timing depends on another seasonal fruit, an Old World fruit, the walnut (called *nuez de Castilla* in Mexico to distinguish it from the pecan, which is simply *nuez*). Fresh walnuts and cream bathe the stuffed green chili while ruby-red pomegranate seeds, also Old World in origin, provide the third color of the Mexican flag.

Some people believe that the patriotic appearance of this Old World sauce for New World chili stuffed with Old World pork is not happenstance. They say that *chile en nogada* was invented in Puebla for a banquet honoring Agustín de Iturbide, the self-styled emperor of the newly independent Mexico, on August 28, 1821. Once again, it doesn't matter if the whole story is true; it only completes the symbolism of a great dish that is the epitome of a mestizo culture and its mixed cuisine.

CHAPTER II

PUERTO RICO

THE FIRST permanent Spanish settlement in what is now the United States (and therefore the oldest European footprint on our soil) ought to be a Mecca for history buffs and patriots. Since it has had as long to develop a modern cuisine as most Western European countries, it should attract the same gastronomes who haunt regional restaurants and make polenta from Navajo blue cornmeal in their homes. Puerto Rico, moreover, has more than just a few exotic chilies and pine nuts to show for itself. Its cosmopolitan past and welcoming climate have made it a "melting pot" for food plants from Europe, Africa, South America, and Asia. With such a larder to draw from, its cooks invented dozens of new dishes, so many, in fact, that this place should probably be considered the home of the most fertile and diverse of all our regional cuisines. Of all the post-Hispanic New World cuisines, Puerto Rico's (along with the Dominican Republic's and Cuba's) should be considered the most original because island chefs, starting essentially from zero after the savage decimation of the indigenous Tainos, were able to concoct an entirely new roster of dishes with foods brought in from all points of the compass subjected to an essentially Spanish culinary point of view.

The results of this brilliant improvisation could not have arisen anywhere except in the Spanish Caribbean. The climate was ideal for experiments in eclectic agriculture. There was no powerful local cuisine to compete with the spirit of invention that always inspires cooks confronting new foods in frontier situations. In Mexico, Aztec cookery was a powerful shaping force that engulfed the cuisine of the conquistadors to produce Mexican cuisine. In Puerto Rico and the other Spanish islands, a world empire poured its ingredients into an empty bowl and whipped up a menu unlike any that had existed before.

Many of these dishes are widely available on a daily basis in the

Puerto Rican diaspora in New York and other major American cities. And yet almost no one who is not from Puerto Rico ever eats its cuisine or thinks of it as a source of interesting food and food ideas. This neglect is not new. Outsiders have always turned their backs on Puerto Rico.

On his second voyage, propelled by favorable winds, Columbus discovered the island. He named it San Juan Bautista and never returned.

In 1508, Juan Ponce de León set sail from nearby Española (Hispaniola, now divided between Haiti and the Dominican Republic), site of the first post-Columbian European settlement. Ponce de León colonized the smaller island, which its indigenous Taino inhabitants knew as Borinquén. But Ponce de León did not fall in love with Puerto Rico. He decamped for the mainland in search of the fountain of youth and died from an arrow wound acquired in Florida. Today there is a statue of him in San Juan but, as Puerto Ricans are fond of pointing out, it gazes west toward Santo Domingo. Disdain and contempt have colored the outside world's attitude toward Puerto Rico ever since.

After almost four centuries of Spanish hegemony, four hundred years in which the Tainos all but vanished from European diseases and intermarriage, four hundred years in which gold deposits were exhausted and African slave labor manned the ranches and grew the sugar and coffee that kept this colonial backwater economically afloat, the United States took over the island during the Spanish-American War in 1898. Puerto Ricans have been U.S. citizens since 1917, and the island has been called a commonwealth since 1952, but most non–Puerto Rican U.S. citizens still have to be reminded that people from the island were born in the same country that they were.

The Justice Department maintains an immigration check at the San Juan airport for passengers boarding flights to New York. This route has already brought hundreds of thousands of Puerto Ricans to the mainland, and their presence has dramatically changed the face of New York. With the help of other Spanish speakers from many other places but overwhelmingly through their own numbers, Puerto Ricans have made New York a bilingual city. This is a fact that almost everyone in the anglophone so-called master culture does his best to ignore, hoping that it will disappear or that New Yoricans will finally join the rest of us by switching to English.

Perhaps they will. Thousands are already bilingual, and their Spanish has evolved into Spanglish, with hybrid words such as *el super*.

But for now, English-speaking New Yorkers and people in other cities with Puerto Rican and other hispanophone neighbors are mostly neglecting the best opportunity Americans have ever had to pick up another language from native speakers. Instead of fighting proposals for bilingual education in public schools as a sop to Hispanics, we ought to be pressing for it as an opportunity for our own children to learn the other major American language. Similarly, we ought to be pursuing the food of Puerto Rico in Puerto Rican restaurants, just as we flock to the restaurants of other cultures in our midst. But have you ever heard anyone say, "Let's eat Puerto Rican tonight"?

Why is this? Why do our two cultures go merrily on their two ways with so little of the usual contact you would expect to occur between them? Why is it, for example, that most people I know have never cooked the plantains or true yams or other tropical vegetables always present in our supermarkets? Why is it that when I buy Oriental ingredients in Chinatown or at a Korean grocer on upper Broadway, the cashier shows no surprise, but when I make a purchase at a Hispanic butcher two blocks from my house on the Upper West Side of Manhattan, the man behind the counter asks me if my wife is Spanish?

C. P. Snow spoke of two cultures that kept their distance and didn't understand each other—humanists and scientists. Puerto Ricans and other citizens of this country have a similar problem, and I don't think we can explain the almost universal lack of non–Puerto Rican interest in Puerto Rican food by invoking class or race prejudice. After all, most whites have not hesitated to eat soul food in black restaurants. Their bias does not seem to run against Hispanic food per se. Cuban restaurants draw non-Cubans both in Florida and in New York, but I have never heard of a Puerto Rican restaurant north of San Juan that was a success with the general population.

Come to think of it, I have never heard of an ethnic Puerto Rican restaurant in San Juan that was a hit with Anglo visitors even though those same Anglo visitors do not hesitate to seek out Jamaican food in Jamaica or Martinican food in Martinique. Indeed, on the island of Manhattan at this moment there is a small vogue for the food of the Caribbean. Several restaurants have sprung up, but they ignore the food of Puerto Rico.

As I embarked on my trip to Puerto Rico, I hoped to experience the island's post-Columbian foods by roaming about in the hinterland. In this way I might avoid the deadening international food of major resorts and observe the more traditional life of the western highlands. From San Juan it took over three hours to reach Parador Hacienda Juanita in mid-jungle along the Ruta Panorámica that winds by giant bamboo sprays and teams of men with machetes slashing away at vegetation to keep the shoulder clear.

Hacienda Juanita is part of a network of inns maintained by the government. In addition to its lush gardens it offers examples of *la cocina puertorriqueña* in its dining room. For example, its menu features *serenata,* a "serenade" of flaked salt cod served cold as a salad on one plate and with a combination of starchy vegetables on another. *Serenata* is a strange adventure in connoisseurship, flaunting the unexpected differences between green and ripe plantains, *yautías* (taro), yams, *yuca* (manioc), and breadfruit—those diverse vegetables brought here from all over the world by Spanish galleons, naturalized, and now considered separate and fundamental parts of the diet and classified as *viandas hervidas,* boiled foods.

In her learned and thorough *Rice and Beans and Tasty Things, a Puerto Rican Cookbook,* Dora Romano lists some fifty recipes in a chapter on vegetables dominated by preparations for roots and tubers—fritters, purees, salads, chips, and many more. The ingenuity is impressive, but it is the profusion of plants from around the world brought by Spanish colonists and African slaves to this one island that makes Puerto Rican cuisine so special.

The parador turned out to be a rare example of a full-scale restaurant serving full-blown dishes of a traditional nature. Demotic Puerto Rico does not lack for public eating opportunities—far from it—but most of what I found of indigenous food in the western highlands, on roadsides, or in the village of Maricao and in the western port of Mayagüez was in locally rooted fast-food emporia.

Along the western end of the Ruta Panorámica one typically came upon a simple building that doubled as bar and standup, open-air restaurant with a small number of specialties, most of which were deep-fried *cuchifritos,* ranging from pork-and-plantain *mofongo* to more straightforward pork oddments. One place served suckling pig. The "restaurant" I most lusted to try out was Willy's, a shack at a bend in the road between Mayagüez and Maricao. Willy's opened in the afternoon and advertised as its specialty *cuajito*—pork stomach.

Unfortunately, Willy did not serve *cuajito* on the day I passed by, only beer and coconut juice straight from the whole fruit. I did much better wandering around Mayaguez, dropping into storefront snack bars, sampling the never redundant array of fritters of various description, *piononos,* cod *empanaditas,* and *pasteles* of this or that. Apart from the beer, the rum, and the relaxed welcome, the common link between these places was hot lard sizzling in the background and handwritten signs that said NO HABLE MALO. RESPETE QUE HAY DAMAS. Don't swear. Respect the presence of women.

As I had expected from hearing many similar reports before I left, the height of this informal but diverse public Puerto Rican dining takes place at the beach. You will go far before you find a food scene livelier than the three restaurants at the western edge of the beach at Piñones Forest just to the east of the San Juan airport. Here, with the dunes and the Atlantic on one side and a piney woods on the other, the glamorizing hand of resort development has not yet squeezed out local culture. Food stand after food stand pops up along the road for miles. There are also graffiti threatening to fight the big builders. But for now the women next to the hot fat are grating *yautía* for the next batch of giant land crab *alcapurrias,* and islanders drop in for a beer and some solid nourishment.

Another way to observe the lingering indigenous food culture is to wander among the stalls of the central market in town, south of the University of Puerto Rico campus. Many San Juanians now live in suburbs and shop in supermarkets. In the market the fruit sellers will pour you *refrescos,* cold drinks made from *guanabanas* (sweetsops), and the butchers have *gandinga.* What is *gandinga?* It is a mixture of cubed pork offal—liver, heart, and kidneys. The basic dish is a ragout and has, shall we say, a strong taste. Some people on the island favor it for Christmas Eve dinner. I found it on the menu at El Obrero, a truckers' restaurant down the street from the San Juan central bus station and a short walk from the central market. El Obrero is not some dirty truck stop but a well-run restaurant, a local institution with humorous place mats and militantly traditional and unpretentious local food. El Obrero's *gandinga* comes with rice and beans. It isn't veal Orloff, but that's the point. It is what it is, very gutsy food that stands for the place it comes from. You won't find *gandinga* in Spain or Mexico, but you will find it at serious Hispanic butcher shops in New York.

I felt a lot better about the future of the city when I learned that. Hundreds of thousands of New Yoricans don't have to settle for burgers; they can still get *gandinga.* At the supermarket in my neighborhood they have their choice of *yautía* or its cousin, *malanga.* There are white sweet potatoes (*boniatos*), true yams plus plantains, the bottled leaf-coriander condiment *recaito,* and *sofrito* (more on this shortly). Perhaps somewhere someone is flying in mangrove crabs, but even without them I'm no longer down in the dumps about the future of Puerto Rican food in New York. There are no important restaurants because that is not the way it works back on the Isle of Enchantment either. What we ought to have on our island, though, is a little place where you can get a beer and a plate of *cuajito* on your way home from work, as you drive past the beach just to see what's happening.

There never will be such a place in New York City, of course, and no sane person would expect a North Atlantic megalopolis to look or feel like San Juan. But those of us who live in New York side by side with millions of Hispanics might well ask ourselves why virtually none of us Anglos shows any curiosity about them as people or in the food they eat.

For years I have wondered about this state of affairs, wondered why the only Puerto Rican restaurants in New York were either fast-food outlets for *cuchifritos* or lunch counters with limited menus. Could it be that lard-fried pig parts and a few unspectacular dishes common to the whole Hispanic Caribbean were all that Puerto Ricans ate? I couldn't believe it, and from time to time I would make an experimental visit to some unprepossessing little place with a Spanish name. My biggest success was at a now defunct hole-in-the-wall in the wholesale textile district below Canal Street. It opened for lunch only and served laborers who moved bolts of cloth in and out of trucks and lofts. There was no menu. I asked the old woman behind the counter what she had. "*Mollejas,*" she replied. In standard Spanish, *mollejas* are sweetbreads. The woman returned with a plate of gizzards, twelve of them. Not wanting to hurt her feelings, I ate them all. Then I told her what the English for *mollejas* was, on the off chance that another greenhorn would wander in. She thanked me and urged me to come back the next week—for octopus.

Recently I extended my Puerto Rican research in another direction. I acquired three Puerto Rican cookbooks, all in English, and quickly discovered that our Caribbean commonwealth has an extremely original food heritage, one it shares to a great extent with geographically and historically similar islands such as Cuba and the Dominican Republic. All of these places display their common Spanish heritage with omelets called *tortillas* and blood sausage called *morcilla*. And they share a basic vocabulary of tropical flavors and ingredients, notably the bewildering array of tubers and roots, from cassava to taro to yam.

In the end, however, only Puerto Rico has truly Puerto Rican food, and the reasons for this are not trivial. The conditions that produced such brilliant hybrids as *alcapurrias de juey*—in which Spanish technique is applied to African, non-Caribbean, New World, and indigenous ingredients, and given an obsolete and apparently inappropriate Moorish name—obtained throughout the entire Spanish Caribbean. Indeed, the factors that produced Puerto Rican cuisine must have been more or less available to the entire Spanish empire, from Seville to Manila.

In the tiny but cosmopolitan world of the Caribbean in the heyday of European colonization, the culinary turbulence of San Juan could be found in any of the island capitals, Spanish-ruled or not. The processes of influence and invention, of transplantation and cross-fertilization that marked the Puerto Rican kitchen were also at work in Martinique, Jamaica, Curaçao, and Trinidad. And in each of these places, dishes evolved that the modern traveler encounters as signposts of distinct cultures. Just as historically minded cooks in Puerto Rico will serve you *asopao* (from Spanish *asopado*, souped), a liquid rice stew of chicken or shellfish, so the Martinican epicure will flaunt *patte-en-pot* (paw-in-pot), an indigenous lamb ragout that includes the feet.

The Dominican chef at La Sartén on Amsterdam Avenue in Manhattan, not far from the Museum of Natural History, serves *asopao* on a menu identifiable as Dominican by the presence of *chicharrones de pollo* (small fried chicken pieces named because of their resemblance to pork cracklings, *chicharrones*). Does this make *asopao* less Puerto Rican or *chicharrones de pollo* less Dominican? Not at all. Their juxtaposition on the same menu may simply represent a wish by the restaurant to attract a pan-Hispanic clientele. But this is not the first time that *asopao* has been served in a non-Puerto Rican context. Victor's, the avowedly Cuban restaurant a few blocks away, has also offered New Yorkers *asopao* in its time. The Caribbean is not so large, and its denizens travel and take their recipes with them. It would have been impossible for islanders to be completely insular, especially in the formative days of these cuisines when all the Spanish islands were truly Spanish. What we perceive today as typical of one island or another is often a dish that, after four hundred years, has emerged as a local favorite rather than an exclusive local invention with a pedigree that can be clearly established.

When one speaks of Puerto Rican cookery, one makes a necessary but an imperfect generalization about a group of dishes with a common history and a current life on one island where those dishes are more prominent than elsewhere. Some are almost never found anywhere else, perhaps, but it is difficult to prove a negative. It is safer to say that Puerto Rican dishes are those that most especially mark the gastronomic life of the island. Many of these same dishes are also available on the islands closest to Puerto Rico in history—the Dominican Republic and Cuba. But the emphasis, the style, the flavor, the frequency—all these factors vary in the three places, vary enough so that one can speak sensibly about different, if related, cuisines.

Furthermore, if you were to compare Puerto Rican and Dominican cookbooks, you would immediately be struck by the differences in the names for the same or similar dishes. The broad-leafed "coriander" (*Eryngium foetidum*), which looks roughly like a bay leaf but tastes like a stronger, bolder relative of European coriander (*Coriandrum sativum*), which it is, is known in Puerto Rico as *culantro, culantro de monte,* or *recao,* which is also the name given to a mixture of *culantro* and regular coriander, known locally as *cilantrillo, culantrillo,* and *culantro.* (*Recao* derives from standard Spanish *recado,* which means the day's shopping.) The mixture, bottled and commonly available in New York as *recaito,* is an essential part of the cooked condiment Puerto Ricans call *sofrito,* a mixture of *recao,* fatback, ham, lard colored with *annatto* (the seed of *Bixa orellana,* also called *achiote, bija,* and *bijol*), garlic, onion, tomato, green pepper, and oregano that is the starting point of numerous soups and stews.

They order things a bit differently in the Dominican Republic. Ligia de Bornia in *La Cocina Dominicana* speaks of *recado verde, cilantro ancho* (wide cilantro), *cilantro sabanero* (cilantro of the savannah, evidently *E. foetidum*), and *cilantro de España* (probably *C. sativum*). The dialectal differences between these two islands cannot be exaggerated, and there is a useful task awaiting some sun-loving soul who compiles a glossary of food words in use in all the islands of the Caribbean (as well as the countries of Central and South America). School Spanish is no help in a world where *plátano* does not mean banana but plantain and where some but not all people say *guineo* when they mean banana.

Fortunately, Dominicans and Puerto Ricans mean the same thing when they say *mofongo* (not to be confused with *mondongo* or tripe). I assume this is an African word brought to both islands by slaves. It is a puree of plantain mixed with bits of crushed pork crackling (*chicharrones*). Even more complex and original is the *alcapurria,* a fritter whose dough is a clever mixture of two purees, glutinous plantain and starchy white *yautía* (*Xanthosoma saggitifolium,* an aroid root related to taro), stuffed with the standard Puerto Rican meat filling, shaped into fritters, and deep-fried.

Like other Spanish words beginning with *al,* the Arabic definite article, *alcapurria* must have come to Puerto Rico from Spain where it would have begun as an Arabic term brought in by the Moors. Spanish dictionaries don't mention it, and its apparent connection with the Spanish word for caper, *alcaparra*, is mystifying. But no one worries about this at the Piñones Forest beach near San Juan where, in steamy bars competing for the world fritter title, I saw women grate *yautía* for *alcapurrias de juey*, which are *alcapurrias* stuffed with the meat of the mangrove crab (*Cardisoma guanhumi*).

Alcapurria is only one of the mystifying food names in active use in Puerto Rico. *Apio (Arracacia xanthorrhiza)*, a tuber of the carrot family native to northern South America, now grows in the highlands of Puerto Rico. Puerto Ricans give it the standard Spanish name for celery, but they also retain the original Andean name, *arracacha*. Such confusing multiple names are typical of Puerto Rican foods. The Central American fruit most commonly known as *sapodilla* (from Spanish *zapotillo*, a small *zapote*—which is still another Central American fruit—but known in Mexico as *chicozapote* or just plain *chico*, reflecting the original Nahuatl name *tzicozapotl*, or gum *zapotl*) is usually referred to in Puerto Rican parlance as *nispero*. In Spain, *nispero* is the name of the European medlar, *Mespilus germanica*, and the loquat, *Eriobotrya japonica*. Puerto Rican cooks have added still another layer to this nomenclatural palimpsest with a dessert called *nisperos de batata*, which is prepared from sweetened mashed sweet potatoes shaped to resemble *sapodillas* and given *sapodilla* "stems" made with a green thread tied around a whole clove.

Puerto Rican cookbooks written for English speakers always include glossaries to help us Anglos over the significant hurdle of these exotic names. These lists not only identify local flora and fauna such as the *mabi*, an indigenous tree whose bark is the basis of a fermented drink, but also lay out the local lingo for plants known by other names in other places. As one glances down these lists and discovers that in Puerto Rico the common orange is a *china*, the realization grows that Puerto Rico is a place unto itself. Even the cooking vocabulary of so similar a place as the Dominican Republic, with its *mangú* (plantain puree), *mapuey* (a variety of yam), and *galleticas* (cookies), is easily distinguishable from that of Puerto Rico.

I have been taking this tack—focusing on the food of Puerto Rico as a separate cuisine—because the evidence was there to support it. Puerto Rico does have, arguably, the most fully developed and distinct, most diversely original cuisine in the Americas, but its origins as part of a culturally coherent world empire and its regional ties with other islands, even those with ties to England, France, and the Netherlands, link it with other microcuisines of the region and make it part of a pan-Caribbean kitchen.

To begin with, there are the indigenous ingredients and fish and to some minor degree the lingering Carib-Arawak-Taino traditions for preparing them. But the more remarkable defining traits of the pan-Caribbean cuisine are the dishes that merge continents and hemispheres. All of these influences help give the Caribbean its special culinary texture, but the major force, the dynamo that made the system run and that moved foods and ideas across water and land, was the Spanish empire. The so-called Manila galleons brought back many things to Mexico, including those ivory crucifixes executed by Chinese artists with western teachers in the Philippines that are now part of the baroque sculpture collections of Spanish museums. But these same galleons, returning from Mexico, brought, inter alia, foods and food ideas from Spain itself and from Mexico.

Perhaps no food better exemplifies this circumglobal aspect of Caribbean gastronomy than salt cod. Long before Columbus, this tasty preserved fish of northern waters had spread to Iberia and Italy and made itself at home. Salt cod travels well and was an obvious candidate to be in ships' holds carrying provisions to the colonists of the New World, hungry for familiar tastes and just plain hungry in the early days. The transatlantic cod trade never stopped, and today at food stands on Puerto Rican beaches you will be happy to find salt cod fritters known as *bacalaitos* (from standard Spanish *bacalao*, salt cod). But you will also find salt cod fritters on other islands under other names.

As Elisabeth Lambert Ortiz observes in *The Complete Book of Caribbean Cooking* (1973), *bacalaitos* are members of the same family as *accra* in Trinidad, "stamp and go" in Jamaica, *acrats de morue* in the French islands, and *marinades* in Haiti. Mrs. Ortiz also notes that there are differences among them, and her recipes show these differences. Some have raising agents in their batter (yeast or baking soda), some don't. Seasonings vary from place to place, as do additional ingredients. On Trinidad, fried yeast biscuits called floats are served with cod accra. But the basic idea—salt cod shredded and fried in batter—does seem to descend from a universal archetype, and that archetype seems to be West African, a fritter called *accra*.

The fritter vocabulary of the Caribbean is immense, unprece-

dented in Europe and certainly in Spain where the idea is mostly
limited to desserts. But in the French islands one finds fritters based
on taro, hearts of palm, chayote, breadfruit, pumpkin, black-eyed
peas, minnows, crayfish, and of course salt cod. Jamaica calls its fritters, which are made from black-eyed peas (much like the West African original of these colonial fritters) or soybeans, *akkra*. On Curaçao
they call black-eyed pea fritters *calas*. Are these related to the New
Orleans rice fritters of the same name? I bet they are. And then there
are Trinidadian *phulouri*, split-pea fritters.

Similarly, most islands have their fried leaf-wrapped or dough-
covered pastries—*pasteles, pastelitos, empanadas, empanaditas*, codfish
and ackee patties. Another trans-Caribbean combination is avocado
and salt cod in a salad or canape spread.

And let's not forget *coo-coo*, also known as *funche* and *fungi*. This
is a chameleon of a dish, really a concept—a cooked side dish based
on a starch, usually cornmeal. People with a European background in
cooking will be thinking that this is some sort of cousin of polenta,
but I think we have a case of spontaneous culinary generation here,
sometime around 1600 or so, as maize became available all over the
world and cooks discovered how to use it. Polenta and its Romanian
neighbor, *mamaliga*, are not the archetypes from this perspective but
simply two among many early modern notions of how to serve cornmeal mush. In Barbados they add okra, a sure sign of black African
inspiration. On Jamaica it's served with cod. Grenada, Puerto Rico,
and other places dress up their *coo-coo* with coconut milk. Many places
substitute other starches—flours derived from plantains, breadfruit,
and manioc. Since manioc is native to Brazil and a cassava *coo-coo*
existed among the Indians of Brazil before European colonization,
perhaps this is the original form of *coo-coo/funche/polenta/mamaliga*.
In Brazil it is known as *angu de farinha de mandioca*. Mrs. Ortiz speculates that it might have migrated to the islands of the Caribbean
before Columbus arrived and before Cortés made the spread of maize
around the world a possibility.

I propose the following scenario for the birth of polenta in the
New World: Corn comes to Barbados in the sixteenth century and
falls into the hands of an indigenous cook accustomed to processing
manioc to make cassava flour for *coo-coo*. This culture hero(ine) substitutes cornmeal and eureka! The world has a new dish. Barbados is the
likely place for this since it is the major center for *coo-coo* in the
Caribbean and is the nearest large island to the South American
mainland.

I should also call attention to East Indian and other Asian immigrants to the Caribbean who also contributed to its menu. From them, Martinique gets its various curries (*colombos*). The Chinese brought their own cuisines to the region and adapted them to local conditions, while some local dishes took on a Chinese tinge. *Chicharrones de pollo* are often prepared in a soy sauce marinade, and the characteristically small nuggets of chicken (cut with the bone left in) imply the Chinese chef with his cleaver and the Chinese diner with his chopsticks.

By a similar process of substitution and analogy, the word *tamales* entered the standard culinary jargon of Manila, as did that typical dish of Madrid, tripe with chick-peas. Filipinos, according to our leading authority Reynaldo Alejandro, also eat a rice chicken soup, *arroz caldo con pollo*, which looks to me like the grandchild of Valencian *arroz caldoso* and the first cousin of Puerto Rican *asopao de pollo*, made Asiatic with the addition in Manila of fresh ginger and the fermented fish sauce known locally as *patis*.

When I say that a Filipino rice-chicken soup has its origins in Spain, this may sound perverse. Why should an Asian country, while preserving so much of its indigenous rice-based food heritage, learn a rice recipe from Europeans? But why not? With the arrival of the Spanish in the Philippines in the sixteenth century, the world migration of rice had come full circle. Rice had reached Spain long before, moving westward with the Moors. The rice-growing center of Spain in Valencia developed its own rice cuisine whose classic achievement, *paella*, capitalizes on the limitations of what can be done in a finite space with rice and liquid and a few other solid ingredients. *Paella* is quantum cookery, the triumph over a restricted, inelastic cooking space in which the dry (rice and lima beans) are transformed into the moist and what begins as liquid is totally absorbed.

There is, however, a whole category of equally traditional rice dishes in Valencia that are inclusive where classic *paella* is exclusive, various where *paella* tends toward the monochromatic, and unrestrictive in cooking space and liquid where *paella* is almost dry. These multifarious dishes are the *arroces caldosos*, literally soupy rices. They are rice stews and really ought to be made in flameproof earthenware pots called *pucheros*, but the main point is that the finished dish has a broth with rice and other ingredients floating in it. There is too little broth to call *arroz caldoso* a soup; it's just soupy. Spanish cuisine has many dishes in this category. Almost no one outside Valencia talks about them, but that has not prevented this versatile food idea from cropping up all over the Spanish-speaking world under one name or another, linking Valencia with the *asopaos* of San Juan, and San Juan with similar rice-and-broth dishes in that farthest-flung outpost of the Hispanic kitchen, Manila.

CHAPTER III

THE PHILIPPINES

BEFORE I WENT to the Philippines, I read everything I could get my hands on about Philippine food, and I pestered everyone I met who had ever been there for information. As so often happens when one tries to do research about gastronomy from a distance, my two-pronged inquiry clarified nothing. I boarded the plane for Manila more confused than I would have been had I done nothing at all to prepare for the visit.

The old Asia hands had given me pitying stares. "It's the worst food in Asia," said one seasoned journalist. "I never had a good meal in a Manila restaurant," said the Princeton-minted Orientalist.

They shrugged when I told them that my reason for flying through thirteen time zones and across the international dateline to a sweaty third-world capital where Americans had been held hostage in a recent coup d'état was to investigate the culinary results of four hundred years of Spanish and American colonization in this Southeast Asian republic.

Their position was the gourmet position: Philippine food did not appeal to their taste, as defined by their background in eating and by the criteria for excellence they had evolved, with or without conscious effort, over a lifetime of consuming cuisines outside the Philippines.

My position, insofar as I could divorce myself from the dictates of my palate and from the standards of my own gastronomic past, was that of the impartial ethnographer. It didn't matter to me (or shouldn't, I told myself sternly) if Philippine food tasted like motor oil. I was going as an impartial observer with a lifetime of professional experience in the gauging and preparation of food from other cultures. I would work my way through Philippine food like a whale through krill, tasting as I went, noting ingredients of dishes and their presentation, not in order to give the cuisine a star rating on some ten-point scale that implied a comparison of value with other cuisines, but to see it for what it was in its native context and to analyze how it got that way.

But why the Philippines? Because it was the most remote beachhead of European civilization in the sixteenth century, Spain's entrepôt for the China trade. It was here that East first met West as a modern colonizing force. From the foundation of Manila in 1571 to the Spanish-American War 327 years later, a vigorous Southeast Asian culture lived under the rule of a single European country. The Philippines emerged from this Hispanic yoke as the only Catholic country in Asia. During the early years it had been administered by the Spanish viceroy of Mexico as the colony of a colony, connected to the mother country by a global system of commerce.

When the Spanish colonists first arrived in the Philippines, they encountered an island society that fed itself from fish and rice. Like the rest of Southeast Asia, the Philippines flavored its food with a fermented fish sauce, *patis*, which is a first cousin of Vietnamese *nuoc mam* and Thai *nampla*. Most of the indigenous foods that anyone in 1571 could have found in what is now Thailand and Malaysia and Indochina could have been found in the Philippines. Overseas Chinese were also a factor, and they had brought their food with them.

Even back then, however (indeed, especially back then), it would have been a crude bit of ethnographic generalization to lump together Filipinos and mainland Asians whose cultures had developed separately over centuries. The concept of Filipino culture itself is reductive, a political convenience that gives a Spanish name (the name of a Spanish king, in fact) to an extremely diverse population that speaks many languages even today and finds itself split between Christianity and Islam. It is still possible, however, to talk about the Philippines as a unified collection of historically linked Asian cultures. For centuries this polyglot archipelago was dominated by Spain, then, for the first half of this century, by the United States. But today, as I discovered when I went there, Filipinos are coming out as Filipinos for the first time since the sixteenth century. They had just been biding their time, allowing the small and mostly transient colonial elite to think that it had Europeanized them.

To be sure, the Spanish did transplant their religion with lasting success, and Filipinos continue to be serious Catholics. But the Spanish did not manage to graft their agriculture or their cuisine onto the Filipino rootstock with anything like the completeness they had achieved in Mexico or even in Peru. They could not begin to grow wheat or most vegetables that required a temperate climate, and unlike Mexico, they were not starved for protein and did not lack domestic animals.

The Asian water buffalo, the carabao, supplied the horsepower needed for plowing fields and paddies, and it also supplied the cowpower that produced a rich milk. Coconuts and bananas flourished in the Philippine climate. Chickens and pigs were already available. This was not an economy of scarcity, an ingredient vacuum into which European foods rushed as if unaided. But of course, in over three centuries of symbiosis, there had to be a mixing of traditions, hadn't there?

Any menu, any book on Philippine cooking that I looked at was full of Spanish words. These people eat *lechón* (spit-roasted suckling pig) and *paella*. They use tomatoes and chocolate and maize. The influence of Mexican administration and all those decades of transpacific commerce were not for naught in their cuisine. The national dish of the Philippines, or the one usually given that title, is apparently the offspring of all those influences: *adobo*. The name is Spanish, but the style of cooking it implies in the Philippines is not what you would expect in Madrid or in Acapulco. *Adobo* of chicken starts with a cut-up chicken that is then stewed in soy sauce, vinegar, lots of garlic, and peppercorns. But this is not at all what they mean by *adobo* in other parts of the Hispanic or post-Hispanic world.

In standard Spanish the verb *adobar* means to marinate, and this has been variously interpreted around the world. In metropolitan Spain the basic method involves wine and spices. In Mexico an *adobo* is a medium of chilies, vinegar, garlic, and other seasonings. Often it is a pastelike marinade for meats that will be barbecued. Sometimes it is more liquid, a stewing medium as in the Filipino *adobo*.

One is tempted to stress the similarities here and say all these *adobos* are really flavoring mediums descended from an original concept brought from Spain. But I wonder. Isn't the Mexican *adobo*, with its carefully roasted and milled chilies, really more Mexican than Spanish in taste? Does the vinegar really define the dish?

Certainly if we look at the Philippine dish called, in the predominant indigenous Tagalog language, *adobong hipon sa gata* (shrimp *adobo* in coconut milk), we find ourselves with at least one foot in Malayan tradition. The shrimp are marinated in vinegar, garlic, and pepper, then stewed until the sauce almost evaporates. Coconut milk is then added and reduced.

Philippine food is full of these mixtures and borrowings. Monina A. Mercado acknowledges this in *The Culinary Culture of the Philippines* (edited by Gilda Cordero-Fernando, 1976), where she compares the multifarious food of her country to the "multiracial features of the Filipino—a Chinese-Malayan face, a Spanish name, and an American nickname." In the same essay she points out all the leading foods that have been borrowed: the Chinese egg rolls naturalized as *lumpia,* the Malayan dishes cooked in coconut milk, the American pies, and most of all the myriad dishes with Spanish names and, sometimes, Spanish origins—*paella,* tortilla (the Spanish omelet, not the Mexican corn bread), ox tongue with chick-peas, *caldereta.*

Reading this sensible, learned essay, one expects a kind of cosmopolitan, international feel to the eating experience in the Philippines, but this is not at all how it actually strikes you. On the ground in Manila, the food seems, well, very Philippine. What can this mean?

First of all, I have never encountered a food world more complex and diverse yet more of itself. Almost immediately one begins to ignore the obvious borrowings and the Spanish nomenclature because the food is a harmonious panoply cobbled together from everywhere and transmuted, Filipinized into a comestible alloy with its own special properties. Not everyone has seen this so clearly; perhaps it was not so obviously and easily available to the visitor before the recent boom in Filipino restaurants. Ten years ago, I am reliably told, proper restaurants of the sort that international tourists frequented offered a truly international menu. Filipino food was eaten mostly at home or in very simple restaurants, *turo-turos* (point-points, because they consist of a row of aluminum pots, and you point to what you want to eat) and *carinderías,* somewhat higher up the social ladder but a little too third world to attract the jet set.

Manila is still very much a third-world capital, with ragged squatters and beggars—and armed guards everywhere, even in fast-food restaurants. There is an extremely vivid street cuisine that probably will never move up to restaurant status. As you stroll along you see people selling slices of green mango sauced with anchovy paste. Most notoriously there are *balut,* fertilized duck eggs with extremely duck-like embryos inside them, which are eaten on the run. The list of these street dishes could be extended almost indefinitely, but the newest ones, those that have cropped up since Philippine poverty went into high gear in the eighties (the birth rate is the second highest in Asia after Nepal's), deserve special notice for their desperately ingenious use of previously discarded protein sources and for their sardonic names.

The peripatetic diner in the streets of Manila will encounter

Adidas (chicken feet), *Walkman* (pig's ears), and *IUD* (chicken entrails wrapped around a stick and barbecued). If these don't appeal, almost no one could object to *buko*.

When you see a *buko* seller for the first time, you, as an uninformed newcomer, think this is some local-color act. You have had fresh coconut before, after all. You have watched someone with a machete knock off enough of the husk of the fruit so that you could hold it and drink the water through a straw from a hole punched in the shell. But that was not the Philippines, and *buko* is not just a fresh coconut waiting to be made into a coco loco. It is a fresh young coconut. Its meat is soft and flexible, and has a flavor infinitely superior to the coconut meat we get out of the mature fruit we buy here in the United States.

The Filipino playwright Nonon Padilla spent a year in Manhattan and couldn't believe that people would actually eat the dried-out coconut he found there. "It's really copra," he told me, "not much good for anything but industrial oil production." Padilla now runs the cultural center of the Philippines in Manila, and he can buy the real thing any old time, trucked in from Laguna just south of the city. He is spoiled.

The *buko* man knocks off the husk just like any beach boy in Barbados, but then he shows his real stuff. He lops off the top of the husk, revealing moist white meat, then he takes out a long strip of black, flexible carabao horn and inserts it delicately between meat and shell, completely separating the meat all around and leaving it intact. He inserts a straw through the soft white flesh and hands you the *buko*. You drink the cooling and delicious water, then you eat the meat. It is wonderful and quite unlike other coconut flesh you might have eaten. (*Buko* meat retains a lot of its allure even when baked in a pie with an unsweetened boardlike crust made from soda crackers—*buko* the American way.)

Buko connoisseurship is not complicated or hard to understand, but if anyone wants to bark his gustatory shins up against the essential mystery of Philippine cuisine, he or she should try *sinigang*. *Sinigang* is a lightly sour broth usually flavored with tamarind and garnished with almost anything from pork bits to swamp cabbage. It seems to arrive as a side dish almost anywhere, with *pancit malabon* (Chinese noodles cooked with seafood) or next to a heaping plate of *paella* topped with slices of *lechón* at Lydia's *Lechón* restaurant next to the Baklaran flea market.

In *Sarap* (Mr. & Ms., 1988), the brilliant study of Philippine cuisine she wrote with Edilberto N. Alegre, Doreen G. Fernandez begins by asking, "Why *sinigang?*" Mildly but firmly she states: "Rather than the overworked *adobo* (so often identified as the Philippine stew in foreign cookbooks), *sinigang* seems to me the dish most representative of Filipino taste. We like the lightly boiled, the slightly soured . . ."

Other people do not react with wild enthusiasm to such culinary minimalism. They get off a plane fresh from the big bang of food in Thailand or Indonesia and miss the softer music and the hundreds of nuances of sourness in the dishes of the Philippines. They wondered why Filipinos, with their long history of Mexican administration, were the only major culture in Southeast Asia not to embrace the chili pepper with abandon. Filipinos, it turns out, could embrace almost anything from abroad and make it their own. They could, for example, grate processed cheese into rich carabao-milk ice cream to produce a horrible-sounding but seductive contrast between the unctuously rich sweetness of the ice cream and the tangy chewiness of the cheese—something I tasted in a coconut thatch dining room at the Villa Escudero resort in Laguna, south of Manila.

But Filipinos do not seem to be much attracted by extreme flavors and extreme seasonings. They do eat chili peppers, but not often and usually not immoderately, as they would see it. They have their own standards, quite wonderfully intricate. But you will miss the point if you are not willing to compare in your mind twenty theoretical ways of making fish taste sour. Into such a mental/sensual framework, the whole of world cuisine can fit and end up Filipino.

One of the best ways to savor Philippine food at its most essential is at Christmastime. You might expect that in this former Spanish colony with its strong current commitment to Catholic worship, Christmas dishes would reflect the islands' European heritage more than at other times of the year. But you would be wrong. The Philippine Christmas is, in fact, an emphatic example of the oddness of gastronomic life in this idiosyncratic Asian republic. The religious setting could not be more pious and orthodox, but the special Christmas menu, which occupies a central place in Philippine foodways— more central, if such things can be compared, than Christmas foods in America or Europe—is overwhelmingly indigenous.

For Christmas, Filipinos eat rice cakes in panoramic variety. Many of them are pre-Hispanic, to judge from their mode of preparation, in bamboo tubes and banana-leaf packages. They form a minicuisine served outdoors in a traditional manner as ritualistic in its way as the early morning masses this ambulatory meal customarily follows. In *Sarap*, Doreen Fernandez devotes a special chapter to Philippine Christmas. It is a small masterpiece of culinary ethnography, evoking the atmosphere of the seven dawn "rooster" masses *(misas de gallo)* followed by sweet feasting at the food booths outside church. She quotes a nostalgic Filipina who wrote her from New York, yearning for a green Christmas and "the sweet lavender rice sprouting out of little bamboo tubes, topped by a generous sprinkling of grated coconut meat and brown sugar"—*puto bumbong.*

> She was, of course, remembering the makeshift stalls that sprout like mushrooms the week the dawn masses begin. Along the streets leading to the churches, and especially in the patios—at Las Piñas, under an ancient tree lit by a galaxy of lanterns—are built lean-tos made from bamboo poles and roofed with old blankets or coconut leaves, with a *dulang* [low table for dining] in front serving as a counter. From them cooking smells tantalize the churchgoers and render children impatient to get through mass.
>
> Not only is there *puto bumbong* made from violet-colored *pirurutung* rice, but also *bibingka* [rice cake], flat and soft and fragrant in banana leaves a mite singed by the charcoal fire above and below. Sometimes these have a bit of native [carabao milk] cheese on them or a sliver of salted egg—but always they come with freshly grated coconut meat for sprinkling on the hot, moist, and golden cake. With it is served a cup of hot tea or *salabat* [ginger tea], ambrosia on a cold morning.

These are only a few of the standard Christmas dishes in the Philippines. Ms. Fernandez also mentions sweetened *suman*, glutinous white rice steamed in a banana leaf or palm-leaf package and a so-called tamal filled with rice, coconut milk, ground roast peanuts, achiote, and slivers of meat, all wrapped in banana leaves or corn husks, depending on the region.

Indeed, each Philippine region seems to have come up with its own menu of Christmas delicacies, centering on rice but also including ham and other European-style Yule foods.

Still, the central dishes—*puto bumbong, bibingka,* and *salabat*—are almost aggressively non-European, as if the pious were saying to the Church: You can have my soul, but my body stays Filipino. Or should we see this panoply of Asian dishes as a particularly heartfelt tribute of native treasures for the naturalized god?

Anyone interested in trying *puto bumbong* and *bibingka* on a normal day will find them at the cafe attached to Manila's most elegant restaurant, Via Mare. This is Glenda Barretto's home base, but she is making an even grander and more sophisticated statement about Filipino food in her Nielson Tower restaurant at the other end of the fashionable Makati district. Makati is today a spectacle of high rises, but it was once the site of Manila's airport, whose runways are now Makati's thoroughfares, and Ms. Barretto has converted its control tower into an art deco laboratory for evolving a native nouvelle cuisine.

Ms. Barretto's cooking experience ranges from classic European food to the cutting-edge kitchens of Paul Bocuse and Fredy Girardet. When Imelda Marcos would return to Manila from a trip to New York, she used to call Ms. Barretto and describe a dish she'd had at La Côte Basque, and Ms. Barretto would reproduce it through educated guessing in the private presidential kitchen at Malacañang Palace.

Her menu at the Nielson Tower, written in Spanish and English, reflects this cosmopolitanism, but even its most ostensibly classic Spanish dishes have a local tinge: Fried bananas garnish the *lengua estofada* (braised ox tongue), the *paella* has a fluffy egg topping, and the purely indigenous items have been raised to new heights of delicacy.

At the Nielson Tower, *balut* is served out of the shell under puff pastry, and Ms. Barretto buys the duck eggs a day or too younger than usual so that the embryo is not so visibly a duck. Her *kare-kare* (oxtail stew) comes with a fermented shrimp sauce and toasted *adobo* flakes. In her version of *bangus* belly, the prized delicate fish's midsection is wrapped in a leaf and presented in cylindrical form. She makes a sabayon of mango flavored with *ilang-ilang*, the plant essence used in perfume making, and garnishes the dish with fried *sampaguitas*, the highly aromatic little white flowers sold everywhere in the country in the form of leis.

"I'm trying to refine our cuisine," she says, "to lighten it and to work on its presentation. For chicken *adobo*, I debone the chicken and roll and wrap it in cheesecloth. Then I braise it and serve it sliced. The sauce is lighter because I use light soy sauce. I've done it in red wine too."

Despite all the deliberate emulation of modish French models, which extends to decorative fans of sliced fruit, Ms. Barretto never loses sight of the cuisine she began with (those fans are cut from green mango). And to an outsider, at least, she fits smoothly into the Filipino food boom that is happening all around Manila, but especially in the raffish district of Ermita.

Waiters and hostesses in embroidered Filipino traditional shirts and dresses preside over a menu of regional dishes at Kamayan, where no utensils are provided. The idea is to scoop up the food from its banana leaf-covered plate with a rice ball—by hand. A line of sinks on one wall is for cleaning up afterward. At Pinausukan there is traditional seafood and deep-fried banana buds. At Barrio Fiesta they serve pork *paksiw*, cooked in vinegar with salt, ginger, and garlic.

At Ang Bistro Sa Remedios in the nearby Malate district the menu is entirely in Tagalog and restricts itself to the dishes of the gastronomically celebrated Pampanga region north of Manila. There is eel cooked in coconut milk, flavored with chili and *kamias* (a sour fruit), stuffed frog, and much more.

This big-city bistro is not a cunning resuscitation of vanished country fixin's. I was able to eat some of the same dishes in Everybody's Cafe, a big, cheerful place on the MacArthur Highway just outside San Fernando, the provincial capital of Pampanga. Like many Filipino restaurants, this one preserves the informality of *turo-turo* service in a more dignified setting. The food is arrayed in a line at a counter where guests enter and point to what they want, just as they would point at the aluminum pots in an outdoor *turo-turo* place.

The proprietress, Carmen N. Santos, is on hand to explain the dishes, which include crickets from the rice paddies (cooked *adobo* style and then deep-fried), snipe *adobo* (with head and beak), and *chicharrón bulaklat*, deep-fried sections of the large intestine of the pig that have exploded into little blooms (*bulaklat* means flower).

On another day trip out of Manila I got a taste of pre-Hispanic cuisine at Villa Escudero. The proprietor, Ado Escudero, presided over an open fire and demonstrated the ancient method of braising inside a bamboo tube containing coconut water.

I have been running through this list of indigenous dishes I ate in the Philippines to stress how completely and variously the non-European foodways of the country have survived four centuries of colonization. But the overlords from Spain and Mexico did leave vestiges of their dominion in the Philippine kitchen, just as they left traces of their language in popular speech (*kumusta* is a standard greeting); these traces survive even when only a tiny senescent elite continues to speak Spanish.

Dozens of ingredients now popular in the Philippines came in with the Spanish and stayed, especially Mexican ingredients such as corn, tomatoes, avocados, achiote (*achuete* in the Philippines), and jicama. Dishes such as *caldereta* (goat stew), Spanish omelets, and *bacalao a la vizcaína* (Basque-style salt cod) are common. And some basic techniques seem to have been imported, notably frying and that combination of sautéing and simmering called *gisar* in Tagalog, from the Spanish word for stew, *guisar*.

These influences are not negligible, but they are surprisingly peripheral to the way Filipinos eat, more peripheral than most Filipinos are ready to admit. There is no obvious explanation for why people who eat a remarkably local and unique array of dishes every day should think that they are part of a seriously mixed culinary tradition such as exists in Mexico and elsewhere in Latin America or in Africa and the United States, not to mention Western Europe. But it is possible to point to some probable causes for the confusion.

The authentically Spanish dishes in the Philippines are prestige dishes brought in by a mostly transient ruling class, and those dishes often involve expensive ingredients such as beef. In the Philippines, authentically Spanish food is frequently fancy food or holiday food, while, as Doreen Fernandez points out, the other major foreign influence came in from the street and was easily absorbed everywhere. I mean Chinese food, which was truly naturalized. For example, fried rice became simplified and universalized as the garlic rice of the Filipino breakfast table.

But Spanish food did not mix or spread in the same way to the overwhelmingly Asian population of the islands. I say this fully aware that most Philippine food experts believe that many foods from Spain and Mexico have been "adapted" by the local genius. There is, for instance, *bringhe*, assertedly adapted from *paella* by the substitution of coconut milk for olive oil and saffron. And, of course, there is the most important case of all, *adobo*, the so-called national dish supposedly descended from Spanish and Mexican dishes of the same or similar names.

To an outsider these "new" dishes do not look like adaptations. All the essential ingredients for *bringhe* were present in the Philippines before Magellan. Ditto for *adobo* and for the Filipino *tamal*. What is new here is the name for the dish or, in the case of *bringhe*, the notion that it is somehow based on *paella*. This hypothesis must have originated with Spanish colonists who naturally made connections between *bringhe* or other native Filipino dishes and ones they remembered from Spain. When a Spaniard came upon chicken and pork cooked in vinegar, soy sauce, and garlic, it reminded him of a Spanish *adobo* cooked in a wine marinade, a dish whose name he had previously grafted on a chili-laden marinade in Mexico.

Similarly, I theorize, when the Spanish reached the shores of Manila Bay, they saw leaf-wrapped, steamed rice cakes filled with meat strips and other oddments. These they called *tamales,* by analogy to what they knew from their prior experience in Mexico. And a big festive dish in which rice was cooked with a spectrum of foods became *paella* or, if it kept its old name *bringhe,* it was viewed as a local variation of the more authentic *paellas* seen in the big house of the Spanish plantation owner.

This is not a theory that can be proved with hard evidence. At least I know of no documents in which a sixteenth-century Spanish friar or chronicler says he came upon a local cook making something that reminded him of *tamales* or *adobos* from back East. But there is certainly no good reason, in the face of the thriving and vigorously independent cuisine of the Philippines that has survived uncontaminated through the centuries, to assume that anything devolved from Spanish cooking just because it has a Spanish or Mexican name—especially when all crucial ingredients for the supposedly adapted dishes were in place before Magellan.

Even ingredients that were imported by the Spanish have been completely Filipinized. We might have expected, when corn came in from Mexico, that the myriad Mexican corn recipes would have come with it, but instead of adopting this ready-made cuisine of corn *tortillas* and *tamales,* Filipinos worked corn into their own traditional food syntax. In Cebu, the only part of the country where corn is preferred to rice, the corn kernels are ground to resemble rice and then are steamed as if they were rice. *Ginataang mais,* corn steamed in coconut milk, is another example of how the Filipino cook completely de-Mexicanized corn.

Another factor that argues for Filipino originality here is the absence of intermediate steps. Take the case of *adobo.* Full-blown Filipino *adobo* stands by itself, fully formed and always distinct from the *"adobo"* dishes of Mexico and Spain. But where is the transitional Mexican-Filipino *adobo* with hot chili paste, soy sauce, and vinegar? Where is the Hispano-Filipino *adobo* with wine in the cooking liquid? It exists only in Glenda Barretto's kitchen where she is deliberately manipulating Filipino *adobo* with knowledge of Spanish cookery.

Perhaps the best way to think about the Spanish cloak of words disguising the blatant originality of Filipino food is to look at the great Filipino houses of the colonial period. As Fernando N. Zialcita and Martin I. Tinio, Jr., make clear in *Philippine Ancestral Houses* (Manila: GCF Books, 1980), the great mansions of the colonists had a stone exterior at street level to make them look Spanish. But these were not bearing walls. The real structure of these two-storey houses was a traditional Filipino bamboo post-and-beam skeleton inside the stone skirt and rising visibly above it on the second storey, topped with a palm thatch roof. Such essentially traditional structures would withstand the frequent earthquakes and let air flow in to combat the tropical heat. The Spanish stone at ground level was a skin that often cracked and fell away when the earth shook. The Filipino underpinnings within survived, like the superficially hispanified Filipino cuisine.

For Filipino *tamales* and *paella* and *adobo*, the cloak of names covers an indigenous reality. The rest of the cuisine—the huge repertory of dishes with Tagalog and other Philippine-language names—is obviously a thing unto itself, with a huge indigenous vocabulary of food names and ideas that even Filipinos, isolated from one another by their many local languages and their island geography, are just beginning to learn about in their multifarious totality.

CHAPTER IV

THE SPANISH MAIN

ON THE BEACH at Cartagena, Colombia, I thought about the peculiar business of black Americans and watermelons. Black women walked up and down the sand with flat baskets of delicious cut fruit on their heads—mangoes, papayas and, yes, watermelon. Much ostensibly genial racist humor revolves around blacks and their allegedly ravenous attachment to watermelons. I'm not trying to say that blacks don't like watermelons. Why shouldn't they? Indeed, food history suggests that they have a better reason than the rest of us for being attached to watermelons. Watermelons are roots food, so to speak, for blacks all over this hemisphere because watermelons are indigenous to West Africa. When black slaves arrived in Brazil, Jamaica, and Charleston, they brought watermelons with them. Cartagena was a major slave area, and the women I saw selling watermelon there are the *palenqueras,* direct descendants of slaves who settled there when Cartagena was the main port of the Spanish Main— Cartagena de Indias, a massively fortified warehouse for the commerce of the Americas.

What we call the Spanish Main is the mainland of the Caribbean coast of South America. The Spanish called it Tierra Firme in the sixteenth century to distinguish it from the islands of the West Indies and from Nueva España (the New Spain of Mexico and Central America). Cartagena was settled in 1533, named after the port in southeast Spain that was named New Carthage by Hasdrubal in ancient times.

In its heyday, Cartagena de Indias (hereinafter simply Cartagena) was a swashbuckling place captured briefly by Sir Francis Drake. It was the pearl of the vast new Spanish colonial state that came to be called New Granada and that then devolved, during the sterterous process of liberation in the early nineteenth century, into the modern countries of Venezuela, Ecuador, Colombia, and Panama. Because of this outcome, the country we call Colombia has two coasts, a Caribbean and a Pacific, seemingly bisected by the Panamanian isthmus where it abuts South America. This is not the only geographic obstacle to the physical unification of modern Colombia. The Andes, as well as various tropical forest regions and a still uninviting road system, have divided the country into distinct isolated regions.

Cartagena and the other *costeño* cities of the Caribbean coast have retained much of the architecture and spirit of their colonial origins through almost five centuries. Cartagena today is an overwhelmingly black city with its own cuisine based on African and local ingredients, Spanish cooking methods, and Spanish ingredients. This Ibero-African mixing happened in the Caribbean islands and in northeast Brazil. And there are parallel examples of so-called Creole cooking in the non-Spanish Antilles and even in New Orleans and the rest of the U.S. South. But Cartagena (and in its different way, northeast Brazil, see page 72) crystallizes the African adaptation to the Spanish-American empire. Perhaps it is simply a matter of population and geography—a large black population evolving a new way of life under Spanish dominion but without significant intermarriage, on the shore of a large land mass, not an island. Conditions were ideal for Cartagenans and other blacks on that warm coast to work out their own culinary identity, substituting African foods in Spanish recipes they learned from their masters and adapting local foods to the traditions of Spanish and African cooking.

It goes without saying that seafood is the dominant source of animal protein on the Caribbean coast of Colombia, but the more important basic element of the cuisine of Cartagena—I am tempted to call it a staple—is the coconut. Everywhere you go there are producing trees. On the beach people drink the sweet clear liquid (*agua dulce*) right through a punctured coconut eye. There are dozens of coconut recipes in Teresita Roman de Zurek's classic *Cartagena de Indias en la Olla* (Gamma, 1987; this is the revised edition, which is far superior to earlier Spanish editions and the clumsy English translation). There are desserts of every description—puddings, cakes, candies. There is soup. There is chicken with coconut. But the standard, the most characteristic dish of Cartagena is rice cooked in coconut milk, *arroz con coco.*

The basic recipe is a brilliantly simple idea once you have laboriously grated and squeezed out the six cups of coconut milk from the coconut meat. Then you are in effect simply substituting coconut milk for the water you might normally use to cook rice. The result is, of course, different. The coconut milk turns caramel brown and is absorbed by the rice, which takes on a delicate coconut fragrance and a richness of texture. The cholesterol content of *arroz con coco* does not recommend it to first-world peoples with life spans long enough to make them concerned about coronary disease. No doubt this caveat should apply to modern Cartagenans as well, but it does not seem to prevent them from indulging in *arroz con coco* as a side dish with meat, poultry, grilled fish, or fish stewed with plantain, manioc, yam, and potato in the bouillabaisse of the Caribbean, here called *sancocho. Arroz con coco* even appears as a dessert with chocolate.

Arroz con coco is not only ubiquitous, it is a minicuisine, including many variations. Even a brief visit to Cartagena will turn up more than one. In the simplest sort of palm-thatched restaurant called La Caimana in the black fishing village of La Boquilla, a short drive over the sand from Cartagena's Rafael Nuñez International Airport, I watched local fishermen row out through the surf to retrieve their nets while I ate a classic *costeño* shore dinner: grilled red snapper steak, *patacones* (flattened, fried slices of green plantain), French fries, home-made hot sauce, and *arroz con coco y pasas,* coconut rice with raisins.

Roman de Zurek also lists *arroz con coco* with pumpkin, manioc, ripe plantains, black-eyed peas, shrimp, cheese, or salt beef; there is also *con coco aguado* (swimming in thick coconut milk) and, most intriguing of all, *con coco frito.* This is a final refinement of coconut milk cookery whose only parallel known to me is a West Sumatran dish called *rendang,* in which water buffalo is cooked for a long time in highly spiced thick coconut milk until the meat is coated with a dark brown residue of the sauce. For *arroz con coco frito* in Cartagena, something similar happens. The coconut milk is boiled until it appears to caramelize, and browned solid matter sinks to the bottom of the pan. Then the rice is added and cooked in the "fried" coconut milk, which has by then lost its whiteness and turned to a transparent oil.

For the itinerant gastroethnographer this is not only a treat but food for thought. How did coconut milk come to preoccupy the cooks of Colombia's Caribbean coast? For that matter, how did coconut get there? Was it native to those shores? Did slaves bring viable coconuts, the world's largest seeds, from West Africa to their new homes in this hemisphere? In general, this is a good question without a good answer. In the enormously detailed *Perennial Edible Fruits of the Tropics* (USDA Agriculture Handbook No. 642, 1987), Franklin W. Martin et al. give a terse, if not actually evasive answer. They say, in a word, that the origin of *Cocos nucifera L.* is "pantropic."

That certainly describes the status quo. By one estimate there are 600 million coconut palms distributed around the world, mostly in warm places. But where did this all start? The Indo-Pacific is an attractive choice, given the evidence: fossil coconuts in New Zealand, a rich panoply of coconut-specific parasites in Southeast Asia, and records of coconuts in India going back three thousand years. In 1280, Marco Polo reported seeing coconuts in Sumatra and in India. Vasco da Gama may be the first person to mention a non-Asian coconut. He sighted some in Mozambique in 1498, which leads to two speculations. First, that *C. nucifera* was brought to East Africa by Arab spice traders. Second, that the Portuguese introduced the plant to West Africa and Brazil after 1500, taking its name, *coco*, from the Portuguese word for monkey, supposedly because of its eye pattern and brown furry skin. On the other hand, there is no good reason to think the coconut had not been grown in West Africa for eons, especially since it plays a fundamental role in West Africa and did from the earliest days of colonial contact.

But how did this invaluable seed get to the Caribbean and non-Portuguese South America, including Cartagena? Frederic Rosengarten, Jr., states in *The Book of Edible Nuts* that early Spanish explorers found coconuts growing in Panama but that no indigenous people were eating them; and that the Spanish introduced coconuts to their American empire in the early 1500s. There is also the theory of oceanic migration in which prevailing currents transport viable coconuts across the Pacific and wash them up on idyllic New World beaches where they germinate under favoring suns.

None of this conjecture much impressed Thomas H. Everett. In his authoritative *Encyclopedia of Horticulture,* he takes a dim view of the oceanic migration theory, pointing to the paucity of recorded instances "of the successful establishment and spontaneous development of washed-up nuts into trees" and citing saline water in beach soil and the ravaging of young shoots by crabs as the chief deterrents to such a pattern of transmission. Everett also states that no "truly wild" coconut palm has ever been found anywhere, and he quotes the British palm authority E. J. H. Corner, who pronounced unequivocally that "there is no island or shore where its presence is not due directly or indirectly to its having been planted by man."

Well, then, which men brought *C. nucifera* to South America? For me, the evidence of culinary practice, both in Colombia and in northeast Brazil, points most suggestively toward introduction by the Spanish and the Portuguese as part of the process of colonization in an economy based on slaves imported from West Africa. Two facts are not in doubt: Both the Colombian Caribbean coast and northeast Brazil were and are centers of transplanted West Africans, and both areas also continue to base much of their traditional cooking on coconut milk, a predilection not shared by contiguous centers of non-black African heritage on the South American coast, even places of equally old colonization such as Venezuela. Furthermore, a notable number of the dishes of Cartagena and northeast Brazil are almost exact equivalents of dishes popular in modern West Africa. Brazil's rice porridge cooked in coconut milk is called *acaca*, the name of an identical dish in Benin and Nigeria. Cartagena-style coconut rice is common in West Africa and northeast Brazil.

This set of facts can be explained in several ways:

1. Slaves with a common coconut-cooking heritage in West Africa were distributed among Spanish and Portuguese colonies and found coconuts already there.

2. These same slaves knew nothing of the coconut until they found it in the New World and experimented with its cultivation and use in cooking. Their fabulous success led eventually to the export of the coconut and coconut recipes to Africa along with other useful American plants such as manioc and the peanut, which are now crucial to African agriculture and diet.

3. Coconut-wise slaves and/or their masters brought the coconut to the Americas, as they did okra and watermelon. This last scenario makes the most sense to me, especially if it includes Arab traders and slavers as the coconut emissaries from East to West Africa at some point during the fifteenth century or even earlier. If they brought the coconut to Mozambique, why not elsewhere when they were much more established on the African continent and much earlier than the Portuguese or the Spanish? This timetable allows for the establishment of mature trees in West Africa and for the creation of dishes (or were they also brought in by the Arabs?) before the American slave trade began.

But even if this theory is wrong and the slaves in Cartagena and Bahia either applied earlier knowledge to indigenous coconuts or invented coconut dishes in the New World, we can certainly say thanks to them as we eat our *arroz con coco*—thanks for sponsoring if not actually inventing this and all other delicious coconut dishes that now grace the tables of postcolonial South America's northern coasts.

It is the Spanish, however, who deserve credit for inventing *bocadillo,* the food Colombians miss most when they are away from home. In English we have to settle for saying guava paste. We don't eat much guava paste, of course, but it is ubiquitous as a dessert sweet with white cheese at meals all over the Caribbean and in Mexico. One of many such fruit pastes sold in Spanish-speaking markets everywhere, guava paste probably strikes most people not born to it as overly sweet. But it commands our attention for two reasons: It is a pure case of the most important mechanism of creative evolution in culinary history, the substitution of one ingredient for another, and an enormous amount of fascinating information is available to show exactly how this substitution in rural Colombia of native guava for Old World quince led to a home-grown food-craft industry whose variation on an age-old theme is now the edible emblem of a culture.

The guava *(Psidium guajava L.)* is an aggressive, commonplace, small tree of tropical America. A member of the myrtle family *(Myrtaceae)*, which also includes nutmeg, allspice, cinnamon, clove, eucalyptus, and the feijoa, the guava produces a round, ovoid, or pear-shaped fruit in the general size range of the apple. The color of its rind develops from green to yellow. The flesh is aromatic and ranges in color from white to deep pink or salmon-red, with a great many small, hard, kidney-shaped seeds in the center. At the end opposite the stem is a little black "crown" that will remind you of a medlar if you've ever seen one. The guava is high in vitamin C and in pectin, the natural substance that makes jelly gel. By the time the Spanish noticed the guava, it was well established from Mexico to Peru. The name guava seems to derive from a word in use by the indigenous Tainos of Hispaniola. The first real account of the plant was by Gonzalo Hernández de Oviedo in his *Natural History of the Indies* (1526). He does not seem to have tasted a guava but reported that the best ones he'd seen were in the area of the isthmus of Darien (Panama) and that people accustomed to guavas preferred it to the apple.

Although it is hard to imagine how anyone could want to compare the apple and the guava, perhaps shape was the main consideration. This seems to have been the case in ancient Europe with the apple and the quince—"apples" in ancient literature may actually be quinces and true apples just late arrivals on the European horticultural scene that usurped the quince's Latin name *(malum).* At any rate, the same word was classically applied to a whole range of fruit, and we can hardly point fingers at the early Spanish amateur botanizers for picking a familiar fruit as a model to help identify an exotic fruit.

Spanish colonists definitely had no trouble growing the guava. Livestock and birds spread the seeds, and the plant behaves like a weed on cleared, plowed ground. Tropical farmers fight a constant battle to keep guava saplings from taking over their fields. So, with the importation of sugarcane around 1550, the manufacture of guava paste was, it now seems, inevitable.

I say inevitable because the Spanish came to the New World with a taste for sweet fruit pastes instilled in them from childhood. Quince paste, literally quince meat (*carne de membrillo*), is still a common dessert in Spain today, a solid jelly-cake sold in flat tins. This is a survival of a standard Spanish dish that came in with the Moors from North Africa in the low Middle Ages.

Quince paste is a standard part of Near Eastern cuisine today. In *A New Book of Middle Eastern Food* (1985), Claudia Roden recommends serving it with coffee, and she mentions a variant in which chopped or halved blanched almonds are spread between two layers of hot quince paste, creating a sort of sandwich that may be the visual ancestor of the Colombian *bocadillo*. But I am anticipating my story. By mid-sixteenth century Spanish settlers had created the ideal setting for a guava paste industry. They had disturbed the ground of the primeval tropical forest with plows and then introduced cattle who ate wild guavas and dispersed their seed in pastures with their dung, aiding the traditional guava-proliferating efforts of frugivorous birds, bats and, with Darwin as our witness, Galapagos turtles. Soon some of those pastures were overrun with guavas and became guava thickets, called *guayabales* in Spanish.

These volunteer groves sprang up in the vicinity of sugar mills. To the quince-paste-hungry Spaniard, here was the hand of Providence: Guava paste, the result, was impossible before the arrival of Old World sugar; it was a new food in a region where guavas had been domesticated for millennia (according to archeological evidence, preserved fruit dated to 2500 B.C. in coastal Peru).

Exploitation of the guava reached its zenith deep in the interior of Colombia in the mountainous *departamento* of Santander. Two hundred commercial producers of paste were active in the area in 1970, shortly before the intrepid Klaus J. Meyer-Arendt began looking into the subject for his M.A. thesis in geography and anthropology at Louisiana State University and Agricultural and Mechanical College. This unpublished study, *The Guava in the Upper Suarez Basin of Southern Santander and Adjacent Boyaca, Colombia: A Geographical Perspective*, paints an unforgettable picture of a regional food in every conceivable aspect, from the horticultural to the technological, social and historical.

The Santander guava industry, reports Meyer-Arendt, produces not only paste, jams, and jellies but also *manjarblanco,* a caramelized paste made of guavas, sugar, and milk, pastries filled with guava paste, *puche* (a marmalade and milk concoction), an array of candies, candied guava shells in syrup, juices, yogurts, and wines. But paste is the jewel in this particular crown, and its manufacture has traditionally centered in the town of Velez, once a trading center for the aboriginal Chibchas, then the second city founded in the area by the Spanish, then a backwater of provincial obscurity after trade shifted elsewhere. Only recently has Velez emerged from its isolation since paved roads have brought it into contact with the rest of the country. But Velez is still not to be found on many maps.

Nevertheless, this highland boondock of mestizo peasantry has developed a very sophisticated, very sweet guava paste based on the color difference between the fruit's two leading varieties and celebrated throughout Colombia. The trademark Veleño *bocadillos* are, according to Meyer-Arendt, "made of pink guava paste coated on the top and bottom with white guava paste . . . formed into a small rectangle, and wrapped in the leaves of the bijao plant. (These long, wide, flat, and lightly waxy leaves are used all over the American tropics for wrapping food, after they've been boiled and dried. Bijao is the name given to two plants, the wild plantain, *Heliconia bijai,* found in Boyaca, and *Calathea lutea,* which is common in the upper Suarez Valley and therefore is the dominant wrapping material in Velez.) The current harlequin form of the Veleño *bocadillo* is said to have been invented in 1925 by Doña Maria de Tellez in a small family factory. In those days *bocadillos* were made with the crude, locally produced raw sugar called *panela.* Nowadays refined sugar trucked in from the south is the overwhelming choice. Plastic wrap is replacing bijao leaves, and containers in thick plastic and clay printed with neo-Chibchan motifs are ever more common, according to Meyer-Arendt.

It would be pretentious for me to lament the passing of bijao-wrapped Veleño *bocadillos* since I obviously never had the chance to earn nostalgia for them through actual experience. But Meyer-Arendt does make me vicariously wistful for a hand-stirred, *panela-*based *bocadillo* from the Tellez factory. And he makes me feel guilty for having taken guava jelly for granted as a child in the forties when it seems to have been widely available during shortages of other fruit conserves. According to Jane Grigson, this was the case in England where the abundance of South African guava jelly in wartime made most people avoid it after local fruit came back into production.

Ms. Grigson did not share this aversion to guavas and extolled the room-filling fragrance of the cooking fruit in *Jane Grigson's Fruit Book* (1982). She also quoted, without attribution, the most beautiful description of the exterior of the guava I have ever seen, a French couplet by someone who may have experienced the fruit in his youth on the French colony of Réunion in the Indian Ocean, where guavas were introduced in the nineteenth century. He wrote:

> *C'est trop peu que des fleurs: je veux t'offrir encore*
> *Goyave au court duvet que le safran colore.*
> (Flowers just won't do. I want to give you guava, too; guava covered with short down, painted with saffron.)

Whoever the poet was, his sensuous passion for guavas would come as no surprise to a Colombian, for in this violent country where the Andes slope down to the Caribbean, this guava, which began its popularity here as a quick local fix for the Spanish settlers' quince nostalgia, has turned into a special Colombian enthusiasm rivaled only by the coconut. Perhaps the Colombian flag should be redesigned to represent the favorite fruits of its main ethnic groups. The guava would be on one side as an emblem of Spanish settlement (with a buried suggestion of all-but-vanished indigenous peoples, Chibchas and other Indians who knew the guava long before anyone thought it resembled a quince), and on the other side a coconut palm would rise, symbol of the adaptation of African slaves to life in the Hispanic New World.

CHAPTER V

NORTHEAST BRAZIL

THE PORTUGUESE did not settle Brazil by accident. As relative latecomers to American colonization, it was all they could wrest from the entrenched Spanish. No precious metals lured them to this immense wilderness. They came to settle and to command immense plantations. Slaves shipped across the Atlantic from West Africa did the physical work in the fields of the earliest fully settled part of the country, the northeastern state of Bahia. Its main city, Salvador, remains an outpost of African life in South America. Its cuisine, famous around the world, shows the influence of Portuguese ideas, of the indigenous Tupis, and of local ingredients (manioc, cashew), but it is primarily African in flavor and in many other details.

In Salvador one thinks about slavery every minute. One tastes it and smells it. What had seemed almost a myth of a distant bad past turns real and near. Centuries melt away in the heat of the palm oil bubbling on every street corner. The women cooking fritters in those big iron pots could just as well be in Nigeria or Ghana today, or in those same places in the sixteenth century. Or even long before.

They are continuing the lost history of African food whose origins stretch back beyond the Middle Ages. In Bahia it is easy to begin speculating about early Arab trade routes across Africa and about West African dishes built on very old Asian or Egyptian models and somewhat more recently made more various with manioc and sweet potatoes brought eastward in empty slave ships returning for more human cargo.

When I was in the brightly painted square called Largo Pelourinho in the raffish old section of Salvador, black women in gauzy white dresses were singing "Happy Birthday" in Portuguese in the colonial church. They were celebrating the 441st anniversary of the founding of the city, which was the first Portuguese settlement in Brazil. But this was no routine commemoration of the dawn of a now-vanished empire. It had a special flavor and complexity about it

since Largo Pelourinho is literally the Place of the Pillory, the whip-
ping post where African slaves once were publicly punished. The
church, with its planked, perspectively painted ceiling is A Igreja dos
Pretos, the church of the blacks. The singing women wore the costume
of *candomble*, the African cult widely practiced in a city notable for
its creative continuation of its West African slave heritage, most tangi-
bly in its famous food.

The cuisine of Bahia mixes Portuguese, Amazonian, and African
foods and food ideas deliciously but perhaps dangerously. It is preemi-
nently a cuisine based on tropical oils, palm oil and coconut oil, which
zealots in the fight against heart disease have lately been indicting as
coronary culprits lurking in our packaged baked goods.

Brazil's leading novelist, Jorge Amado describes Bahia's *moquecas*
and *vatapas* with zest in his writing, especially in his best-known book,
Dona Flor and Her Two Husbands. Dona Flor, as readers and the many
more millions who saw the film starring Sonia Braga in the title role
know, is a cooking teacher in Bahia specializing in Bahian dishes. For
me the most memorable of her culinary lessons in the film was the one
in which she demonstrated how to prepare a crab dish flavored with
dendê oil.

Dendê is the most common Brazilian name for palm oil, the oil
pressed from the fleshy part of the fruit of the West African oil palm
(*Elaeis guineensis*). Its color is a deep red-yellow, and most of the
popular Brazilian food, especially Bahian food, would be emasculated
without its powerful aroma and flavor. In a story not short on sensual-
ity, *Dona Flor*'s most prurient moment is the image of Flor's first
husband, the playboy, not the pharmacist, emerging from a bout with
her crab dish, his teeth dripping yellow from *dendê*.

Before I went to Brazil I tried cooking with *dendê* myself. I had
probably eaten it before in Brazilian restaurants in New York, but I
had never known for sure what its specific taste was, had never seen
it separate from other food, and so I bought a bottle at that ware-filled
little emporium, International Latin American Products, at 142 West
46th Street, that briefly stepped into the void left by the disappear-
ance of Casa Moneo before succumbing to the urban renewal of the
Times Square area.

Here, I thought, was a rare chance to get to the bottom of a
cuisine I barely knew. *Dendê* oil, by all accounts, was the heart and
soul of one of the hemisphere's great postcolonial food cultures. Perhaps the best way to approach this potent liquid was to taste it plain,
right from the bottle.

I snapped off the metal cap with a bottle opener and tilted it toward my mouth. It flowed with a grand viscous languor. Finally, a few drops fell into my mouth, and I ran them around my tongue. I was underwhelmed. There was something there, but it was too subtle to have launched a whole cuisine. Still, what did I expect? I didn't much like olive oil neat either. Cooking media required food to show their stuff.

I heated some *dendê* oil in a skillet with an equal amount of corn oil (Brazilian recipes seemed to do the same kind of mixing of media) and proceeded to fry a few chicken legs. In a short time, their skin turned yellow and the kitchen filled with a heavy aroma. After a few minutes the drumsticks were cooked and I ate them. They had acquired a somewhat more intense degree of the same flavor I had detected when I quaffed *dendê* oil from the bottle, but this was still small beer, not worth flying down to Rio for.

The morning after, I saw the light. Not wanting to throw out the oil left from the past night's experiment and wanting even less to clean the skillet before breakfast, I decided to reheat that complicated residue of *dendê*, corn oil, and chicken fat, and fry bread in it.

Nirvana. Valhalla. Fat City.

But Dona Flor had been there before me, as I discovered while looking more analytically at some Bahian recipes, which almost always incorporated the *dendê* oil used in cooking as part of a sauce, often a sauce given extra richness and body with coconut milk.

So much for aesthetics; now a bit of *dendê*-oriented gastroethnogeography.

Dendê oil came to Bahia with slaves who were transported from West Africa by the Portuguese to work the sugar plantations. They must have brought along seeds for *E. guineensis* or cuttings. At any rate, a plant crucial to the cuisine of West Africa crossed the Atlantic and enabled Yoruba or Hausa slaves to recreate the essential smell and taste of their homeland in the New World.

Palm oil continues to be the basic cooking medium of West Africa, and the connections between Bahian and West African dishes is a rich potential area of culinary research that could link two continents in a strong material way. Indeed, the food pathways between Africa and the New World spread much farther than Bahia, to the Caribbean, to Mexico, to New Orleans, and to the whole eastern United States. Some day someone will trace all these connections and show in detail how an African cuisine radiated through the Americas in the sixteenth and seventeenth centuries and merged with the cuisines of Europe, America, and Asia, yielding different dishes from place to place but leaving a strong trace of black Africa everywhere.

Even where *dendê* oil is not available, people of African heritage have found ways of coloring their cooking oils red to resemble it. The standard substitute for *dendê* advised by cookbook authors is any other vegetable oil colored with paprika. All over the Caribbean, however, there is a red oil valued for itself but which must have begun as an ersatz *dendê*. This is *annatto* oil or *annatto* lard, the cooking fat tinted red when heated with the seeds of the New World tree *Bixa orellana,* known in commerce as *annatto* or *achiote.* The seeds do add their modest flavor to the oil, but it makes much better sense to think of *annatto* oil as a *dendê* substitute cobbled together from local ingredients by exiled West African slaves after they had been cut off from any direct commerce with their Portuguese-controlled homelands and from their oil palms in French and British island colonies. By now the people who use *annatto* oil in their cooking no longer connect it with the naturally red oil of *E. guineensis* that had been used by their ancestors in Africa.

The oil palm did reach the outside world eventually and came to flourish as never before in what is now Malaysia. Today, Malaysia is the world's leading producer of palm oil and earns 11 percent of its gross national product through palm oil exports. Some of this Malaysian palm oil reaches the United States as a bleached, neutralized solid white substance used in the American food industry in a minor but not negligible way as a constituent of certain brand-name foods.

For manufacturers of crackers, shortening, and nondairy creamers, Malaysian processed palm oil has definite advantages. It has a shelf life of several months, it remains solid at room temperature, and its relatively low melting point gives it a good "mouth feel." These virtues are the result of the same chemistry that is also palm oil's biggest liability in this country. Palm oil is high in saturated fat, to the tune of 51 percent, and this is not a happy tune in a society worried about cardiovascular disease. In Salvador da Bahia, however, there is nothing fearful or guilty about the consumption of palm oil. Walking along the street you can smell its pungent odor. Not for nothing do the locals call it *azeite-de-cheiro,* odorous oil.

Palm oil is a basic ingredient in most of the classic Bahian dishes that even tourists in Salvador can enjoy in their hotels or in the many restaurants featuring Bahian regional food. The palm oil that perfumes the streets of the city is being heated by the Baianas, the local black women who are cooking *acarajé*. These fritters, made from black-eyed-pea flour fried to a golden crisp, then slit open and stuffed with a peppery sauce whose main ingredient is dried shrimp, are the central food of one of the world's outstanding transplanted cuisines. To stand on the street in Salvador looking out over the beach and the Bay of All Saints while eating an *acarajé* is more than an ambulatory snack in a hot place at the edge of the South Atlantic. *Acarajé* is an emblem of the slave experience in the New World and of the enigma of African history.

Without any doubt this is the same basic black-eyed-pea fritter sold on streets in Nigeria as *akara,* and it is a certainty that Africa is where *acarajes* started out since black-eyed peas are indigenous to Africa, palm oil came to Brazil via West Africa, and *akara* is a native West African (Yoruba) name that was apparently Brazilianized into *acarajé.* In other words, *acarajé* is a pure case of African export to the New World with a broad penumbra of fritter/croquette descendants including the *buñuelo* of Colombia, *akkra* in Trinidad, *acrats* in the French islands, and hush puppies in the United States South. This minicuisine encompasses a wide variety of fritters and beignets made from salt cod and cornmeal and much else, fried in peanut oil and lard where palm oil is not available. Even where the two basic ingredients of the original Yoruba fritter, the black-eyed pea and palm oil, have given way to substitutes, the connoisseur of the black cooking heritage in former centers of New World slavery knows that fritters of almost any kind are a vestige of this simple but influential West African food. Indeed, I am prepared to argue that so-called southern frying and other forms of deep-fat frying now associated with plantation life in the antebellum South are echoes of the palm oil cooking still so basic to the old slave coast of Africa.

What other contributions did African slaves make to the cuisines of the Americas? To attempt to extend the list much beyond okra and watermelon is an abstruse undertaking, part of the whole controversial business of sorting out which foods were indigenous to Africa, which ones came in medieval times with Arab caravans and with traders sailing into East Africa from India, which moved south and west across the Sahara, and which reached West Africa in the same European ships that carried away the slaves. For some people the very idea that anything useful came to Africa as a result of the slave trade is repulsive. On the other hand it is clear that significant ingredients in the current diet of black Africa did originate in the New World, and the most scholarly summary I know of the sources of food now eaten in West Africa shows how the overwhelming majority came from somewhere else, a great many from the Americas after Columbus.

In his unpublished manuscript about the African heritage of American blacks, Stanley B. Alpern painstakingly sorts through the evidence in diaries, memoirs, and official documents to support his claims about how the West African market basket came to contain the things it does. Perhaps West African is too vague a geographic designation for the area that Mr. Alpern surveys. The region that "sent more slaves to the New World than any other part of Africa" he calls Kwaland because it is "inhabited mainly by tribes speaking Kwa languages, a subfamily of the Niger-Congo linguistic group." The region subsists on a basic yam and palm oil agriculture. It is a three hundred-mile-deep coastal region stretching from eastern Ghana to eastern Nigeria with "a highly developed market system, lost-wax brass casting, pantheism, and urban traditions. It gave rise to relatively large and complex kingdoms such as old Benin, Oye, Dahomey, and Asante."

What were the original crops in Kwaland? Mr. Alpern says that for two millennia farmers in the region have probably been "growing native yams, millets, sorghums, rice, cowpeas [that is, black-eyed peas], okra, gourds, watermelons, fluted pumpkins, groundnuts, malaguetta, and Benin pepper, and protecting numerous native trees including the oil palm, raffia palm, kola, shea butter, locust bean, akee, baobab, and silk cotton." But since, by one estimate, Africans grow 90 percent of all plant varieties known to man, the list of indigenous Kwaland crops is short compared to the list of borrowings and imports now cultivated. Yet, as Mr. Alpern notes, "some regions of the world, including Europe, imported nearly *all* their crops. In their willingness to accept and ability to adapt new crops, Africans were second to no one."

Even before Columbus, Europeans, notably Portuguese, made inroads on the Gold Coast and set up slave-run plantations on various islands. Later they had to feed the slaves sent to the New World. Mr. Alpern estimates they introduced some seventy new Mediterranean crops to Kwaland: figs, melons, pomegranates, sugarcane, citrus fruit, eggplant, chick-peas, members of the onion family, cucumbers, cabbage, lettuce, carrots, herbs.

The most important contribution of Europeans to the African diet were crops imported from the New World. Maize, cassava, and peanuts became basic African foods. Crucial, too, were sweet potatoes, *tannia/yautía/malanga* (the New World cocoyam), common and lima beans, *Capsicums,* pumpkins and squash, tomatoes, pineapples, papayas, guavas, avocados, and cashew nuts. Europeans also introduced plants of Asian origin to Kwaland. Indonesian, Arab, and

Persian ships had long since brought these plants to East Africa, but few of them, besides the Asian cocoyam or taro and probably bananas and plantains, had made the tough trip across Africa to Kwaland, argues Mr. Alpern. The Portuguese brought many things in by boat, including sugarcane, citrus fruit, Asian rice, Asian yams, coconut, mango, breadfruit, and possibly several spices. A small number of crops—the best known is tamarind—originated in Africa, traveled to India, and then were reintroduced to Africa by Europeans.

Of course, all the foods listed here didn't come into wide use in Africa at the same time, but certainly in our day the legacy of Columbus is a crucial bounty for black Africans. Much can be said against cassava as a source of nutrition, but in the end, poor food as it is, this wonderfully viable plant is a lifesaver for millions.

Africans have certainly taken it to their bosoms. In *Things Fall Apart* (1958), his moving portrait of traditional Ibo village life under pressure from outside forces at the turn of the century in what is now rural Nigeria, Chinua Achebe makes food a central trope for the culture whose crumbling he laments. And cassava is one of the main foods in his recurring banquet scenes, along with yams and palm wine:

> Obeierika's compound was as busy as an anthill. Temporary cooking tripods were erected on every available space by bringing together three blocks of sun-dried earth and making a fire in their midst. Cooking pots went up and down the tripods, and foo-foo was pounded in a hundred wooden mortars. Some of the women cooked the yams and the cassava, and others prepared vegetable soup. Young men pounded the foo-foo or split firewood. The children made endless trips to the stream.

A century ago cassava had taken its place in this corner of Kwaland, as elsewhere in the region, among absolutely basic foods. It fitted seamlessly into a cuisine built on roots and tubers and the starchy banana, all of them originally imported from somewhere else except the yam. But the indigenous yam opened the way for the taros of Asia and the Americas (grouped, significantly, under the same name, cocoyam, in Kwaland), cassava, sweet potatoes, and plantain. By the principle of substitution through which cuisines so often grow and change, the knowledge of one starchy vegetable made Kwaland cooks receptive to others as they became available.

The arrival of cassava in Africa is not a mystery. It crossed the

Atlantic in the sixteenth century. It couldn't have come earlier because there was no significant, documentable contact between the two sides of the Atlantic before Columbus. But controversy does divide historians over the arrival of Old World foods in Kwaland. No one denies that many Asian and Near Eastern foods and ideas came to East Africa and Africa north of the Sahara first. These coasts were accessible to Europeans from the Mediterranean as well as to Arabs traveling overland from Arabia and across the Indian Ocean. The great question is: How did foods shipped to East Africa and North Africa reach West Africa? One theory is that they could have moved across the continent by caravan across the Sahara or through the even more arduous direct east-west route.

Mr. Alpern takes a dim view of this possibility for most plants. He thinks the trip was too hard, and he has a lot of evidence to support his notion that most things from the outside reached Kwaland by ship after the Europeans began visiting and then settling West Africa in the later fifteenth century.

This makes sense to me, but I want to propose an exception. Food plants may have been prohibitively difficult to move across Africa, but ideas were not. And while the basic cooking techniques now found in Kwaland may be assumed to be native, deep-frying—the least obvious and most technologically advanced of all cooking methods—could have been brought in by Arabs who inherited a tradition of deep-frying centuries old. Arab traders, however early they may have reached Kwaland, probably would have encountered the basic ingredients for *akara* as we know it—black-eyed peas and oil palms. Putting one and one together, they could then have "invented" a dish closely resembling a beloved fritter they had left behind in the Middle East: the *falafel*.

In the Middle East they use chick-pea flour instead of black-eyed-pea flour, and they fry with other fats and oils. But the *falafel* is so close in concept, technique, and appearance to the *akara* and *acaraje* that it is very tempting to point out the similarity of these fritters and the cultural symbiosis they suggest, without of course denying that *akara* might just as well have been first fried before any outsiders penetrated the pristine kitchens of Kwaland.

I prefer, however, the romantic hypothesis of a family of fried starch croquettes stretching from the streets of Salvador da Bahia to Lagos to Cairo and Haifa all the way to India, where chick-pea dough and deep-frying even now produce the basic fritter batter for *pakoras* and where, in the city of Agra, as Julie Sahni tells us in *Classic Indian*

Vegetarian and Grain Cooking (1985), they make deep-fried vegetarian patties out of split-pea batter. India has also learned to make croquettes with New World tapioca (cassava) and peanuts. And Sahni writes that black-eyed peas "are almost a staple in the southwestern area of Coorg, Maharashtra, and Gujarat. . . . They are also ground into flour for crepes and pancakes." By a similar process, in the southeastern United States, we eat hush puppies, *akara* from cornmeal. Call it the transmigration of soul foods.

Wherever this dispersal and evolution of foodways began, we know that in the last four centuries Africans and their descendants have impressed their inherited traditions on the Americas while transmuting what they learned from their masters and what they found in their new homes into dozens of dishes forged out of sheer necessity with the improvisational genius of a jazzman putting his mark on a new tune.

PERU

P E R U ' S relatively greater isolation from Spain and North America—compared to the relatively greater accessibility of Mexico and the Caribbean Islands—put all its foods except the uniquely valuable potato and sweet potato at a competitive disadvantage with similar foods from the more convenient parts of the Spanish empire. Thus Mexican maize became a plant of world significance while large-kerneled *choclo* stayed at home. Ditto for Andean chilies in a world already growing the full panoply of Mexican varieties. But this neglect and isolation has allowed Peru to develop its Creole cuisine in peace since the sixteenth century. The isolation of the Indian population in the Andes, until the fateful migrations to Lima's shantytowns of the last few years, has preserved traditional agriculture and ingredients.

In Lima I also experienced traditional Peruvian food at its most indigenous in the plush suburb of Miraflores, a sort of Peruvian Malibu, where I had dinner with Carlos Raffo. He is a man of refinement, a man who speaks nostalgically of the Ligurian coast of Italy and his British golf club. When I met him in the spring of 1989, he had just returned from a posting as Peru's ambassador to England to be minister of industry, integration, and tourism. (Integration means furthering the cause of cooperation between the Andean nations.) On the minister's shelves were complete sets of Aristotle and Plato in Spanish. He poured French wine, this fanatical gourmet who orders rare titles in gastronomy from Cooks Books in Rottingdean, Sussex, and served me the purest Andean meal it is possible to imagine: corn on the cob.

This was not the eccentric part of my dinner with the minister of tourism of Peru. What could be more appropriate to serve a visitor on a gastronomic mission to Peru than this world-changing local grain in its most elemental form. Nor was I in a position as a North American used to corn multifariously since infancy to feel blasé about Raffo's offer. The corn of the Andes is not our corn. The kernels are much bigger, the taste and texture different. *Choclo* is just one of a hundred fundamental things that make Peruvian food a world apart. So I accepted this Spartan meal, meant graciously as a tribute from one eater of discernment to another. Remarkable but not strange. No, what was odd was the pistol stuck in the minister's belt, visible against his trencherman's belly.

There were also armed men at the door and a hoarse thug of a driver for the minister's Volvo. You see a lot of guns in Lima these days because of the Sendero Luminoso (Shining Path) Maoist guerrillas and other forms of violence and crime provoked by economic chaos. The minister, ever jovial and not one to admit that his tourism portfolio is a bad joke in times when no traveler to the interior of Peru is safe, is an obvious target for assassination. It occurred to me that to dine with him on *choclo* was to take a seat in a potential crossfire. Even to stay in his house finishing my wine after he left to meet his wife at the airport was to prolong the risk. The airport itself is an emblem of the precariousness of Peruvian life. Named after Jorge Chávez, a Peruvian pilot who made the first flight from Switzerland to Italy in a small Bleriot plane in 1910—a flight that ended in a fatal crash—the airport is surrounded by the hovels of Lima's dreary port, Callao, a cloacal safety hatch out of the present danger.

Lima perches a taxi ride away on the foggy cliffs of Peru's Pacific coast, where Francisco Pizarro founded it as a stronghold against Inca rebellion and unrest on January 18, 1535. The Andes stand off a short distance, filled with treasure, menace, and a biological wealth that changed the rest of the world more than all the gold raped from the Incas and the bowels of Bolivia to the east. Through Lima, once glittering outpost of empire, the potato escaped from the frigid Altiplano and transformed itself into shepherd's pie, *omelette à la Parmentier, pommes Anna,* the plum-filled dumplings of Szathmar, *Kartoffelnsalat,* French fries, potato chips.

We could probably go on naming potato dishes invented outside Peru for pages without even consulting a reference book, but I doubt that most people can come up with a typically Peruvian potato dish although some of the world's most original—and certainly the oldest—potato dishes are still in current use at Peruvian tables.

In the rough-and-ready dawn at Lima's central market, a woman called *la reina de papas* (potato queen) reigns supreme over the capital's potato trade, and so it is within the sophisticated Miraflorean's reach to cook the air-dried potatoes (*chuño*) of the cordillera in his walled mansion by the Pacific. Indeed, it is possible to buy *papas secas* in a freezer bag in the New York metropolitan area, most specifically at Inca's Foods on Broadway in Passaic, New Jersey, where refugees from troubled Peru have taken to settling. Reportedly eighteen restaurants in Paterson and Passaic serve such typical dishes as a potato-thickened shrimp stew called *chupe* or *ají de gallina* (chicken in a sauce of milk, bread crumbs, and pureed red hot chilies, called *ají* in South America).

I went to one of these places, La Furia Chalaca, at 87 Broadway in Passaic, next door to Inca's Foods. The name means the Mad Woman of Callao, but it was a calm, friendly place with a fairly large number of typical dishes. It wasn't really necessary to leave Manhattan to have this kind of experience, though. Falcon's Peruvian Restaurant (466 Amsterdam Avenue between 82d and 83d streets), a well-appointed place only a short walk from the Museum of Natural History, offered an excellent cod seviche, the dish made of raw fish, citrus juice, chilies, and onions common to most of Spanish America. There was *papa à la huancaina,* cold boiled potato in a cheese sauce; *carapulcra,* bits of pork and *papas secas*; fish *chupe*; tripe dishes that probably descend from recipes brought to Peru by black slaves from Africa; and for the gastronomic adventurer, *mazamorra morada,* a viscous purple gelatin made with dried purple corn.

In Lima I went to some trouble to try the widespread, nonalcoholic purple drink made from this same corn, called *chicha morada,* and eventually risked dysentery or God knows what by downing a glass of it from a street vendor stationed at the city's main square, Plaza San Martín. He served his *chicha* in real glasses, rinsed in a communal bowl of water. Happily, I suffered no ill effects. Although *chicha* is so popular in Peru that supermarkets sell powdered *chicha* mix (something I found out only after risking my health by buying it in the street), taking the (very) long view it is not a purely native beverage. Corn originated somewhere in what is now Mexico and migrated southward at some unrecorded moment in history. Peru returned the compliment, however, by sending the original tomatoes and chili (*Capsicum*) peppers north to Mexico. Today, Mexico gets the credit for tomatoes and chilies in the world at large, having cultivated the versions of them that entered other cuisines after Columbus.

No doubt Mexican tomatoes do deserve fame in the world and not the wild little green ones growing in Peruvian river valleys that started the world's love affair with tomatoes. No doubt Central American corn deserved its role as the hybrid of preference almost everywhere since it was the oldest. But how can we explain the continued insularity of Peruvian hot peppers, the aggressively delicious *mirasol* and the big red *rocoto*, which combines the suavity and juiciness of the red bell pepper with the heat of Mexico's finest? How, indeed, can we explain the continued isolation and obscurity of Peru's traditional dishes that comprise the last great cuisine undiscovered by a world gone mad for new tastes?

To a degree, the nature of the food itself explains this. Roast or stewed guinea pig has no future in the non-Andean world. Even in Lima this primordial source of protein in the aboriginal cooking of the country is not normally available. But in the countryside, poor Indians still raise guinea pigs *(cuyes)* as a major meat source just as their ancestors did before the Conquest brought in the domesticated meat animals of Europe. In shacks all over rural Peru, miniflocks of *cuyes* scamper on the floors, waxing fat at the feet of the people who share the same roof and will eventually eat them.

The other nonexportable Peruvian standby is *anticuchos,* a vigorously spiced preparation of marinated, cubed beef heart barbecued on skewers. The name sounds as though it is a Spanish word related to *antipasto* and *cuchifritos,* an appetizer or snack, but Elisabeth Lambert Ortiz reminds us that it is an indigenous Quechua term meaning "a dish from the Andes cooked on sticks" and that it was probably first made with llama hearts in the days before beef.

I can attest that the modern recipe, even when done with non-Andean chilies, is very delicious, but I doubt that it will win the hearts, so to speak, of offal-squeamish non-Andean cooks.

Various other Andean foods do not look like good bets for the wide world because the niche they fill in Peru and Bolivia is already satisfactorily occupied elsewhere. We in the first world already have access to enough potato varieties not to feel more than titillated by the unexploited cornucopia of Andean types in all their many colors and shapes. Perhaps if the *papa amarilla,* the yellow potato, with its lusciously waxy texture that does not turn mushy, glutinous, or starchy when cooked, has a future, but the demand would have to be carefully nurtured. Other Andean tubers (except the sweet potato) stand no chance at all, not even the thumb-shaped, iridescent yellow-green-fleshed *ulluco.*

Peru, on the other hand, is continuing its historic openness to foods imported from the wide world. Lima has recently attracted a serious Japanese population, one of whom was elected president in a surprise victory in 1990 (Lima has had a big Chinese contingent for a long time and many Chinese restaurants, called *chifas*). The most visible culinary result of this Japanese influx is the Peruvianized *sashimi* called *tiradito* (little strip). It consists of thin slices of raw fish very slightly cured in citrus and served without adornment, not even onion—just seasoned with chili. I experienced this newest culinary wrinkle at a spectacular lunch in the hills at a glamorous new restaurant next to the Gold Museum. The restaurant, El Pabellón de Caza (the Hunt Pavilion), is decorated with big game trophies and has parrots, a jungle garden, a French chef, and an ebullient man at the helm, Arturo Rubio. He is a dynamic enthusiast for the dishes of his country and offered me a *tiradito* of octopus and another of *lenguado*, a white-fleshed Pacific fish that is conventionally identified in English as sole.

I was able to experience this extremely pure-tasting hybrid on its home ground two days later, at Rosita's, one of innumerable small, cheerful, extremely informal restaurants scattered through scruffy Callao. It is in such inelegant surroundings that Limeño businessmen lunch, seeking authenticity and inverse chic. Not everyone goes in for this sort of thing, of course, and when my meeting with Minister Raffo was under discussion, he expressed the hope that I would not insist on going to Callao to *comer sucio* (eat filthy).

As far as I could tell, sanitation was well maintained at Rosita's (Avenida Colonial, Cuadra 30, Callao) by the amiable proprietress, Rosa de Yimura, and her husband, who did card tricks and other conjuring in the al fresco dining room, while his wife and daughters prepared *tempura; tiradito;* two kinds of octopus *cebiche,* one in olive cream; *tacu-tacu,* a patty of rice and baked beans with stewed goat; and a *shangai* of *lenguado,* peaches and scallions. Rosa de Yimura's cooking, half Japanese, half Peruvian, embodies the latest stage in a millennium of genetic and culinary mixing and adaptation in Peru. To merge *sashimi* with New World *cebiche* (itself probably once a Moorish contribution to Andalusian menus) and to compound the Creolizing effect with an olive cream is nouvelle cuisine (really *nueva cocina*), but the fancy term isn't necessary in Callao, the dilapidated melting pot and dauntless slum on the foggy southeastern edge of the Pacific rim.

My first direct recognition of the complexity of Peru's culinary life came in the form of an olive. Of all the olives I had ever eaten until then (1986), this black, hard, wizened fruit was the strangest. The taste was extremely bitter and the texture gritty and dry, like stale cake.

Actually, I acquired a whole jar of them at the now sadly vanished

Latin food emporium on 14th Street in Manhattan, Casa Moneo. The elusive César Morales had imported these unprepossessing olives from Peru—packed in an ordinary jar, not vacuum-sealed, not covered in oil or any other preserving substance. Indeed, no foreign substance had apparently ever touched these olives after the harvest. They were, in the normal sense, uncured, never had been soaked or salted or treated in any of the myriad ways worked out millennia past in Europe and the Middle East to remove the naturally occurring bitter gluco-sides and stabilize the purified flesh of the fruit. No, these were Peruvian olives prepared for a long shelf life in the Peruvian manner. They had been preserved in the same way that Andean people have preserved food since long before the Spanish brought the olive to Peru in the sixteenth century. They had been air-dried in the cool, dehy-drating breezes of the Altiplano, like the naturally freeze-dried potatoes (*chuño* or *papas secas*) and air-dried, salted meat (our word jerky is derived from the Quechua *charque*) that native Peruvians survive on in their marginal environment.

Or so I reasoned. If any documentation of the history of this adaptation of immigrant olive to indigenous Peruvian food processing methodology exists, I haven't found it. The most convincing support for the idea is the dried olive itself. The Spanish olive experts, Alicia Rios and Lourdes March, tasted some of these olives, which I brought to the Oxford Food Symposium, and found them highly unusual, similar to a type of olive produced in a remote village in the mountains of Spain. Rios saw immediately that the extreme dehydration had left the apparently crumbly olive saturated with oil, so much so that she was able to make it stream with oil by rubbing it lightly against her arm.

These Incaicized olives are a peculiar relic of the Spanish system of colonizing Peru, a system that sought to impose the agriculture as well as the culture and religion of the *madre patria* on the Andes and its peoples while exporting their mineral wealth. In the end it was the agricultural part of the program that had the most lasting effect. Until very recently the ancestral peoples of the Peruvian highlands stayed largely put and unassimilable while the people of Spanish heritage and their mestizo offspring conducted a Europeanized life in Lima. Lately, millions of deracinated mountain people have come down to the capital, trading inherited forms of misery for new ones in the shanty-towns that pullulate at the edges of the city. So at last the vastly different societies left from the confrontation of the Spanish and Inca empires in the sixteenth century have become extremely uncomfortable next-door neighbors without much prospect of happy relations soon.

The seeds for this culture war were literally sown in the first decades after the foundation of Lima in 1535. Contemporary sources document in surprising detail the swiftness of the transplantation of European crops and domesticated animals to Peru. Pedro de Cieza de León composed the first eyewitness chronicle of the conquest of Peru (*La Crónica del Perú*) between 1540 and 1550, basing it on his experiences from 1535 on.

In his chapter on "the fertility of the plains and the many fruits and root crops that are in them and the excellent arrangement they have for irrigating the fields," Cieza de León proudly calls attention to crops flourishing "now" (his way of implying that they were introduced by the Spaniards):

> Now, in many of these valleys there are large vineyards, from which they harvest many grapes. Up until now they haven't made wine, and for that matter it can't be said for sure that it will ever be done; presumably, because it would be grown with irrigation, it will be thin. Also there are big fig groves and many pomegranates, and in some parts they are already getting quinces. But why am I going on with this account since people think and consider it certain that they will produce all the fruits that Spain grows.

Before restraining himself completely, however, he does point proudly to fields seeded with wheat and barley and to groves of all the citrus fruits popular back home.

Some sixty years later, in 1609, the mestizo son of a conquistador and a noble Inca woman, Garcilaso de la Vega, el Inca, published his *Comentarios Reales* in Lisbon. This was, of course, eleven years before the establishment of the first Pilgrim settlement at Plymouth Plantation and five years before Galileo became embroiled with the Church. The Spanish crown, however, had long since been making excellent progress with its plans for the hispanicization of farming in the lee of the Andes.

Garcilaso de la Vega informs us that wheat was first brought to his country by the noblewoman María de Escobar. She brought it to the city of Rimac, in what year he didn't know, but it took three years before there was enough seed to divert any grain to making bread flour. As late (!) as 1547 there was still no wheat bread in Cuzco,

although wheat was already being grown there. He is sure of the date
because he remembers that in their house in Cuzco his father fed corn
(maize) bread to soldiers fleeing the battle of Huarina. They were so
hungry, they stuffed handfuls of raw corn flour in their mouths as if
it was "candied almonds."

As for vines, Francisco de Caravantes, a nobleman from Toledo,
had plants sent to him from the Canaries, and by the time Garcilaso
de la Vega himself witnessed a neighbor trampling on grapes to make
wine, in 1560, it had already been produced "much before" in Hua-
manca and Arequipa. The impetus, he claims, was not thirst or commercial profit but pride. Their Catholic majesties back in Spain were
offering two bars of silver worth three hundred ducats each as a prize
to whoever was the first in each town to produce Spanish things not
available in Peru. To qualify for the award as a vintner you had to
produce at least four *arrobas* (100 pounds in liquid measure) of wine.
An award was also available for pioneer producers of four *arrobas* of
olive oil or a half *cahíz* (about 770 pounds) of wheat or barley.

Garcilaso de la Vega's most dramatic story of horticultural imperialism concerns the introduction of the olive. It is worth repeating:

ABOUT THE OLIVE AND WHO BROUGHT IT TO PERU The
same year, 1560, Don Antonio de Ribera, our neighbor at
Los Reyes, having gone to Spain years before as procurator
general of Peru, brought olive plants with him from Seville
when he returned home. And despite the care and diligence
he invested in bringing over two big pots containing over a
hundred cuttings, only three plants arrived at Ciudad de Los
Reyes alive. These he sent to a very beautiful walled farm he
owned in that valley, whose grapes, figs, pomegranates, melons, oranges, limes, and other fruits and vegetables of Spain,
when sold fresh in the main square of that city, went for a
large sum of money, which is definitely thought to have
surpassed 200,000 pesos. In this farm Don Antonio de
Ribera planted his olives, and so that nobody would be able
to have even a single leaf to plant somewhere else, he had
them guarded by a great army consisting of more than 100
blacks and 30 dogs, which stood watch over his new and
precious plantings. It happened one night that other people,
who stayed up later than the dogs or got help from one of
the blacks, who was suspected of being bribed, stole one of
the three plants, which surfaced within a few days in Chile,

600 leagues from Ciudad de los Reyes, where it produced offspring so successfully for that kingdom during the next three years that they did not plant a cutting, no matter how scrawny, that didn't take root and in short order turn into a handsome olive tree.

At the end of the three years, although the men who stole Don Antonio de Ribera's plant had had to read many letters of excommunication directed at them, they returned the same olive tree they'd taken and put it in the very same place from which they'd removed it, with such ingenuity and stealth that the owner never found out who had taken it or who had put it back.

This story could easily have been an episode in a Spanish picaresque novel of the same period, but in Garcilaso de la Vega's hands it fits into his quite lengthy paeon to the successes of viceregal horticulture in Europeanizing Peru. His catalogues of newly introduced fruits and vegetables are of stupefying length and are not just lists; they also contain detailed accounts of splendiferous achievements in field and orchard.

We hear of Spaniards who amazed the Indians by grafting several kinds of exotic fruits to native trees:

After pomegranates were available, they took one along in the parade of the feast of the most holy sacrament. The fruit was so big that it excited the admiration of those who saw it. I don't dare say how large people claim it was, for fear of shocking the ignorant, who won't believe there can be greater things in the world than they have in their village; but it's a pity not to write about the marvelous works of nature there have been in that land just so as not to frighten the simpleminded. And returning to them, we say that they have been of extraordinary largeness, especially the first ones; that the pomegranate was bigger than one of those earthenware jugs they make in Seville for bringing olive oil to the Indies, and many grape clusters have been seen that weighed eight or ten pounds, and quinces as big as a man's head and citrons half as big as pitchers.

The most remarkable thing about Garcilaso de la Vega's Bunyanesque descriptions is that in his dithyrambic puffing of the triumphs of the

Spanish settlers' transplantations, he pays no attention to the achievements of native agriculture. Throwing all his rhetorical energies behind the official agricultural campaign to transform Peru into a better Spain, he has nothing to say about indigenous farming. The ensuing centuries inevitably brought about a mixture of the two in fields and on tables, which is what we call Peruvian cuisine, Bolivian cuisine, and Ecuadorian cuisine. And in a reversal that offers rich opportunities for ironic musing, today the rest of the world looks to Peru and the other Andean countries for miraculous new foods and horticultural innovation.

The Andean grain *quinoa* is the darling of the health-food world. Other Incaic roots and tubers, *ulluco* and *oca*, have captured the imagination of gastronomic futurologists. Newspaper feature writers have lately been goggling over the low-energy farming methods of ancient Andeans. In Peru advanced methods of biology, including gene splicing, are being applied to those fabulously adaptable local plants, the potato and the sweet potato, while a hungry world waits for the results.

PART III

THE NEW WORLD
RESHAPES THE OLD

THE FIRST PHASE of the food revolution started by the discovery of America took place in the new European colonies. The second stage took place everywhere in the world as the foods of the Americas dispersed to the four winds and found new fates. This process began when Columbus returned to Spain with strange seeds, and it continues today.

The most dramatic phase took place in the early modern period when American ingredients were infiltrating Europe, Asia, and Africa, before those Old World civilizations had evolved into the nations, cultures, and cuisines we know today.

Sixteenth- and seventeenth-century Europe was in the midst of coagulating modern countries out of fiefdoms and principalities just at the time that New World foods arrived on the continent through Mediterranean ports of entry. When the potato and the tomato crossed the Atlantic in Spanish boats and were offloaded at the port of Seville, they entered a Spain unified under Isabel and Ferdinand only a few years before. Italy, the next place they migrated, did not coalesce into a true nation with a true national language until the nineteenth century. France did not really shake off its feudal raiments until the revolution of 1789, really not until Napoleon superimposed a central administration after 1800.

The national cuisines we find in European countries today evolved out of a pan-European medieval way of eating at about the same time that France, Italy, and Spain were defining themselves as nations in the modern sense of the word. New World ingredients influenced the growth of these cuisines every step of the way. They were not oddities grafted onto a full-grown, gnarly tradition of national cooking stretching back to the Caesars. Rather, they were naturalized into everyday cooking in an atmosphere of universal experimentation and invention.

Different places adopted different American foods with differing degrees of enthusiasm, and some national cuisines were quicker than others to assimilate the exotic foods from the Western Hemisphere. The tomato, for example, moved quickly into the larders of Mediterranean Europe but had to wait much longer before it found a place in countries farther north.

But in the end all the cuisines of Europe (and Asia and Africa) ended up with an important American component. So when we speak of culinary authenticity, we are talking about foodways that began with a heavy influence on them from the New World. Eventually, as I'll be demonstrating in later chapters, Europe repaid the compliment by sending its foods to the North American frontier, there to be put through another culinary redaction. And, most recently, the whole world has been trading recipes and ingredients under the postmodern aegis of nouvelle cuisine.

This outward spiral of evolving foodways began around 1500. In France and China, now considered the world's most highly developed and distinct cuisines, we can see clearly how the national styles we now honor as authentic and traditional evolved after Columbus, in crucial contact with foods his discoveries brought to their shores.

CHAPTER I

FRANCE

IN THAT yeasty time in the mid-sixties when I went to work as a reporter in Paris, the world was about to pop. The global temblor that for a while was taken to be a lasting cultural revolution filled the air with its heady vapors. In 1967 I interviewed the rector of the Nanterre campus of the University of Paris, the tinderbox where the student revolt of May and June 1968 started its convulsions. Even a year before, it was obvious that trouble was brewing, that the static minuet of traditional French education was going to break into a frug. The signs of impending change were everywhere—in fashion, in popular music, in attitudes toward sex and work—but there was one part that seemed especially unlikely to change: the life of the table. Professors of literature might abandon their Racine and Milton texts and turn to the analysis of Beatles lyrics, but those of us seriously interested in food, and particularly those of us interested in French food, did not foresee gastronomic change of any kind.

Speaking for myself, at any rate, I thought of food as the one important part of life in which change did not play a fundamental role. While music and art presented themselves to my sense of them as historical developments, from Bach to Boulez, from Masaccio to abstract expressionism, food was different. Unlike the other arts where the originality of an individual creator lay at the heart of our enjoyment, in the art of food, originality was most often a sign of vulgarity. Original recipes were to be found in American women's magazines, concoctions of "clever" new sauces made on the quick from canned mushroom soup and new casseroles "conveniently" dressed up with pineapple rings.

Serious cooks shunned these grotesqueries, and serious eaters shunned hotel food, international and continental menus. Gastronomes of the late sixties ran from originality and instead beat their brains out trying to reproduce the tried-and-true recipes of French and sometimes Italian tradition.

I can recall spending a day following every step in Julia Child's voluminous recipe for the French regional bean casserole, *cassoulet*. The result was delicious, confirming my prejudice that carefully and laboriously copying classics, with no substitute ingredients and no new wrinkles added by me or anyone else, was the only acceptable way to cook well.

When I thought about it, I justified this doggedly conservative outlook by invoking a theory of food history not unlike modern science's vision of the history of glaciers. In a past so distant as to brook no contemplation, an unimaginably slow process had ground out our food heritage and left the recipes behind, like eskers and drumlins—stony relics to be accepted as part of the landscape, respected and enjoyed as they were.

In effect, this meant that people like me were acting as if food had no history at all. Cooking on a serious level was a form of practical anthropology in which the food rites of various cultures were noted down and then reenacted. The English food writer Elizabeth David epitomized this approach for many of us. She had lived in Italy for extended periods, and after World War II she tramped about the devastated countryside gathering recipes from, as it were, native informants.

In a less peripatetic but basically similar way, Julia Child, while resident in Paris in the late fifties, collaborated with two French women, Simone Beck and Louisette Bertholle, on the crucial text for American cooks of the next decade, *Mastering the Art of French Cooking* (1961). In their foreword they do not ever discuss history or change. Typically for the time, they approach their subject as if it were a known body of knowledge such as the complete works of Dickens. They had to make a selection from the classic corpus for reasons of space, but it was all written down in an orderly way somewhere and had been inscribed there presumably forever.

Child, Beck, and Bertholle speak in Platonic terms of recipes as ideal types not brooking alteration: "A perfect navarin of lamb . . . requires a number of operations . . . and if any is eliminated or combined with another, the texture and taste of the navarin suffer." And it is just such mucking about with proper ingredients and canonical steps that produces "pseudo-French cooking, with which we are all too familiar" and which "falls far below good French cooking" in taste and texture.

In this certitude about the fundamentally immutable structure and principles of French cooking, process by process and dish by dish,

Child, Beck, and Bertholle were themselves following a tradition of French culinary historiography. The greatest figure of the professional French kitchen in their parents' generation, Auguste Escoffier, had left a bible of haute cuisine, begun in 1898 and still in print today with its five thousand recipes of traditional cookery. Escoffier thought of himself as a reformer, but he meant only that he had eliminated the most elaborate decorative architectural fantasies of his forefathers from his banquet tables. While acknowledging that cooking must change with the times, he nevertheless wrote: "But that which existed in the time of Carême [the early nineteenth century], which exists still in our day and which will exist as long as cooking itself, is the basic essence *[fonds]* of this cuisine."

Similar semimystical claims can be and are made for all of the world's important cuisines and for the lesser ones. But what do they mean? What can they mean? How far back in time does authentic French cooking go? How was its basic essence created? Clearly there must be a limit. French cooking must have a history. But in their zeal for purging their cookbooks and their kitchens of "pseudo-French" ideas, the anthropological gourmets of my youth naturally adopted the ahistorical, Platonic stance so beloved of other anthropologists working in other areas with scant or nonexistent written records.

It was especially convenient for food writers to take each national or regional cuisine as a given. Their main goal in the sixties and seventies was to make it possible for jet-age gourmets to reproduce at home, with reasonable accuracy, exactly what they had eaten on vacation. History, if there was any for these dishes, was beside the point. Authenticity was what mattered.

And by authentic these anthropological food authors meant whatever their informants cooked for them. But it was implied that these dishes had been made in exactly the same way since man first strode upright on French soil. No one ever said this, of course, but it was the unspoken assumption of hundreds of otherwise excellent books.

When did French cooking begin to resemble what we call French cooking? There will never be a simple, good answer to this question, but all available evidence argues that there never was a time when French food had a Platonic essence. A continuous record of recipes going back to the Middle Ages shows a dynamic, evolving process— not immutable granite traditions. Authenticity is yesterday's orthodoxy.

Look at the recipes in the oldest French cookbooks, the *Viandier*

of Taillevent and the anonymous *Ménagier de Paris,* both set down in
the 1390s and reflecting court practice somewhat earlier. This is a
world of caldrons and open-hearth cookery, of spits and of food that
sounds like nothing we would eat today, food in bizarre combinations
with lots of Oriental spices—ginger, cardamom.

Historians have noted similarities between these recipes and the
highly spiced "Oriental" cooking of ancient Rome. It has even been
suggested that the food of modern India gives a good idea of what
medieval French people ate.

The oddity of fourteenth-century French cookery is undeniable.
It was, one might say, not French, not even for its time. As everyone
who looks at the surviving records for Europe then has observed,
court food all over the continent was much the same. There were no
meaningful national traditions. Recipes in England's earliest cookbook, *The Forme of Cury,* are first cousins of recipes in Taillevent.

So when does French cooking become French? In her authoritative *Savoring the Past, the French Kitchen and Table from 1300 to 1789*
(1983), Barbara Ketcham Wheaton states flatly: "French cooking did
not begin to take on its present character until the end of the seventeenth century." Stephen Mennell goes into this question in great
detail in the introduction to his edition of four documents relating to
a mid-eighteenth-century culinary dispute about "la nouvelle cuisine"(!).

Mennell wants to locate, as closely as possible, the moment in
time when the French broke with pan-European medievalism and
adopted the fierce culinary nationalism so remarkable in the texts
Mennell has collected as *Lettre d'un pâtissier anglois et autres contributions
à une polémique gastronomique du XVIIIème siècle* (University of Exeter,
1981).

He begins by dismissing the cliché theory that Italian chefs
brought modern cooking with them to Paris when Catherine de
Medici married Henri II. Italian cookbooks published in France in the
sixteenth century, he observes, do not show any revolutionary modern traits. Mennell points out that when Montaigne describes his
conversation with the Italian maître d'hôtel of Cardinal Caraffa, he
treats the man's inflated prating with the mild irony suitable for an
essay entitled "On the Vanity of Words."

Mennell goes on to dismiss the French cookbook literature of the
sixteenth century as scant and mostly a repetition of Taillevent and
another cookbook from 1350. "No written proof of the appearance
of a specifically French kind of cooking exists before the publication

in 1651 of La Varenne's *'Le Cuisinier françois,'* " argues Mennell. This is the book usually picked as the sign of a sharp break with the past. But Mennell points to medieval survivals among the recipes for dishes that have survived until modern times (omelets, *beignets, boeuf à la mode*). In other words, La Varenne is an example of evolving modernity, not the complete thing.

Mennell summons text after text to show how chefs began creating the structure of haute cuisine at some point in the seventeenth century. Whether a revolution took place or not is hard to say and seems doubtful, but one thing is sure: It makes no sense on the basis of real evidence to talk about French food as we know it, even in an embryonic sense, before 1651.

By this date the Spanish had been exploiting the New World for more than a century and a half. Most of the foodstuffs that were going to cross oceans, westward and eastward, had already done so, yet few of them had thus far made their now-indelible mark on French "traditional" cuisine. As they percolated northward and eastward, the potato, the tomato, and all the other New World plants met a conservative culinary world, but it was a world in flux, a world in which no cuisine resembled the ones we know today. Here, for example, are two pre-Columbian recipes of Taillevent, translated and adapted for the modern kitchen by Barbara Ketcham Wheaton in *Savoring the Past*.

BLANCMANGE OF CAPON
FOR A SICK PERSON

2½ *pounds breast meat of capon*	*[½ teaspoon cardamom]*
2 *quarts good chicken stock*	6 *blanched almonds, slivered*
1 *cup finely ground almonds*	*Pomegranate seeds*
[1 teaspoon ginger]	*Sugar*

1. Poach the capons in the chicken stock until they are cooked (about 20 minutes or a little more). Let cool.

2. Cut up the meat and pass it through a food mill fitted with a fine grid. Beat in the ground almonds and, if desired, the spices. [Wheaton added the ginger and cardamom to the recipe with justification from a reference elsewhere; they are not mentioned in the Taillevent text.]

3. Dilute with as much of the cooking broth as is necessary to

make the mixture agreeably moist but still rather stiff. Stick the slivered almonds into half of the top and the pomegranate seeds into the other half; sprinkle the second half with sugar.

HYPOCRAS

3 cups dry red wine

2 ounces fresh ginger, sliced and
    peeled

1 tablespoon whole cloves

2 ounces stick cinnamon

1 tablespoon cardamom

3 1/3 cups granulated sugar

1. Put all the ingredients in a stainless-steel, enamel, or earthenware pot to heat, without boiling, for about 15 minutes, stirring to dissolve the sugar.

2. Strain through a fine sieve, repeatedly if necessary, to remove all spices. Let cool and serve at room temperature or slightly chilled.

The period after 1492 would have been a time of great if gradual change in European eating patterns even without the New World imports. As modern nation states evolved, their cuisines evolved with them. But during the entire time of this extraordinary development in the daily habits of every living person, Europe was also coming to terms with the exotic ingredients brought from the Americas. From this perspective, to call any dish authentic is to take a freeze-frame still from a moving picture.

CHAPTER II

CHINA

A N Y O N E searching for a culture with a long and still-potent history need look no further than China. Despite all the atrocities committed in the name of throwing off the imperial Confucian past by Red Guards or by the Chinese Army in Tiananmen Square, the overwhelming weight and length of Chinese cultural continuity persists as a major force in modern China. And even the most vigorous proponents of change—Communist, pro-Western, Democratic—while inveighing against the evils of one intellectual orthodoxy or another, have never suggested that cultural revolution should include the suppression of traditional Chinese food.

As far as I know, at any rate, no Chinese futurist has indicted chopsticks or rice as the source of his society's decadence. Perhaps the standard of dining in China since the triumph of Mao Tse-tung forty years ago has declined for the populace and the elite as well, but I am not at all sure of this; in any case, neither nutrition nor the putative state of banquet life for the Chinese party mandarinate is my subject here. I want to consider something simpler and less controversial: the enduring Chineseness of Chinese food and its paradoxically chameleonlike relation to the changing material conditions of Chinese life over the past twenty-five hundred years.

As outsiders we necessarily get a distorted impression of Chinese cuisine, but I think that we are not fundamentally mistaken in our attempts to define it for ourselves as a cuisine based on rice consumed in tandem with other foods. We know other things, too, about Chinese food that are surely not wrong; for instance, because it is eaten without knives, the entire cuisine involves either small pieces of food precut in the kitchen or large things—buns, for example—eaten with the hands. We can also assert with confidence that Chinese, when dining as Chinese, do not ingest chocolate or cheese although they do eat an abundance of foods, from bear's paw to *bêche-de-mer*, that we approach with a tremor at best.

All I mean to say is that we, you and I who have devoted serious time to eating Chinese food in our own country, feel confident that we know it when we see it. By the same token I think almost no one among us presumes that she or he has the multifarious subject of Chinese food under control. It is as if we had a working fluency in Albanian, enough to conduct business in Tirana without being able to read the national epic, and yet our minimal competence allowed us almost unfailingly to spot someone speaking Albanian. By this account Chinese cuisine has a language recognizable even by its dilettantes.

This means that you and I, if confronted with an unfamiliar dish, could tag it as Chinese, which is to say, not French, not Italian, not even Thai or Korean or Japanese. I believe I could do this, and I make this claim without believing that it is much of a boast. On the other hand, when I sneaked in the word *language* in the previous paragraph, I did not do so idly for it seems to me that what we take to be the Chineseness of Chinese food is not primarily its vocabulary of ingredients (although these may indeed mark it off from Aleut food or even the cuisine of Ortonville, Michigan), but its grammar, its underlying structure.

To prove this would require much detailed argument and comparison with other cuisines, something I hope to do in the future when endowed with greater wisdom, but I am prepared even now to contend, as a corollary to this grander theory, that the unifying identity every one of us grants to Chinese food cannot possibly be the result of our sense of its ingredients as a defining set. We may think that the Chinese have always stir-fried *bok choy* as they do today in peanut oil or that from the Bronze Age on they have eaten sesame noodles. But we would be wrong. *Sesamum indicum* has been in China for a long time but not as long as the Chinese language, in which it is known as foreign hemp. Peanuts arrived from the New World much later—as recently, by Chinese standards, as the sixteenth century—with the Spanish through the Philippines or with the Portuguese through Macao or India.

These are not isolated examples. Throughout its very long history the cuisine of China has absorbed new ingredients. Anyone who doubts this should read E. N. Anderson's *The Food of China* (Yale, 1988). Mr. Anderson, an anthropologist who has lived in Hong Kong doing field work, proceeds methodically through the millennia of Chinese civilization showing how the larder evolved over time.

It is not necessary to comb the evidence from deep antiquity—

the arrival of soybeans around 1000 B.C. or the predominance of millet over rice in the Han dynasty (beginning 206 B.C.)—to find dramatic change in the foodstuffs available to Chinese cooks. As late as the Tang period (618–907) tea was a novelty, "a new, exotic drink," says Mr. Anderson, probably brought in from the Burma-India border country by Buddhist monks, "a major example of westward influence at the time."

Only during the Sung dynasty (960–1279) did China's agriculture and food take "definitive shape." Mr. Anderson speaks of the creation of an "elaborate cuisine" and regional specialties, but getting down to cases, he says that "the only really revolutionary innovation in Sung . . . was the introduction of new crop varieties"—drought-resistant rice from what is now Vietnam, mung beans from India, sugarcane, watermelons, and sorghum.

The evidence for regional cuisines seems spotty, but Anderson mentions regional restaurants in the capital and alludes to Sung accounts defining a northern cuisine based on meat and dairy products and a southern cuisine marked by rice and aquatic foods.

"Sichuanese cooking, set apart already by its spiciness and use of mountain products and herbs, was also distinctive." What Anderson means is that Sichuan food was definable as Sichuanese even without the ingredient that is most crucial to its identity as a cuisine today—the chili pepper. That essential source of heat did not reach China until the Iberian traders brought it in from the New World in the later Ming period. Before then the pepper in this peppery cuisine was the native spice called *fagara,* the brown or *Xanthoxylum* or Sichuan pepper that plays a central part in the cuisine to this day. But *fagara* is not what any modern person familiar with *Capsicums* would call hot. In *Bruce Cost's Asian Ingredients* (Morrow, 1988), an indispensable compendium, *fagara* is described as "strangely numbing" rather than torrid to the tongue, with a "clean, spicy-woodsy fragrance." But was this entirely dissimilar non-*Capsicum* enough of a precursor to prepare the way for the post-Ming Capsicomania of Sichuan and Hunan cuisines?

It is tempting to think so. As a theoretical proposition this rests on the notion that cuisines can evolve by substituting one ingredient for a new one that surpasses its precursor. Undoubtedly this has happened. In southern China rice replaced millet. In England wheat flour replaced barley and oat flour for breadmaking since wheat was physically superior to the other grains in containing lots of gluten that let it rise.

Capsicums provide an entirely different advantage. They make food hot, which *fagara* does not do in any dramatic way. Furthermore, chilies so completely took East Asia by storm that the pressing question for China is not why Sichuan and Hunan embraced it but why the rest of the culture did not, while Thais, Burmese, and Indians jumped on the chili bandwagon.

Perhaps these non-Chinese Asians also had pre-Columbian cuisines with a predilection for dramatic spice. But I think it makes more sense to see them as societies in eager, direct, and open contact with the trade opportunities brought in by European imperialism. China as a whole was not closed to these influences, as Anderson's chapter on the Ming makes clear, but Sichuan seems to have been particularly ready to accept novelties passing through it from the West. The peanut is another New World plant product that is now a signpost of Sichuanese cooking.

Eclipsing all of this borrowing from Europe and the Americas—the guavas, the papayas—is the Chinese embrace of the sweet potato and maize. The enormous Chinese production of these plants has not been a matter of taste but of survival. Despite a basic aversion to the sweet potato, the Chinese now consume more of them than any other nation, and maize is the third Chinese grain.

Meanwhile, Chinese and other Asian immigrants to America have brought their foods with them in a profusion no one would have dared predict even ten years ago. Cost's book is the best available testimony to this. He has written a Baedeker to all those confusing greens and bottled delicacies cropping up more and more in U.S. markets.

I vividly recall my feelings of triumph after I successfully hunted down imported dried leaves of the kaffir lime (*Citrus hystrix*) in a Thai grocery on upper Broadway in the late seventies. Cost writes that kaffir lime trees are now growing in Florida and California, sometimes in the backyards of Thai restaurants.

Most of the new arrivals are, expectably, from Southeast Asia (that's where the newer immigrant communities come from), so now it is relatively easy to buy Vietnamese rice-paper egg roll skins and Philippine palm vinegar.

From a gastrohistorical point of view, however, the most fascinating of these new "arrivals" are really natives. Cost includes sweet potatoes in his roster because of their significance to the Chinese, and he also devotes a page to that currently chic native of the United States Southwest, jicama. The Spanish took these tubers to the Philippines where resident Chinese farmers adopted them. Today the Chinese raise jicama primarily as a source for thickening starch. Americans won't find jicama at Chinese markets, but it is sold by Vietnamese who sometimes put it in spring rolls or stew it.

My favorite Cost novelty is a native Asian vegetable that got a real American name fifty years ago. Seeds for *Lactuca sativa var asparagina* (aka asparagus lettuce and stem lettuce) arrived at the Burpee Company from China in 1938. After giving it scrutiny for four years, Burpee released seeds to the United States gardening public in its 1942 catalogue under the name celtuce.

Celtuce sounds more like celery than lettuce, whence, no doubt, the name. You throw away the leaves and eat the giant stem, three feet tall. Peel it, slice it, and boil or sauté it. The best place to look for celtuce is, Cost advises, at stands owned or patronized by northern Chinese or people from Shanghai. On second thought, perhaps trying to buy celtuce is not a really good idea. Cost does not give the Chinese name for the plant, and if you are in Boston, the danger of getting confused in front of a bevy of Shanghainese shoppers as between celtuce and Celtics, not to mention Boston lettuce, is probably not worth it just to be the first in your set to taste a yard-high stem.

PART IV

INGREDIENTS
FOR CHANGE

C H A N G E S like those in China and France happened all over the world at different rates of speed and with radically different results. Yet every cuisine we have inherited from those days shows the results of the Americanization of eating. Most cookbooks today are the end result of this process, codifying the "traditional" recipes of one country or one culture. But the story of food after 1492 can also be told as a global saga that transcends national borders and national cuisines, a saga whose "heroes" are ingredients. Here are the stories of some of the most important of these wayfaring foods.

Potatoes and manioc are basic to dozens of cultures outside their place of origin in South America. Their migrations are a fundamental part of human history and human survival. Chilies and tomatoes are also of global significance even though they don't count as staples. Instead, they radically alter and enhance the spirit of cuisines that employ them. Hungarian chicken without paprika or a meal in the south of France without tomatoes—these and dozens of other typical foods of cuisines from chili-mad Bangkok to tomato-drenched Calabria would lose their zest and heart without the punch of chilies or the darkening acid addition of tomato. As for chocolate and strawberries, we could all survive without them and they don't form the backbone of any cuisine, but now that we have them, they brighten our lives, add whole dimensions of delight to the ends of meals all over the planet, and their stories are perfect examples of the international nature of the way the world eats after Columbus.

CHAPTER I

TOMATOES

EVERYONE I KNOW seems to have his own story of how the scales fell from his palate and he tasted, really tasted, a real tomato for the first time. My own ecstatic rebirth as a tomatomane took place on a rail siding in some border no-man's-land between Yugoslavia and Greece in early August 1960. After two days of sparse and dismal feeding on the old Simplon-Orient Express passing through Yugoslavia, I was able to buy a large red tomato from a boy hawking them to passengers waiting on the platform. I bit into one; juice spurted on my cheeks, and tears almost mixed in. I quiver still when I recall that moment.

It is impossible to exaggerate the attraction of the tomato, its universal appeal. Of all the New World foods it has traveled farther and wider and changed the face of more cuisines. The potato may have entrenched itself more deeply in the cold climates of northern and eastern Europe. Manioc may have transformed the subsistence economies of Africa. And corn, too, is a staple of life, or at least barnyard life, in many places outside this hemisphere. Yet the tomato, while it is rarely ever the basic means of anyone's survival, is curiously fundamental on tables from Lima to Naples to Delhi.

Consider the case of Italy. The Greeks and Romans prospered there entirely without benefit of tomatoes. No one in Europe, Africa, or Asia tasted the fruit of *Lycopersicon esculentum* until the Spanish found this Andean member of the Solanaceae family (eggplants, potatoes, deadly nightshade) under cultivation in Mexico in the early sixteenth century. But today it is impossible to imagine the cuisine of Italy without the tomato. Ditto Spain. In the last twenty years the tomato has crossed its last frontier and conquered China. Today, according to Charles Rick, the venerable tomato geneticist at the University of California at Davis, the tomato is now virtually the dominant vegetable in the People's Republic.

In this country the tomato is, of course, ubiquitous, the demand for it insatiable and unceasing. We eat so many tomatoes that they are the number-one source of nutrients among all fruits and vegetables in our diet. In a study done in the late seventies by M. A. Stevens, also of U.C. Davis, the tomato led the list of all crops in contribution of vitamins and minerals although it was only sixteenth in its intrinsic nutritional value. In other words, it would be nutritionally much more efficient to eat broccoli, spinach, Brussels sprouts, lima beans, peas, asparagus, artichokes, cauliflower, sweet potatoes, carrots, sweet corn, potatoes, or cabbage (the first fifteen in nutrient concentration in Stevens's study, in descending order), but Americans prefer tomatoes. (The next fifteen biggest actual nutritional contributors after the to-mato to the national diet are oranges, potatoes, lettuce, sweet corn, bananas, carrots, cabbage, onions, sweet potatoes, peas, spinach, broccoli, lima beans, asparagus and cauliflower.)

And yet when the Reagan administration cost-cutters declared that tomato ketchup could count as a vegetable in school lunches, there was a major outcry. The ironies were multiple. The least of them was the quibble, so beloved of writers of letters to the editor, that the tomato is not a vegetable but a fruit. This is technically correct: The tomato, since it begins as a plant ovary, is ipso facto a fruit botanically, but gastronomically it is always lumped with the vegetables, the non-liquid, nonmeat foods that aren't grains. Green peppers, squash, cucumbers, and okra are all fruits that we have reclassified as vegeta-bles because we eat them in the main part of the meal. Fruits, gas-tronomically speaking, are sweeter and are eaten as dessert or between meals. Exceptions to these distinctions are not lacking, but for the most part the botanist and the cook divide the plant world with two internally consistent systems. Botanists may puzzle over the difference between squashes and melons, but anyone who has eaten them knows that Hubbard squash is a vegetable and cantaloupe is a fruit. We can monkey with the basic qualities, usually by adding sugar or salt, and make a vegetable a fruit and vice versa—tomato ice cream is not unknown, apricots are fine with pot roast—but let's face it: In the real world the tomato is a vegetable, so why shouldn't a tomato puree (ketchup) be acceptable as such in school lunches?

Let's assume that the quantity of ketchup in that hypothetical Reagan-era school lunch was equivalent to the nutrients in a whole raw tomato. I suspect the amount of ketchup used by the average grade-schooler on French fries exceeds a whole tomato in nutritional content, but for the sake of argument, let's suppose they were identical. I doubt very much that the antiketchup people would have been mollified. Nor do I think the outcry against the relatively high sugar content of ketchup was the source of the antiketchup fury.

Ketchup is tainted by its connection with fast food. I myself saw what this guilt by association could do when I devoted a column in *Natural History* a while ago to ketchup, sketching its long and international history as a tomato preserve and an Asian sauce. There was a small revolt among the food snobs who let me know that ketchup was not a fit subject for *Natural History.* So I am inclined to believe that ketchup's low-class current profile had something to do with the school-lunch brouhaha. But the major cause lay at a deeper level and grew out of our very different attitudes toward tomatoes as a fresh, whole, raw fruit compared to tomatoes that have been cooked or processed—tomatoes as salad versus tomatoes as sauce.

Statistically speaking, we consume far more processed tomatoes than fresh. The U.S. per-capita consumption of fresh tomatoes tends to run to twelve or thirteen pounds a year, while tomato products total over twenty pounds, more than half of which is as ketchup and chili sauce. But the numbers obscure the more important difference between fresh tomatoes and processed. Fresh tomatoes are the most beloved and fought-over food in the marketplace. Their abysmally low quality for most of the year focuses the anger and paranoia of the alert consumer as no other outrage foisted upon us by agribusiness and the rapacious middle man. Everyone loves a fresh, red, pleasantly acid, ripe-to-bursting, sun-ripened, fresh garden tomato—and everyone seems to want one not just in August but also in February. So the fresh tomato is the sexy, controversial part of the tomato success story, but the processed tomato, the tomato in its insidious form, blending in with other foods in an underground red river of culinary adaptability, is an even bigger part of the tomato's conquest of the world.

Wherever you go, or so it seems, people have found new ways to add tomatoes to other foods. And since in most of these places the tomato was not easily available before 1800 or even later, the current mass popularity of the tomato outside of Mexico must be the result of active choice by ordinary people. The choice is aesthetic. They eat tomatoes because they like them and especially because they like the effect they have on other foods.

Traditional staples ensure survival; tomatoes are another kind of staple, a sort of culinary catalyst, perhaps, a food whose main appeal is not nutrition or the satisfaction of gross appetite but the way it heightens the gastronomic value of a dish. You could dismiss this notion as a highfalutin way of saying that tomatoes make dishes taste better, but I think that's a shallow way of looking at the power of the tomato in cooking. I think the tomato focuses and improves recipes that were appealing before the tomato was available but that became extraordinarily attractive after it was added. Pizza and gazpacho are two outstanding cases of this. We can all easily think of more examples, but the truly remarkable side to the world's tomatomania is that it was able to develop and spread in an atmosphere of almost universal tomatophobia. Out of initial ignorance and disgust grew ultimate passion.

HOW THE TOMATO WON FRIENDS AND
INFLUENCED PEOPLES

George Allen McCue traced this process in his M.A. thesis at Washington University (St. Louis), which was an annotated bibliography of early tomato references, published in the *Annals of the Missouri Botanical Garden* (1952). The story that emerges from hundreds of statements by botanists, physicians, gardeners, and laymen is a tragicomedy of prejudice and blundering that somehow ends in truth and delight.

The earliest written mention of the tomato was in the commentary on the botanist Dioscorides published by Petrus Matthiolus in 1544 in Venice. He considered the tomato a species of mandrake recently brought to Italy and eaten like eggplant: "fried in oil with salt and pepper." Matthiolus was apparently reporting this secondhand, but the "recipe" was requoted dozens of times by others who also had no firsthand experience of the tomato. One wonders how many Renaissance savants actually tried to cook this proto-ratatouille. Certainly Pietro Antonio Michiel didn't. In the later sixteenth century he wrote: "If I should eat this fruit, cut in slices in a pan with butter and oil, it would be injurious and harmful to me."

Melchior Guilandini looked at the bright side in 1572. He thought that Galen's Lycopersion might be the tumatle of the Americans, and its juice (the Lycopersion's and therefore possibly the tumatle's) was "useful because of its cooling nature for rheumy joints and other such pains." Several other writers, taking off from the erroneous Latin name *pomum amoris,* conclude that it must be aphrodisiac or at least so beautiful as to "command love." How else would it have acquired the name love apple? More circumspectly, Castor Durante opined in 1585 that tomatoes "afford little and poor nourishment."

German authorities claimed certain medical properties for our favorite fruit. Joachim Camerarius (1588) of Frankfurt-am-Main said it was effective against scabies. For his part, J. T. Tabernaemontanus, also of Frankfurt, thought tomatoes "should not be taken internally. . . . Some say that the juice is good for St. Anthony's fire and other fluxes."

The tide turns at Antwerp in 1635. J. E. Nieremberg says the tomato can be pickled and that it brings out the flavor of foods and enhances appetite. But Dominicus Chabraeus paid no attention to this gospel; he listed the tomato under malignant and poisonous plants in 1666, in a book published in Geneva.

By the late eighteenth century Linnaeus knew better and called attention to the fact that people were known to eat tomatoes without ill effect. This bold statement led to a cascade of apparent plagiarism in the next few years, but for most authorities the tomato remained an exotic with a lingering medicinal odor and gave off a whiff of the toxic right into the mid-nineteenth century. Yet right under the noses of these scholastic armchair botanists, ordinary gardeners were growing tomatoes in ever greater numbers and liking them ever better. Eventually some writers noticed. Joseph Sabine reported to the Royal Horticultural Society in 1819 that "great use" had been made of tomatoes for culinary purposes and that plants were being grown in private and commercial gardens. The tomato, he thought, possessed an "agreeable acid" appropriate for use in soups and salads as well as "in the manner of ketchup." According to Henry Phillips (1820), the tomato vanguard in Britain were the "wealthy Jew families" but the habit had spread widely in the "last few years," although not to the middle or lower classes. Phillips mentions a John Wilmot who harvested 433 bushels of tomatoes in 1819 and that some of the tomatoes measured twelve inches in circumference. By 1836 chops with tomato sauce was a dish well enough known to be cited in the *Pickwick Papers*.

The first reference to the tomato in the United States is in William Salmon's *Botanologia* (London, 1710). He talks about tomatoes in Carolina. The next report does not come until 1766. In 1782, Thomas Jefferson noted that his garden produced tomatoes, but not every American was as enlightened as Jefferson. Robert Gibbon Johnson has been declared a hero because he ate a tomato on the courthouse steps in Salem, New Jersey, in August 1820, thereby greatly encouraging public acceptance of the fruit. But as late as 1845 the editor of the *Boston Courier* was quoted comparing tomatoes to "rotten potatoe-balls."

He was an anachronism. It had taken three centuries, but by 1850 the tomato was a successful novelty well on the way to its current popularity and the industrial production of special hybrids genetically tailored to withstand machine picking and gas ripening in interstate trucks.

THE HUNT FOR REAL TOMATOES

Real (as I will call vine-ripened, soft-walled, acid-flavored, summer-grown) tomatoes are an article of faith, a rallying point for the morally serious, a grail. And the real tomato's acolytes are not some ragged little band of malcontents. They are us, brothers and sisters in tomato-mania, converts to the first Western religion since the Stone Age to worship a plant.

This ecstatic enthusiasm, reinforced each summer by new experiences with real tomatoes, have their dark side. They make us picky, unwilling to settle, or at least to settle happily, for false tomatoes. And so we become tomato bores, railing against square tomatoes without taste.

The Tom Paine of this rebellion is Thomas Whiteside who attempted to get to the bottom of the dark lagoon of tomato industrialization in an exhaustively reported article in the *New Yorker* magazine in 1977. It was Whiteside who spread the word about tomatoes being picked green for durability and transportability from Florida fields. It was Whiteside who alerted *New Yorker* sophisticates to the existence of square tomatoes, hybridized by modern plant scientists to accommodate mechanized harvesting. And it was Whiteside who raised the consciousness of upper-middle-class America about artificial ripening of tomatoes induced by ethylene gas.

Of course there were other tomato muckrakers out there building the almost complete consensus of intelligent consumers against the supermarket tomato. But an informal survey indicates that Whiteside was the crucial figure, the tomato Jeremiah behind whom collected a growing throng. All praise to him. He pointed to a great truth: The industrial tomato is a dud. Only corporate executives of tomato companies would disagree with that.

In attempting to think clearly about this matter, it is crucial to keep in mind that the tomato we hate is the one that we buy whole and raw to be consumed whole and raw. We are not talking about tomatoes produced for canning. This means that the square tomato is a red herring. The square tomato is not a tomato you and I can normally buy. It is aimed at the commercial canning market where delicacy of texture and taste is of far less moment than it is for fresh tomatoes on grocery shelves. In any case I have never laid eyes on a square tomato, and I doubt most tomato radicals have. So the square tomato is an illegitimate rallying point. Yes, it exists, and Gordie C. Hanna of the University of California at Davis did engineer the first cultivar suitable for machine harvesting, the VF 145, in the 1950s and 1960s. But to set up the VF 145 as an outrageous example of the perversion of science in the service of agronomic pelf would be a distortion.

So is the hate campaign against artificial ripening. The gas that growers use in storage areas and in trucks hurtling northward to set the process of ripening in motion is the same gas that tomatoes and many other plants produce in the normal course of natural ripening. This gas, ethylene, according to Webster's, is "a colorless, flammable gaseous hydrocarbon of the olefin series, C_2H_4, with a disagreeable odor: it is obtained from natural or coal gas, by cracking petroleum, by the action of sulfuric or phosphoric acid on alcohol, etc., and is used as a fuel and anesthetic, in hastening the ripening of fruits and to form polyethylene."

To the eye of the scientophobe, that definition settles the argument. What could be worse than to asphyxiate tomatoes with the same poison that comes from air-polluting petroleum, puts people out on operating tables, and contributes to the degradation of the environment in the form of nonbiodegradable and unnecessary plastic packaging?

Yes, but ethylene per se is a benign natural organic substance. A ripe apple exudes it into the air and will hasten the ripening of other fruits, including tomatoes. Not all chemicals are bad. It is the use we put them to that counts.

Yet there must be some explanation for those pale and tooth-resistant tomatoes we all hate. My theory was that a plant geneticist/villain had messed about with the genes of "normal" garden tomatoes and concocted a sturdier hybrid fit for long trips in tractor trailers with eighteen wheels on interstate highways. That Dr. Sivana of the plant labs deserved to be the target of a campaign of vilification as a traitor to his science and to humanity. I set out to find him.

Suspect No. 1 was the man who had hybridized Florida's infamous Walter tomato. The Walter won't ripen after picking until it has been gassed, and the Walter was the ancestor of the MH-1, a grower's dream developed by the University of Florida at Homestead. According to Whiteside you could play catch with the MH-1 at twenty paces or let it fall from over six feet without breaking the skin. The Walter and the MH-1 are not cannery tomatoes. They are for the table. They and tomatoes like them, from south Florida and from the state of Sinaloa in Mexico, are what make tomato lovers gnash their teeth and wish for a Senate select committee to expose the whole tasteless mess.

I was one of those people until I met Charles M. Rick, the retired professor of plant genetics at U.C. Davis known in his field as Mr. Tomato. Ruddy, lanky, white-haired, and white-bearded, Rick is a lively, good-humored, and ingratiating, completely unabashed enthusiast for the achievements of tomato science as he has known it since his student days, which ended in 1940 with a Harvard doctorate.

Since then he and his colleagues all over the world have capitalized on the extraordinary genetic malleability of the tomato to increase crop yields manyfold. Rick is not an ethereal lab technician, however; far from it. He is famous for trekking all over Peru in search of wild tomato strains that might enrich the gene pool of cultivated plants back home. He's a home gardener, too, and talks with enthusiasm about Burpee's Better Boy and another favorite variety, Caligrande, which he grows today because of its resistance to tobacco mosaic virus.

Rick has spent a lot of his long career outdoors growing tomatoes, and his modest office at Davis even has an outdoor feel to it. A jay frequently flies in the open window hoping to find a cookie or a doughnut to steal.

For the past six years Rick has been assembling a tomato germ plasm bank, a collection of twenty-six- or twenty-seven hundred tomato lines in the form of seeds. When I was there, two women in his lab were extracting seeds from wild green tomatoes the size of gooseberries. Andean plants like these have been the source of "virtually all tomato disease resistance since the forties," he says.

Although Rick is the epitome of the modern tomato scientist, he is also in the great tradition of untutored green thumbs who long ago hybridized the red fist-sized tomato we think of as normal from the tiny wild fruit nature gave to our pre-Columbian ancestors. By the time Cortés reached Mexico in 1519, cultivation had already produced tomatoes we would recognize today. Hybridization continued in Europe. All the garden tomatoes we love so much are the result of centuries of human meddling. Today's commercial varieties are no more artificial than the "normal" kind. And if Rick is right, they are not categorically worse in quality. He says:

> I don't think it's right to attribute poor market quality to breeding. That's a bunch of nonsense. Unbiased tests have been conducted—at Michigan State, for example—blind tastings of commercial varieties that were all vine-ripened. Most of the criticism is a reaction to what's happened to these tomatoes when they're grown in the off-season. The sad fact is that you can't grow a tomato on the west coast of Mexico in January, pick it green, ship it three or four thousand miles, and expect it to be as good as a garden fruit in summer. Ethylene ripening is not the issue; it's the season, the low light in winter that hurts. And they add a greater handicap by picking them green and ripening them in transit. . . . I'm not sure the best tomato in the world would be a gem under those conditions.

He saw some possible hope in work being done on tomato ripening at a Davis biotechnology firm, Calgene Inc., which just received a patent for an alteration of tomato DNA. The change affects the function of the enzyme galacturonase, which causes softening of the fruit during the ripening process. By thwarting the enzyme, Calgene has created a tomato that stays firm longer while ripening normally in other respects. In principle, the Calgene tomato could be picked mature instead of green, after it had developed flavor.

These are early reports. Field tests are now under way in Mexico. In the meantime, the pressure of a $4 billion U.S. market for fresh tomatoes has finally convinced one bold and energetic New York family named Marcelli to take a great leap forward. They are managing to deliver high-quality tomatoes to Manhattan restaurants and grocers in midwinter. How do the Marcellis do what no one else seems able to manage? They let Florida tomatoes ripen on the vine. They truck them nonstop to New York, and they keep them cool, at 55 to 60 degrees, but don't refrigerate, which would degrade flavor.

"Real tomatoes," as the sticker on each one reads, are not up to the supreme standard of summer garden fruit. They are certainly expensive, but they show that the real obstacle to bringing decent domestic tomatoes to U.S. tables in the off-season was human greed and laziness, not bad science or gas.

Perhaps we should also blame the taste of the American people who were so committed to tomatoes and to getting them for the lowest price that they would buy bad tomatoes out of season. In the world of supermarket grocery departments, tomatoes are sold as conceptual vegetables. Certainly their buyers can't be considering their actual taste since it doesn't take great powers of discrimination to see that a vine-ripened tomato in August surpasses any supermarket tomato in January. Another way of putting this is to say that the sliced tomato has become a necessary presence in certain food situations regardless of taste. It completes a salad or a sandwich; without it the dish is compromised. The sliced tomato, so to speak, adds status to a dish. But if the fresh tomato is a notional advantage at the table, the processed tomato is often a faux pas. Consider how southern Italian food is sneered at by arriviste foodies because it is "swamped" in tomato sauce (while socially acceptable northern Italian food is recommended for its low-tomato-sauce recipes).

Should you wish to correct the balance here and look down your nose at a foodie, wait until she or he serves you gazpacho and say, "Oh, I see, you make it with tomatoes. How up to date."

GAZPACHO, THE SOUP THE TOMATO
OVERWHELMED

That should stop most people right in their tracks because they've come to think of gazpacho as a kind of homemade V-8, served chilled on pool patios. But I have been looking into the matter, and I can report that in all of our Western culinary tradition, you will be hard-pressed to find a dish with so ancient a lineage, so cosmopolitan an evolution, so diverse an identity, and so little fundamental connection with the tomato or the ice cube.

M. F. K. Fisher's gazpacho recipe in *How to Cook a Wolf*—a cold, usually water-based soup of mixed herbs, tomato, onion, and cucumber, spiked with oil and lemon juice, and sprinkled with bread crumbs—stands midway between the dish's ancient Mediterranean origin and its current efflorescence as a breadless liquid salad colored with tomato and filled out with almost anything else the chef fancies.

There are many gazpachos, and I have never, or almost never, tasted one I didn't like. But if we are going to try to find out what this chameleonlike soup started out as, we had better go to Spain, its home base. More specifically, we must travel to the province of Andalusia in the south of Spain, the province of bullfights and Carmen, Cór-doba and Seville, the non-Castilian, nonlisping point of entry for the invading Moors and for the exotic foods brought after 1492 from *las Americas.* Andalusia is the world capital of gazpacho. In any survey of Spanish regional dishes, gazpacho leads the list for Andalusia, and so it makes sense to look and see what an Andalusian cookbook has to say about this totemic soup.

I was not disappointed when I turned to Miguel Salcedo Hierro's *La Cocina Andaluza* (1984). It is a long, literate, serious cookbook, and it contains no fewer than twelve recipes for gazpacho. Some have tomato, some don't. There is one based on fava beans and another on pine nuts. This is not a book influenced by nouvelle cuisine; these are all traditional recipes collected by a hardworking traditionalist. So what makes them all gazpachos? What are the common traits of all these soups. They are oil, vinegar, garlic, and bread. These ingredients are mashed and then diluted with water, then seasonings and other flavorings are added. The soup is served at room temperature.

This is one of the ancestral soups of the Western world, a liquid food made from stale bread. The word *soup* itself shows this origin, since *soup* is an etymological first cousin of *sop,* a piece of bread sopped in liquid and then eaten. A soup, then, is a sop left to soak—and then mixed into the liquid as a thickener.

Gazpacho is obviously an example of a primitive peasant soup of a sort that must have originated over and over again in every place where there was bread. But Andalusian food is heavily permeated with exotic Moorish influences, and the word *gazpacho* looks as though it just might be an Arabic loan-word. Charles Perry has investigated this theory in medieval Arabic sources and finds nothing to support it. All standard Spanish dictionaries include bread as an ingredient of the soup, and none of them refers to an Arabic etymology. Corominas's etymological dictionary of Spanish suggests that the word derives from the pre-Roman *caspa* for fragment, meaning the bread crumbs and chopped vegetable that form the dish. Santamaria's dictionary of Mexicanisms translates gazpacho as the dregs or remnant of food preparation, another possible connection with the crumbs from stale bread and possibly a usage itself left over from the time of colonial Mexico. The *Dictionary of the Spanish Royal Academy* gives, as a second-ary meaning of gazpacho, crumbs made by field hands from a *torta* cooked in hot coals. And a *gazpachero,* it says, was a farmhouse cook for hired hands.

None of this is conclusive evidence of a hard-and-fast etymology, but it certainly does support the notion of a rough peasant context in which day-old bread or the crumbs derived from it play a central role in people's sense of the identity of gazpacho. I have not been able to date the first appearance of the word in a printed text or manuscript in Spanish, but all the evidence points to great antiquity, if not for the origin of the word itself, then certainly for dishes all over the Mediterranean based on soaked bread. The oldest I have found is in the Old Testament. You will recall what Boaz says to Ruth when he comes upon her gleaning among the sheaves (Ruth 2:14): "At meal-time come thou hither, and eat of the bread, and dip thy morsel in the vinegar."

(Vinegar itself was apparently considered a healthy drink by Roman soldiers, according to Spartianus, the ancient biographer of Hadrian. They diluted it with water. And in the Gospel according to John, when Christ on the cross says "I thirst," a sponge soaked in vinegar is raised to his mouth, and after he received the vinegar, he "gave up the ghost." Much the same thing happens in the parallel passage in Mark. To a modern eye this looks like taunting, but scholars see the proffering of vinegar as an act of compassion. Why else would the Roman soldiers have had a good supply of it there at Calvary, with a sponge for applying it? In the version of this reported by Luke, the vinegar is mixed with gall, but this must be a later interpolation based on Psalm 69 where vinegar and gall are the food of despair, when the psalmist is without comforters.)

The Romans also liked to eat bread soaked in vinegar. Apicius gives recipes for salads in which vinegar-soaked bread is the central element, combined with seasonings and olive oil. A version of this dish survives today in Italy, called *pansanella*. To make soup of this salad required little more than water and, for finesse, some work with mortar and pestle. Recipes for a bread soup called *pancotto* are plentiful in the Italian repertoire. *L'Antiartusi* prints four, all of them essentially stale bread boiled in water with oil and seasonings.

I give these ancient and Italian parallels because they show how easily gazpacho could have come to Spain with the Roman legions and Roman settlers. The Italian influence on Spanish cookery reasserted itself in the sixteenth century when the first printed Spanish and Catalan cookbooks began to come out and were either translations of Italian books or heavily influenced by Italian practice.

But the basic food ideas that resulted in gazpacho might easily have evolved separately in Spain without help from the Latin-speaking invaders or from their descendants in Naples and Milan. Frugal peasants anywhere around the Mediterranean would have wanted to make use of stale bread. Soaking it in available liquids was an obvious solution, and depending on what and how much liquid you used, you had either salad or soup.

The special Spanish mark that separates gazpacho from other very plain garlic soups and gruels around the Mediterranean is that it is never exposed to heat but is prepared raw and served at room temperature. And before Columbus made it possible for Spanish cooks to put the tomato in their gazpachos, the dish took on local color with two ingredients combined in no other European country's soups: almonds and grapes.

The paragon of pre-Columbian gazpachos, an improbable but brilliant cold soup still popular in Spain, is a white gazpacho usually called *ajo blanco,* literally white garlic. Medieval Spanish cookery is full of almond-flavored and almond-thickened dishes, and the counterpointing flavor of white grapes is also an idea far from anything we might come up with today. I highly recommend this soup, but I want to stress that, despite its strangeness, at bottom it is really a gazpacho. It is thickened not only with ground almonds but also with stale bread.

This is a far cry from the post-Columbian gazpachos most of us know today, but it is probably the classic soup, the one that Cervantes mentions in *Don Quixote.* He makes it into a symbol of simple enjoyment. In Book II, chapter 53, Sancho Panza tires of being the governor of the island of Barataria, whose name might be translated as Cheapburg. The main problem with his apparently exalted post is that every time he starts to eat something, an official called Doctor Recio snatches the dish from under Sancho's nose, allegedly to protect his health. Sancho resigns eloquently: "Make way, my lords, and let me return to my former liberty. . . . I would rather stuff myself with gazpachos than be subject to the misery of an impertinent physician who kills me with hunger."

We don't really know what Sancho meant by gazpachos. Probably he was talking about *ajo blanco.* Yet the tomato had long since arrived in Spain by the end of the sixteenth century when Cervantes was writing *Don Quixote,* so it is possible that Sancho's gazpachos were red and not white. But it's also worth considering the fact that Sancho talks about gazpachos, plural. Could he mean not a soup at all but the crumbs and fragments and leftovers from which the soup takes its name? He is, after all, retreating from a lordly banquet hall to the food of his lowly past. It may indeed make better sense of the passage to construe its meaning as: "I'd rather stuff myself with stale bread than die of hunger in the lap of luxury."

The evidence just doesn't exist to decide this. We have no dates for gazpacho, either as an evolving word or as an evolving dish, but we do know that today in Spain it refers to a family of cold, uncooked soups based on the ingredients of bread salad.

In the early sixteenth century the tomato was naturalized in Spain and eventually became the dominant ingredient in gazpacho. Before long the soup traveled back across the Atlantic to the tomato's native hemisphere. Mary Randolph in *Virginia Housewife* (1796) speaks of a gazpacho salad—greens, tomatoes, cucumbers, onions, bread crumbs, and salad dressing. According to John Mariani, in an unsourced entry in *The Dictionary of American Food and Drink,* the first American printed recipe for a soup called gazpacho appeared in 1845.

It took more than a century and the arrival of the blender to popularize the gazpacho as we know it in this country. Then, in less than a generation, the nouvelle cuisine seized on this simple salad of a soup and made it a metaphor of its former self.

In California, Jeannette Ferrary and Louise Fiszer have invented seafood gazpacho, a smooth puree of bell pepper, onion, parsley, and garlic, diluted with tomato juice and clam juice, seasoned with vinaigrette, and then garnished with cooked bay shrimp. Garlic croutons are optional.

Jeremiah Tower went a bit further. For a group of food writers junketing as the guests of Campbell Soup in 1984, he invented what he calls lobster gazpacho. It is essentially a puree of tomatoes flavored with lemon and oil, chilled, and garnished with diced cucumber and bell peppers, as well as sliced cold cooked and shelled lobster pieces, chive, and three caviars, each a different color. That is not how they make soup at Campbell's—nor in Spain. All links with the past have been severed except olive oil (here its taste is modified by the addition of sesame oil). There is no bread, no vinegar, and no garlic. The original dish has been stood on its head and almost completely claimed for New World ingredients: tomatoes, peppers, and Maine lobster. Here, as in so many places from Palermo to Petaluma, the once-feared tomato now commands unthinking fealty.

CHAPTER 11

POTATOES

THE POTATO took almost as long as the tomato to achieve international mass acceptance. Two centuries passed before fearful Europeans were persuaded that this exotic relative of the deadly nightshade (and the equally suspect tomato) was fit for more than pigs. Even in Lord Byron's day, a dubious, aphrodisiac aura hung around it, for the poet, in *Don Juan,* speaks of "that sad result of passions and potatoes."

It took roughly 250 years for the potato to make its way from Peru to Spain and then to be naturalized and universally adopted as a popular food. French fries did not reach England until roughly 1870, according to C. Anne Wilson, the British food historian. They really were French in origin, a commercial food from the start, produced by street vendors in Paris in quarter-moon shapes and called *pommes Pont-Neuf.* Since the potato did not "arrive" in France as a staple food until the early 1800s, it seems probable that French fries did not exist until somewhat later. At any rate, authorities agree that they were French and reached England about 1870. This matters to the history of the potato chip because the chip is a special case of the French fry itself. The earliest recipe I know for potato chips comes from Mary F. Henderson's *Practical Cooking and Dinner Going,* published in New York in 1878. I learned this in Susan Williams's remarkable survey, *Savory Suppers and Fashionable Feasts: Dining in Victorian America* (Pantheon, 1985).

Henderson calls her chips Saratoga potatoes. This lends support to the anecdote repeated in *The American Heritage Cookbook* that potato chips were invented by accident at a fashionable resort in Saratoga Springs, New York, in the nineteenth century. The resort was Moon's Lake House, and the chef was George Crum. A patron kept sending back French fries, complaining that they were too thick. The irate Crum sliced some potatoes paper-thin, fried them, and sent them out to a rapturous reception. This mixture of legend and fact does seem to fit into a logical scenario: The French fry reaches England around 1870. A recipe for potato chips appears in an American book in 1878. All authorities agree that Victorian chips were Saratoga chips. So it does seem probable that the French fry crossed the ocean in the early seventies and was further refined by Crum or some other Saratogan soon after.

Or it may be that the deep-fried potato reached England and America separately from France. The English-speaking world does divide sharply in its fried potato vocabulary. "Chips" over there are French fries, but English potato chips, in the American sense, are always called crisps except in one situation: when they are handmade (one wants to say when they are produced in the Hawaiian style) and served with game. This exception supports the idea of a separate invention of the potato chip in England. Someone like Chef Crum must have sliced potatoes thin, but this chef decided to serve them with game. Instead of viewing his invention as a special new thing, he saw it as a kind of French fry (chip). Instead of becoming a popular food in England, the game chip was limited to the aristocratic table during hunting season. Later, when the similar but visibly different (larger, thinner, drier) American chip arrived, it couldn't be called chip, so a new term was created: crisp.

Note well that there is no confusion in England between the two kinds of potato chips. Over here we are rediscovering this difference and in a sense rediscovering our roots. When I was a boy in Detroit in the mid-forties, my favorite "meal" was a large bag of potato chips. Brands meant nothing to me; I liked them all equally well. The very idea that an industrial food product par excellence could vary in quality from brand to brand or bag to bag had never occurred to me. Nor did I expect that even these mass-produced chips were the result of a long chain of transmission that passed overland from the Andes to the Caribbean to Spain, then France, then England, then upstate New York, then Hawaii and, most recently, various U.S. mainland locations including Cape Cod. I was a boy in Detroit, the Vatican of the assembly line of interchangeable parts. And the potato chips I knew fitted in perfectly with this vision of uniformity.

I was never challenged in this "automotive" concept of the potato chip. Indeed, the only claim of brand superiority that I ever heard until quite recently (the only claim, that is, that could not instantly be dismissed as the obligatory boast of an ad) came from a dried-up old man who for a time courted the aged but foxy aunt of one of my own aunts.

When this gaffer came a-wooing, he brought plain brown cartons of potato chips. He was a minor executive at a minor local chip company, and one of his perks was access to chips deemed too large for sale to the general public. I forget if these giant disks were withheld because they were too fragile for bagging or because they would confuse people and destroy the illusion that all chips were identical. It may even have been that management liked them so well they kept them for their own delectation. This is what we were led to believe by my aunt's aunt's beau—not directly but by implication.

The trouble with the suitor's megachips was that they had nothing to recommend them except their size. If anything, they tasted less delicious than the normal kind. This experience soured me on potato chip connoisseurship for a long time. As an adult I was reinforced in this special form of Philistinism by an authoritative-sounding newspaper article which asserted that most potato chips were sold rancid but that consumers were accustomed to the rancid taste and rejected fresh chips. Since I adored commercial chips and found they all tasted alike, I assumed I was one of the millions with degraded palates who preferred rancid chips. So be it, I told myself.

Lately, however, I have been changing my mind. The steady state of the potato chip industry is now a thing of the past. In recent years I have been buying commercial potato chips that are obviously superior to the chips we all grew up with. They are available in regular markets all over the country under several brand names, but the product is essentially the same: a crisper, slightly thicker, slightly greasier chip, tasting powerfully of the spud it was made from.

You might call it the nouvelle chip although, like nouvelle cuisine, it is really not new at all but a return to an old idea, renamed and repackaged. The key word here is Hawaiian. Most of the nouvelle chips refer to Hawaii on the bag. Others identify themselves as hand cooked or kettle cooked. If you haven't noticed them yet, you probably haven't been paying attention to the potato chip racks in your supermarket. This sets you apart from most Americans.

Potato chips are the epitome of mass-market fast food. Open the bag and pop them in. Americans buy nearly $3 billion worth a year, so potato chips account for nearly half the salty snacks sold in the United States. And a single company, Frito-Lay, dominates the industry.

You would not suppose, would you, that the General Motors of potato chips would take serious notice of the emergence of the nouvelle chip. Well, the chip game is not at all like the car business, it turns out. GM might have ignored Japan for years and years, but

Frito-Lay twice tried unsuccessfully to buy the Maui Potato Chips Factory, according to the owners, the Kobayashi family, whose Kitch'n Cook'd Chips started the nouvelle chip revolution. Mark Kobayashi, the grandson of the firm's founder, says he constantly turns down offers from big American and Japanese companies. He is too proud to sell a Maui cottage industry that has inspired imitators from California to Hyannis.

It all started when Kobayashi's grandparents were interned on the mainland with other American Japanese during World War II. Somehow they learned a recipe for cooking potato chips and recreated it thirty years ago on Maui.

Today's Hawaiian chips constitute a return to the original conditions of hand cookery during the Victorian dawn of the chip—unlike the modern, mass-produced chip that is a triumph of cost-effectiveness. By contrast, Hawaiian chips tend to cost a bit more than mainstream, non-Hawaiian. They are certainly fattening, but they taste like the potatoes they started out as. And some of them are appealingly dark.

This is the Kobayashi mark of distinction. The late Dewey Kobayashi reportedly spent fifteen years searching for the ideal chipping potato. He settled on Burbank russets from the Tule Lake area of northern California. Russets contain more sugar, which turns chips brown. Most manufacturers want a light gold chip and avoid russets, but now the careful shopper can buy Hawaiian-style russets almost anywhere.

This is a triumph of marketing, but the story of the rise of the potato has often been a story about overcoming prejudice against a feared tuber through marketing. For example, the potato conquered France thanks to clever promotion by the scientist Antoine-Auguste Parmentier, who is supposed to have given nosegays of potato flowers to Louis XVI and Marie Antoinette, and who otherwise popularized the mysterious tuber by keeping an experimental field outside Paris under ostentatious guard by day; at night, curious Parisians sneaked in, dug potatoes, and ate them with a greed reserved for forbidden fruit.

Once accepted, the potato established itself as the cheap source of food energy. It thrived in the cool climate and poor soil of Ireland and Belgium—thrived so well that entire populations came to depend on it for their survival. Van Gogh's "The Potato Eaters," a grim portrait of a Belgian family at table, is testimony to the wizened subsistence that the potato brought to expanding populations. A marginally valuable nutritional source (7.7 grams of protein per pound, some vitamin C, the rest mostly water and carbohydrate), the potato did sustain life in the new industrial work force, giving them enough energy (279 calories per pound) to drag themselves to their dark, satanic mills. A dog's life but still a life.

Then came the potato blight, the fungus *Phytophthora infestans,* which plunged Ireland into famine in the mid-1840s and forced millions of Irish to seek a less tuber-dependent life in the United States. In addition to the famous blight, other potato diseases, later pegged as viral, cut into productivity. And in North America, the Colorado beetle took its toll. The Detroit River swarmed with these insects in 1871. In 1877 the same pests, still flourishing, inspired a popular ditty: "Take care of your little potatoes, boys, and all your tiny spuds . . . for the Colorado beetle's come to collar the jolly lot."

The situation was perilous. Elizabeth Browning wondered, in her (very) long poem "Aurora Leigh": "And is the potato to become extinct like the moly?" She had reason to worry, but by 1889 French scientists had developed the first effective sprays. The so-called Bordeaux mixture, copper sulfate and lime, was rivaled, appropriately enough, by the Burgundy mixture, copper sulfate and sodium carbonate.

At the same time, horticulturists experimented with disease-resistant hybrids. By the end of the nineteenth century the cross-breeding of potatoes already had a long history in Europe. The Ur potato, an irregular, knobbly affair, had long since given way to the smooth-skinned varieties that are the ancestors of the potatoes we see today. Old records contain dozens of colorful varietal names, including the Irish "Protestant." ("We boil the Devil out of them," was the standard Irish explanation for that curious name.)

Potato scientists have also traced the genetic diversity of their chosen vegetable back to its origins in the northern Andes. Redcliffe N. Salaman, the dean of potato historians, wrote that all of the later varieties of potatoes in England could be traced to the "interplay of characteristics" derived from the two types described by Gerard and Clusius in the sixteenth century.

It was then that the potato first crossed the water from Peru to Europe and began its slow progress toward mass acceptance and universal cultivation. The first recorded confrontation between spud and Western man occurred in early 1537. A scouting party of Spanish soldiers from the expedition led by Gonzalo Jiménez de Quesada pushed their way eastward to the high village of Sorocota in northern

Peru (latitude 7 degrees north). The Indians fled at their approach and, according to the account of one Juan de Castellanos, the conquistadores found their houses stocked with maize, beans, and "truffle": plants with "scanty flowers of a dull purple color and floury roots of good flavor, a gift very acceptable to Indians and a dainty dish even for Spaniards."

Castellanos's enthusiasm notwithstanding, the first potato did not, apparently, arrive in Europe until the 1570s. It was first cultivated at Seville. Shortly thereafter it cropped up in Italy. The old story that Sir Walter Raleigh carried the first potato from Virginia to England seems erroneous altogether. And the best evidence—chromosomal detective work by a Soviet group on Andean wild varieties, comparison with antique specimens in European herbariums, and research on early trade routes—makes it likely that the first exported potato came from the vicinity of Bogotá, was carried overland to Cartagena in the Caribbean, and then was shipped to Spain.

In modern Peru potatoes range in color from pale gray to yellow to red, violet, and even black. In size they run from tiny varieties no bigger than a nut to giants as large as a melon. Perhaps, given this wide choice, we have ended up with an inferior potato (fancy U.S. grocers have started carrying purple potatoes, but they taste much like white ones).

It is certain that Europeans improved on Peruvian methods of preparing potatoes for the table. To begin with, the Indians use an insipid, frost-resistant variety of potato that they then convert into a storable commodity called *chuño* by a five-day process that begins immediately after the harvest. The potatoes are spread on the ground and left to freeze overnight. Each day the people stamp on them to squeeze out the water. The tubers eventually dry out but retain their shape and are eaten like bread. A more refined *chuño*, called *tunta*, is soaked for two months in a shallow pool of water and emerges white and ready to be converted to flour.

In societies with greater technical resources for storage and cooking, potatoes are normally eaten fresh, and they have been prepared by every known process: boiling, baking, roasting, sautéing, and deep-frying. A universally adaptable dish, potatoes go well with nearly all kinds of food, from soup to fish. Russians ferment and distill them into vodka. Schoolchildren in India carry spicy potato snacks in their satchels, and they munch them as eagerly as Americans do potato chips. To my mind the highest point of potato cookery is pureed or mashed potatoes, which reach their ultimate airy sleekness when combined with an unsweetened cream puff dough, the mixture, or *appareil,* known as Dauphine. This rich culinary vehicle can be piped around the border of a serving platter and puffed in the oven or deep-fried as croquettes.

Or if you don't want to bother, you can always settle for a bag of potato chips.

CHAPTER III

CHILIES

MY GRANDMA MARY'S cooking repertoire was purely traditional, which is to say that it included only recipes she had learned from her mother or other women she had met as a girl in rural Lithuania. For us grandchildren who knew her first only as a woman in late middle age, her foods—indeed everything about her—was a reflection of what we assumed was the ancient folk culture that had produced her. And so when she served us bell peppers stuffed with chopped meat, we supposed that this was a dish common to Jewish tables since biblical times. Later, as adults, we came to understand that stuffed peppers didn't go back to the time of Abraham but were part of the general cuisine of East Europe. It was much later still that I reflected on the remarkable connection that this dish implied between my grandmother, Moctezuma, and the Catholic king and queen of Spain, Ferdinand and Isabella, who caused misery to thousands of Jews by expelling them in 1492 but also gave their descendants, including me, much pleasure with the peppers their emissary Columbus brought to European tables.

The story of the transmission of these warm-weather American exotics to the landlocked icebox is retold in a detailed and scholarly account by Jean Andrews in *Peppers: The Domesticated Capsicums* (University of Texas Press). Andrews, who has devoted many years to the study, culture, and painting of capsicums, dates the arrival of the chili in Europe to the landfall of the *Pinta* at Bayona, Spain, in 1493, an event celebrated locally on March 1. Whether Columbus actually brought chilies back with him from this first voyage is unknown. He definitely knew about them, for in his first letter to Ferdinand and Isabella and the treasurer of Aragon, he wrote that the West Indian islanders endured the cold of winter in their mountains "with the aid of the meat they eat with very hot spices."

On the assumption that Columbus took the obvious step of

collecting the source of these spices, Andrews made a pilgrimage to Bayona in 1983 and scattered jalapeño seeds in the churchyard of Ex-Colegiata Santa María in Bayona, where the *Pinta*'s crew gave thanks for their safe return almost five centuries ago.

Written accounts of the chili appeared after Columbus's second voyage (one may even have been written in April 1493), and since a major impulse for these and later voyages of exploration was to bring exotic spices to Europe, it is not surprising that this new "pepper" (which is entirely unrelated to the black pepper, *Piper nigrum,* that Columbus hoped to find) was quickly spread from one end of the Spanish and Portuguese trade routes to the other.

You might guess that with their capsicum commerce in full swing by the middle 1500s the Iberian traders would have been the source for the chilies that started turning up in the Slavic countries about the same time. But this is not how it happened. The Portuguese did bring capsicums to India and China through their colonies at Goa and Macao, making possible hot Indian and Sichuan food as we know it, but the first red capsicums to enter northern Europe came from the Balkans, imported by the Ottoman Turks. Andrews speculates that the Ottomans had latched on to chilies as early as 1513, during their siege of the Portuguese colony at Hormuz in the Persian Gulf. From the Balkan fringe of the Ottoman empire the peppers spread naturally into neighboring spheres of influence, to the German-speaking part of the Holy Roman empire (1543), to the vast territories of the former Byzantine empire, and to Russia. Hungarians, in the middle of this *mitteleuropäisch* pepper pot, started talking about paprika as early as 1569. The Magyar word *paprika* is a variation on a Slavic term for pepper: *peperke, piperke,* or *paparka.*

Hungary was and still is the northernmost major producer of capsicum peppers in Europe. No doubt it is at the upper limit of the plant's range, but even Hungary was slow to work paprika into its everyday cuisine (the rest of northern Europe never assimilated truly hot spices). The first two Hungarian paprika recipes did not appear in print until 1829, in Istvan Czifrai's cookbook. They were *paprikas* chicken and *halaszle,* the fish soup of Szeged, the center of capsicum culture in Hungary then and now.

When I first met George Lang in 1971, on the eve of the publication of his *Cuisine of Hungary,* he served me *halaszle,* a robust soup and an elegant allusion to the history of Hungarian cooking.

For Hungarians paprika is not the innocuous red dust we buy in supermarkets; it comes in several grades, from the sweet to the fiery hot. But paprika connoisseurship is limited to ethnic Magyars and food hobbyists, just as almost all enthusiasm for hot capsicums used to be a very special predilection in this country outside of Louisiana and regions formerly colonized by Spain or Mexico.

In those places there has always been a cult of hot peppers and hot food, but the supermacho aspects of Tex-Mex food, with its jalapeño-eating contests and four-alarm chili, confused outsiders and made them think that chilies were a crude and unreasonable condiment unrelated to the usual culinary refinements: flavor and complexity.

The same confusion muddled American appreciation of Indian food and, most recently, Sichuanese and Hunanese food. Some people insisted on very hot and presumably authentic versions of these exotic cuisines. Others, unused to hot foods, sent back what they had ordered, creating difficulties and embarrassment in restaurant kitchens. Meanwhile the judgment, enjoyment, and presentation of Mexican, Indian, and Chinese food in this country was polarized into an oversimplified matter of hot or cold.

Inexperience with capsicums left most Americans unable to approach these new foods with an open mind. It took almost twenty years for the initial shock of hot capsicum-based cuisines to wear off and for large numbers of people to begin to get beyond the crude fact of hotness to an appreciation of the diverse flavors brought to food by the many varieties of chilies employed with such finesse elsewhere.

The restaurant booms in Mexican, Sichuan, and Thai food have helped. More and more people have habituated their palates to the burn of capsaicin, the chemical essence of capsicum heat. They are now ready to pay attention to the multiform pleasures of the myriad cultivars of *Capsicum annuum*, the chili species responsible for almost all the peppers we encounter.

And we do encounter an ever greater number, even those of us far from Santa Fe and El Paso and the Grand Central Market in Los Angeles. There has been a great change since I first read the section on chilies in Diana Kennedy's *The Cuisines of Mexico* and wondered if I would ever be able to cook most of the dishes in her book at home since they required arcane chilies with names like *pasilla* and *güero* and *cascabel*.

I also wondered if the lady wasn't making a bit of a learned fuss over chili specificity. Then I took a trip to the French islands of the Caribbean and immersed myself in the local Creole cuisine, which, among other fetching characteristics, has a typical flavor that owes much to a crinkly, cherry-sized pepper, hot but not infernally so. It was crucial to the taste of the omnipresent fish stew called *blaff* and to many other dishes impossible to re-create at home without it.

Now I can buy this pepper by the bag in my supermarket. And thanks to Jean Andrews, I can identify it. It is *C. chinense, var. rocotillo*, and I am happy to say that Andrews likes it too. "After growing and tasting peppers from all over the Western Hemisphere for five years," she writes, "my hands-down favorite 'eating pepper' is the rocotillo. This crisp-textured fruit with enough pungency to be interesting but never caustic is not only delicious eaten raw but also beautiful to look at when used as a garnish." Rocotillos are either pale yellow-green or red, and they grow well in central Texas. Eat them on the side as a condiment with beans or roast meat, or throw them in with all manner of foods while they cook. The rocotillos I am buying are pallid in flavor compared to the ones I recall from Martinique, but they are interesting and worth tasting anyway.

That we can buy rocotillos at all in New York is wonderful testimony to the resilience of the marketplace and to the flexibility of the consumer, but at the same time we might also ask ourselves why it has taken half a millennium for chilies to take serious hold in a culture with an Anglo-Saxon, North European base.

Why did capsicums not find a happy home north of the Pyrenees? To an extent, botany was destiny. Peppers were hard to grow in northern climates, but the Hungarian experience is proof that it can be done if the will is there. And the Russian passion for capsicum-flavored pepper vodka is a relatively early example of a low-spice culture acquiring a taste for hot food.

Until our own era, however, the taste for hot spices, of which capsicums are the epitome, does seem to have been deeply embedded in the cultures that had it. Sichuan province already had embraced its local brown pepper before capsicums came in, and India was a proverbial center of spices. Northern Europe, on the other hand, had to import most of its spices, and capsicums seem to have presented too much of a challenge to the palate. This is not really a solid explanation, but the evidence doesn't permit us to say much more than this: The cultures that did adopt chilies shortly after 1500 were cultures in warm enough places to grow the plants and also cultures with a preexisting enthusiasm for bold spices or with a predilection for culinary novelty. (Sichuan and Hungary lay at crossroads of commerce and borrowed heavily from their neighbors in food ideas and in other aspects of life. Hungarian cooks, for example, made Turkish flaky pastry into their very own strudel and spoke Latin in their parliament.) In most parts of this country, for example, chilies did not really catch on with English speakers until the current craze for regionalisms and ethnic food swept over us as part of the general change in taste called nouvelle cuisine. Chocolate had a much easier time making friends with Old World palates.

CHAPTER IV

CHOCOLATE

Yes. It took four men, all four ablaze with gorgeous decoration, and the chief of them unable to exist with fewer than two gold watches in his pocket, emulative of the noble and chaste fashion set by Monseigneur, to conduct the happy chocolate to Monseigneur's lips. One lacquey carried the chocolate pot into the sacred presence; a second, milled and frothed the chocolate with the little instrument he bore for that function; a third, presented the favoured napkin; a fourth (he of the two gold watches), poured the chocolate out. It was impossible for Monseigneur to dispense with one of these attendants on the chocolate and hold his high place under the admiring Heavens. Deep would have been the blot upon his escutcheon if his chocolate had been ignobly waited upon by only three men; he must have died of two.

—CHARLES DICKENS,
A Tale of Two Cities, Chapter 7

IN THE thirty-five years since I first read that luxurious description of an eighteenth-century French chocolate ritual in tenth grade, it has stuck in my mind as a prime example of how, in modern times, privileges and experiences once open only to aristocrats and millionaires have spread and turned into commonplace enjoyments for ordinary people. Chocolate today is no longer a special food. The poorest urchins gobble it unceremoniously in candy bars and junk pastries. It snaps, crackles, and pops in breakfast cereals. Perhaps the last time any civilized human being thought of chocolate as a rare commodity was in Europe during World War II when American GIs won the hearts and minds of French children by passing out Hershey bars. Hitler had not been able to change the fact that chocolate came only from tropical countries not under Nazi domination.

Now produced almost anywhere in the world with a mean annual temperature of 80 degrees Fahrenheit, chocolate was originally "discovered" by the Spanish conquistadors in Mexico. *Chocolate* is a corruption of the Nahuatl word *chocolatl* (a combination of the Aztec root for chocolate and the word for water). Montezuma's household reportedly went through two thousand jars a day. Chocolate spread quickly to Europe in the form the Aztecs used—as a beverage.

It took a while longer for solid chocolate confections to work their way into the Western menu. In any case, chocolate consumption seems to have developed somewhat later in England than on the Continent. The first reference to beverage chocolate in the *Oxford English Dictionary* dates to 1604. Despite his immense working vocabulary, Shakespeare did not mention chocolate at all. Pepys went to a coffeehouse in 1664 "to drink jocolatte" and found this still novel drink "very good." Confectionary chocolate does not appear in English until 1659.

Like many foods imported by Europe at high cost from the New World, chocolate confused people. This is why we have inherited the barbaric word *cocoa*, the result of an ignorant blurring of *coconut* with the generic term for the chocolate plant, which is, properly, *cacao*. Cacao reflects the Nahuatl word for the seeds or beans from which we get chocolate—*cacahuatl*. Today its vernacular descendant, *cocoa*, is normally applied to powdered, partly defatted chocolate and to the drink made from it. This is one time when it might make sense to put the scientific name into general use. Linnaeus chose well: Not only does *Theobroma cacao* pay tribute to Aztec beginnings but the genus name, meaning "divine food," reflects chocolate's high place in everyone's estimation.

At any rate, chocolate does grow on trees. *T. cacao* is fairly short, rarely exceeding twenty-five feet, and produces clusters of small flowers both on its main branches and, strangely, on its trunk. Normally each cluster of flowers turns into a single fruit in the form of a purplish yellow pod, 7 to 10 inches long and 3 to 4½ inches in diameter, with a hard rind marked by ten elevated longitudinal ribs. Inside the pod are five cells, each containing five to twelve seeds embedded in soft, light-pink acid pulp.

The seeds are the valuable part of the plant, the source of chocolate. The Aztecs bagged them in standard quantities and used the bags as a form of currency. It takes five years before a cacao tree will fruit—five years of steady warmth, good rainfall, and shade. In the tropical areas suitable for cacao, shade is the rarest of these necessary conditions, and rows of cacao are commonly interplanted with shade plants such as bananas and cassavas, or permanent shade trees such as the coral tree, known fittingly as *madre del cacao*.

Once the cacao pods are ripe, they are broken open and the seeds are extracted. In the first step of processing, the seeds are allowed to ferment or "sweat" for up to twelve days. This destroys the mucilage on them, reduces their bitterness, and lets their color change to a cinnamon brown. Next, the seeds are dried and cured, after which they are roasted in rotating iron drums at 260 to 280 degrees Fahrenheit. This develops the chocolate aroma, converts natural starch to dextrin, and further reduces bitterness. Finally, the seeds are crushed and winnowed to remove the shells and germs. The result is a rich, dark sort of edible gravel called cocoa nibs.

To make chocolate from nibs, manufacturers add sugar and flavorings such as vanilla (another Mexican native welcomed by the wide world). By then the chocolate has become a semiliquid mass that can be molded into tablets and sold to small, greedy children who like to smear it on their hands and faces, as well as to adults who restrain their avarice only long enough to convert chocolate into a mousse.

Such chocolate is considered too rich to drink, and so hydraulic presses squeeze out some of the fat, or cocoa butter, before beverage chocolate is pulverized into cocoa.

The leftover cocoa butter is not thrown away; it is particularly valued in the pharmaceutical and cosmetic industries because it is solid at room temperature but liquid at body heat.

Not only the fat but also the shells of cacao seeds have a use. They can be brewed with water to make an ersatz coffee, or they can be fed to cattle. The shells also contain theobromine, a bitter, white crystalline compound that is closely related to caffeine and whose salts and derivatives are valued as diuretics.

Cooks, however, are primarily interested in the less exotic byproducts of *T. cacao*, various types of commercially available chocolate, which are officially defined in this country. The cocoas, for instance, are rated according to their fat content. Breakfast cocoa has a minimum of 22 percent; regular cocoa contains between 10 and 22 percent; and low-fat cocoa is less than 10 percent fat.

Chocolate regulation is more complex. Sweet chocolate must contain at least 15 percent chocolate liquor or plain processed chocolate. Milk chocolate must have 10 percent chocolate liquor and 12 percent whole-milk solids. In some varieties the milk-solid component can run as high as 22 percent. Sugar content ranges widely for the various types of chocolate. Semisweet chocolate is usually 40 percent sugar by weight. Instant cocoa can contain 80 percent sugar.

Furthermore, virtually all commercial chocolate has been manipulated structurally so that it will perform specific tasks more efficiently and attractively. For example, chocolate that is used to coat ice cream commonly has vegetable oil instead of cocoa butter worked into it.

Chocolate processing, in one way or another, dates almost from the beginning of its consumption. According to Sahagún, Aztec aristocrats mixed chocolate with honey or purple flowers. In modern Mexico, where grind-your-own-chocolate places still exist—and probably reflect antique custom—the method of manufacture also involved a simple form of admixture and processing. Diana Kennedy writes:

> The townswomen and the peasants from the countryside [of Oaxaca] buy their kilos of cacao beans, and a certain quantity of sugar and almonds to go with them, depending on what they can afford—if they are very poor, then they buy fewer cacao beans and almonds and more sugar. Each woman picks up a zinc tub, which she places under one of the several grinding machines around the store. The cacao and almonds are poured into the hopper, and very soon a satiny, tacky chocolate sauce oozes out of the spout—which has been sprinkled with sugar so that none will stick and be wasted—and falls onto the pile of sugar in the tub below. The women have brought with them two large wooden spoons to mix it all well together, and some even have brushes so that not one speck of the valuable chocolate is left sticking to the metal. Then the chocolate is carried to another machine for a second grinding—this time with the sugar—and it is at this point that you persuade someone to let you stick your finger in and try. It is then carried home and set to dry in small molds in the sun.

Mexican chocolate, even that available commercially in this country, is a wonderful blend of similar elements. I am partial to a kind that is flavored with cinnamon, in the style of Hispanic chocolate every-where. This is the oldest known flavoring for chocolate. I first learned of the cinnamon-chocolate combination reading Elizabeth David's *Spices, Salt and Aromatics in the English Kitchen,* in which she gives a recipe for a cinnamon-spiked, egg-white soufflé called *chocolate chin-chilla.* She also laments the triumph of vanilla over cinnamon as the principal flavoring of commercial chocolate. More recently Miss David wrung her distinguished hands about chocolate once again. In her extraordinary *English Bread and Yeast Cookery,* she laments the passing of the "crude, rather gritty chocolate" of thirty years ago: "Chocolate processing techniques have reached so fine a stage that the remembered texture has gone, and with it some of the character."

Yes, but we can still muddle along with today's sleeker product, using our greater knowledge of the global chocolate repertoire to cook the full historic gamut from Mexican *moles* to Michel Guérard's "melt-ing" chocolate marquise. Perhaps the most "advanced" stage in cross-cultural chocolate cookery was reached circa 1972 at the food conces-sion of Gilbert Lake State Park, Otsego County, New York, where Asia met Mexico in the high-tech form of chocolate-covered frozen bananas.

CHAPTER V

MANIOC

> *Once upon a time men had neither sweet*
> *manioc nor fire. An old woman was given the*
> *secret of the first by the ants; and her friend, the*
> *nocturnal swallow . . . would obtain fire for her*
> *(keeping it hidden in his beak), so that she could*
> *cook the manioc, instead of heating it by expo-*
> *sure to the sun or by putting it under her armpits.*
>
> > *The Indians found the old woman's man-*
> *ioc cakes excellent and asked how she prepared*
> *them. She replied that she simply baked them in*
> *the heat of the sun. The swallow, amused by this*
> *falsehood, burst out laughing, and the Indians*
> *saw flames coming from his mouth. They forced*
> *it open and took possession of the fire. Since then*
> *nocturnal swallows have had gaping beaks.*

—TACUNA MYTH QUOTED BY
CLAUDE LÉVI-STRAUSS
IN *The Raw and the Cooked*

MY DOG'S name is Ilka. She is a kuvasz, which means she is large
and white and descended from a race of surly Hungarian sheep guard
dogs. All of this is lost on the Spanish-speaking staff of my New York
apartment building. Even her name is beyond their ken and their
phonological reflexes. Flummoxed by its Magyar sounds, they call her
Yuca. This would not amuse our Hungarian friends who are already
cross with us because, they say, Ilka is not an appropriate name for
a dog but is for a beautiful woman. Their idea of a good dog's name
is something *we* can't pronounce, like Gyönyörüség (Loveliness). The
members of our Hispanic building staff are highly amused, however,

because they think we have named our elegant white bitch after a homely root vegetable. In the Spanish language, which borrowed it from Taino, yuca refers to manioc, a plant barely known to Anglophone Americans except in one of its processed forms, tapioca.

Because of my gastroethnographic travels, I think I've earned the right to call my dog manioc, particularly since I've grown to like this scrappy plant that keeps so many subsistence communities in South America and Africa alive. I like the way it tastes. I like its distinctive glutinous texture.

In my experience the best place to witness the highest form of manioc cuisine is in Cartagena, Colombia. During my visit to this great Caribbean port (see page 63), I ate many manioc dishes of great delicacy, but the one I remember most fondly was a sort of pastry (except that it had no flour) or candy (except that it was being consumed as a side dish with main courses in a downtown saloon of the most basic variety).

The demotic accent of Cartagena is not easily comprehensible to outsiders, so when I asked the man next to me the name of the dark, thin, wiggling square he was eating, I couldn't make out his answer. After three tries I got a good enough idea so that I was able to match up the anise-flavored oddment with a recipe in a Cartagenan cookbook. *Enyucado* is a mixture of grated manioc, sugar, grated white cheese, butter, coconut milk, aniseed, and cream, baked in a moderate oven for a half hour. It is an unctuous thing to eat and a triumph of man against manioc.

Manioc—the staff of life for some 200 million people in the tropics—is probably the most mysterious and misunderstood of all important foods. By the time the Portuguese discovered manioc among the indigenous Tupi peoples of the Brazilian coast, this shrubby perennial of the spurge, or Euphorbiaceae, family had been under cultivation in this hemisphere for millennia. Manioc roots are depicted on four-thousand-year-old Peruvian pottery, so for at least six thousand years manioc has supported human life, marginally.

In one form or another this prolific, easily cultivated plant supplies the bulk of food energy for the masses of Amazonia and black Africa. Whole cuisines are built on *Manihot utilissima* (alias *M. esculenta*); as *fufu* or *gari* or *farofa*, it is the tropical world's cornflakes and potato chips and bread all rolled into one indispensable, all-purpose, universal starch. But this universality barely extends to tables outside the third world.

Actually, manioc in the processed form of tapioca does occasion-

ally appear in the United States and Europe. Anyone who pays attention to tropical produce sold to Hispanic customers in New York and
other North American cities with Caribbean enclaves will have noticed those bulky, tuberous, whitish vegetables. My Puerto Rican
adventures, as I've said, put me in daily, even hourly contact with
manioc dishes.

Puerto Ricans and other Spanish speakers call manioc yuca; in
English we normally say cassava; the French say manioc; in Asia one
hears tapioca. This chaos of nomenclature, deriving from the vernacular names found by colonists all over the tropical New World, undoubtedly adds to the confusion surrounding a remarkable plant.
M. *utilissima* is an extremely poor source of nutrition. It is roughly
1 percent protein, half as rich as potatoes. The rest is almost entirely
starch, but that is the point.

Like the potato in the diet of the Irish in the nineteenth century,
manioc makes life for millions possible because it provides cheap,
abundant food energy. Protein, vitamins, and other vital nutriments
must come from other sources. This is why most meals in tropical
Africa consist of lumps of cassava paste or porridge dipped in a
protein-rich sauce. If such meals are only a subsistence diet, they do
at least provide subsistence. And there is also good evidence that
people brought up on manioc love it and regard its innumerable
cooked forms with all the fussiness and appetite that we reserve for
lobster or for very thin, pounded white veal.

Nontropical peoples like us don't know much about manioc
because it doesn't grow in our climate. In the zone bounded roughly
by the 30th parallels, north and south, it flourishes in the poor soil
of rain forests. It resists locusts and other pests. It requires only the
most cursory care and the simplest agricultural skills. Since it grows
fast and is a plant for all seasons, it is ideally adapted to the seminoma-
dic, slash-and-burn horticulture of aboriginal Amazonia and West
Africa. As Columbus noticed, manioc is a gardener's dream. Cuttings
mature in only a few months to plants averaging nine feet in height.
Their roots swell into tuberous enlargements one to two feet long and
two to six inches across. These weigh up to ten pounds, and a single
plant can produce fifty pounds of edible root in stump-studded,
crudely cultivated dooryard plots.

But there is a catch: Manioc is often toxic. Some plants generate
lethal doses of prussic (hydrocyanic) acid. No doubt this faculty protects the plant from animal and insect attacks. The poison is not
present in undisturbed plants. Small sacs under the peel or bark exude

a milky latex when the bark is cut. This white juice contains a cyano-genetic glucoside (manihotoxine) that breaks down into prussic acid, glucose, and acetone. The natural enzyme linase frees the acid, and its action can be promoted by soaking the root in water, by cutting up the root to increase contact between linase and the acid, or by heating (but not above 75 degrees Centigrade [167 degrees Fahrenheit] since higher temperatures kill the linase). Once the acid has been liberated into the air by one or several of these methods, the manioc is safe to eat.

Preliterate manioc consumers discovered how to handle poisonous manioc. They also noticed that some plants were not toxic, and so they assumed, as did botanists until recently, that there were two basic varieties of manioc, sweet and poisonous. More careful study has shown that the observed difference is not genetic; it comes from the environment. Researchers have found that clones from poisonous plants will grow up sweet in new settings and vice versa. Indeed, the nature of manioc is so adaptable that varietal names have only limited value, for clones vary significantly under diverse conditions. Perhaps, then, we should not smile too broadly at the fanciful vernacular names for manioc used by the Yoruba of West Africa. The high-yielding *onigbese duro gbowo* ("Creditor, wait to be paid") and the quick-cooking *alejo duro ndana* ("Stranger, wait, and I cook") are probably more practical designations, because they describe specific results, than more technical descriptions that imply something about future generations of plants from the same parent.

Despite such diversity, manioc roots of all kinds are processed in the same basic ways once they have been detoxified. They are pounded, pressed, strained, ground, and dried to form meal, flour, starch, and stock. Meal is the principal product. In Brazil a wooden bowl of raw *farinha da mandioca* is served at every meal as a condiment for rice or beans, and it is still made by a process not far removed from the original Indian technology. The primordial method involved grating the peeled root with a flat, stone-studded piece of wood and then pressing it in a *tipiti,* a cylindrical basket whose diameter and volume shrink when the ends are pulled. The pressed manioc is sieved and then toasted over a fire in a shallow pan.

True manioc flour is made from dried root that is pulverized. To obtain starch, both Indians and non-Indians put grated, pressed manioc in water, stir, and let the starch settle. If the starch is sifted while damp and then toasted, it clumps into tapioca balls. Raw starch is used in laundries and for sizing new clothes.

The toxic, milky liquid, a by-product of all these processes (variously known as *cassareep* and *manipuera*), can be made safe by heating and used as a sauce base.

Finally, like all other starchy substances, manioc can be fermented. Amazonian women and children chew the manioc to impregnate it with saliva and hasten the fermentation along. Although manioc beer probably has no future as a beverage in industrial societies, whole roots and manioc meal are worth trying as alternatives to more familiar starches. Toasted meal, called *farofa* in Brazil and *gari* in West Africa, is a real treat available at Hispanic and Brazilian specialty shops. Perhaps the best way to try it is in a gritslike recipe, *imoyo eba*, brought to Nigeria by ex-slaves returning to their homeland from Brazil, following the same route as manioc itself. First, the manioc meal should be toasted in a pan lightly greased with oil. Stir constantly. Then sprinkle this *gari* into a simmering pot containing 1½ cups of chicken stock and 4 tablespoons of tomato paste. Cook briefly, until firm. Toasted meal can also be stirred into scrambled eggs or mixed with chopped hard-boiled eggs, onion, and garlic to make a stuffing for poultry. You might try heating pork gravy, beaten egg, and *gari* to produce a sort of tropical Yorkshire pudding.

If all else fails, you can fall back on tapioca. Most American markets supply only instant tapioca, finely ground pellets also called grists. The old-fashioned pearl tapioca makes a nice change. These larger granules (or the smaller ones) can be thickened with wine or fruit juice or, in a particularly lush variation, with coconut milk.

Pearl tapioca must be soaked in double its volume of water for at least an hour or until the water is absorbed. Nothing, of course, prevents you from buying a whole root from a tropical fruit and vegetable grocer, chopping it, soaking it, grating it yourself in a processor, and making your own cassava flat bread. But if you are going to embark on so strenuous an act of symbolic solidarity with the third world (where more practical but similarly inclined first-world botanists are now trying to develop high-protein strains of manioc), you should at least be careful you do not mistakenly buy a *casaba* (a melon named after a place in Turkey) or a *yucca* (a member of the lily family whose bloom is the state flower of New Mexico).

CHAPTER VI

STRAWBERRIES

THE SAGA of the strawberry epitomizes the international, hybrid history of the foods we now take for granted. I have saved it for last because that is where the strawberry belongs in a meal and also because its origins in both hemispheres and its debt to all three major colonial powers make an ideal final image, a perfect coda for our odyssey in the world's larder.

Like most Americans I reached adulthood believing that strawberries were the straightforward product of human improvement on a wild plant, a plant native to the United States. There is some truth to this, but only a half truth, maybe just a quarter truth. That was what I believed without taking the matter too seriously, even after I had unwittingly moved within an easy walk of the actual birthplace of the strawberry.

During my stint in Paris in 1966 and 1967, I lived in that part of the Fifth Arrondissement that verges toward the Jardin des Plantes from the eastern slopes of the hill grandly known as the Montagne Ste. Genevieve. One of the neighborhood Metro stops was called Jussieu, but I never bothered to find out why, any more than I stopped to wonder about the etymologies of the other two: Cardinal Lemoine and Monge. During that time in the later sixties I made another nonchalant encounter, with the local wild strawberry, *fraise des bois*, next to the parking lot at the chateau of Vaux-le-Vicomte, subsequently a James Bond location (for *Octopussy*, I believe). I also spent some time interviewing Orson Welles, who was particularly abusive about some large tasteless strawberries we were served at a bad restaurant in the Place St. Michel.

Twenty years later I came to understand the connection between those apparently random events. I was an American in Paris; so, in its day, was the strawberry. Both of us had been significantly improved by contact with the intellectual milieu of Paris. Later experiences caused us to enter a decadent phase. In the case of the strawberry, the tale is dramatic and of worldwide significance.

In the beginning, Europeans had only wild strawberries, those little *fraises des bois* that Diderot Gallicly compared to "the tips of wet nurses' breasts." But enticing as this sounds, the actual berry is awfully small and often "a little seedy on the tongue," as Jane Grigson put it. Even the slightly larger Alpine Hautbois variety is a piker and could not be coaxed to get much larger by the best of early modern European botanists.

Meanwhile, early Virginian settlers battened on their own wild strawberry, grew it, and let it be taken to England and Europe. It held on to its New World virtue, however, and would not cross with Europe's wild strawberries. In 1712 a French navy man named Amédée François Frézier brought back five plants from South America's Pacific coast to Brest, where only one bore viable pollen and managed to produce large pale yellow insipid fruits with a whiff of pineapple flavor.

This gawky Chilean pine or sand strawberry (*Fragaria chiloensis*) was eventually given to the great Parisian botanist Bernard de Jussieu at the King's Garden (his elder brother Antoine had also run what is now the Jardin des Plantes; the Metro stop seems to honor both men). Jussieu shared the wealth, and green thumbs around Europe made these newcomers pop fruits as big as eggs, even apples. It took most of the rest of the century, though, before another French botanist, Antoine Nicholas Duchesne, thought to plant the scrappy little *F. virginiana* near the giant from Valparaiso (actually *F. chiloensis* is native on the Pacific coast continuously from South America to Alaska). The rest is fruit history and a tribute to American vigor, so often sneered at in France, and to American finesse, so seldom admitted to exist. Really, we should confiscate their French fries and send them home to Peru.

Of course we can't, and it probably won't do any good to tell this story to French friends. Most won't believe you; the better sort will see it as another example of America as a wild place needing to be tamed and refined by French civilization. Without Jussieu, without Duchesne . . .

It is true that the strawberries we now produce by the carload, from the Hudson Valley to the verges of Disneyland in fields mulched with vinyl, owe their existence to French and British cleverness. The first examples of the modern variety, now called *F. ananassa* because of their pineapple fragrance, were produced in England in 1819 and sold as Keen's seedlings. We reimported the big and tasty hybrid back across the Atlantic, but we still have a right to feel proprietary over strawberries and to feel sensitive if ribbed about them.

PART V

REDISCOVERING
AMERICA

Y O U   D O N ' T have to be French to dismiss the whole notion of an American cuisine with your nose in the air. None of the standard theories for explaining the origin of cuisines in other places fits the food of this country in whole or in part. With the possible exception of Amerindian foods, we in this new-found land have not had time to accrete a coherent body of dishes and food customs that could properly be called a cuisine in the European or Asian sense of the word. We've had no tradition of royal and noble cookery to perfect a haute cuisine. Similarly, we've had no settled peasant population on the same land under the same conditions for centuries evolving their own regional cuisines. In this country we honor century farms—farms worked by the same family for more than a hundred years. What most of us tend to eat is an eclectic mix of foodstuffs and food ideas gathered from a hundred places and never given the undeniably national stamp that a meal in France or in Italy usually has, regardless of region.

The Old World—Europe, Asia, the Middle East, and North Africa—had been assimilating the larder of the New World for well over a century before European settlement continued the process in North America. Since, by legend, the Pilgrims invented what we would now call United States regional food with the first Thanksgiving in 1621, it is theoretically possible to talk about a food tradition going back almost four hundred years now. But for the United States outside New England and the East Coast, the frontier period, when food creativity was highest, took place later, stretching into the nineteenth and even the twentieth centuries in the West.

It was with thoughts like these in mind that, to my subsequent regret, I mocked James Beard in a review of his magnum opus on

American food (*James Beard's American Cookery*). Mr. Beard claimed that corned beef sandwiches, tacos, and roast beef with Yorkshire pudding all belonged together in this country and qualified collectively as a cuisine. At the time I said I was reminded of what the critic John Simon had said about C. P. Snow: "He sees two cultures where I see barely one." Mr. Beard saw one cuisine where I saw either none or dozens, depending on how you defined cuisine.

I have come to realize that Mr. Beard did not think that johnnycakes and kielbasa fitted into a seamless whole. He meant that they were the survivors in a winnowing process that had left large parts of traditional cuisines behind in their homelands. Here in this unmelted pot some very disparate things had floated to the top and looked to be staying there for the duration. He meant that America's cuisine, like America, was not to be understood by referring to an Old World model of coherence and longevity, which didn't exist anyway. American food's coherence was in its incoherence. Diversity made it whole.

If you detect a mystic tone there, you are not mistaken. I only half believe what I just said. When my head is clearer, as I hope it is now, I tell myself that America's traditional cuisine, if we have one, is the result of many separate collisions between immigrant groups applying what they knew from the old country to what they found in the new.

Stated in the abstract like that, my definition probably sounds like a simpleminded cliché. So let's come down to earth a bit. Maybe it will help if I tell you what I think should be excluded from the gastronomic universe I'm defining as specifically American. Obviously I don't mean French food or other traditional dishes brought here by skilled native practitioners and reproduced more or less authentically, without substituting local ingredients that significantly alter the result to a point where a visitor from the country of origin would be justified in disowning what he's served. In fact, I want to exclude all ethnic or imported foods that haven't changed on these shores. Mayonnaise, even Hellman's, is not American by this definition. Homemade mayonnaise is an import, and so is the bottled kind, invented in England within the past one hundred years or so. The only pasta that I'd call American is probably the commercial kind known misleadingly in one version as Franco-American. But that is a trivial exception.

High principles also force me to reject hot dogs and hamburgers and apple pie. All of them came here from other places and didn't change except in the way they were appropriated to the American myth and grew popular because they suited local conditions of food service so well.

So what am I willing to call American food? I see two general categories. The first includes all the plants and animals native to this hemisphere and unknown to the Old World until Columbus opened the way to their discovery and to their spread throughout the world. In this category belong the turkey, the American persimmon, black walnuts, sassafras, chili peppers, blueberries, Olympia oysters, and wild rice. The second category includes everything that settlers in what is now the United States did with these new foods under the pressure of frontier conditions as well as what they did with the recipes they brought with them from the old country. A French fish soup was turned into New England chowder by substituting available ingredients for the original ones and by anglicizing its name. Early Hoosiers took the tasty little wild persimmons they picked up off the ground and used them in fudge and other European dessert recipes.

Both these categories—the found, indigenous larder of foods new to Europeans and the new dishes created by Europeans in the United States before World War I—make up the first half of this section. They are the foods and foodways we can rightly regard as the specially American foods in our national gastronomic inheritance. Many of them are now regional curiosities, like mulberry fruits or filé. Some have faded away almost completely, such as key limes and hundreds of commercially unviable apple varieties. But the selection discussed in the first part of this section illustrates the historical and social forces at work in the United States in its earlier years, creating the last of the important European colonial cuisines.

While North Americans were inventing traditions for themselves in the kitchen, some native ingredients spread to other hemispheres and then came back again with a new wave of immigrants or in the notebooks of U.S. tourists. As I've shown earlier, jicama traveled to the Far East (probably from Mexico to the Philippines first, with the Acapulco galleons) and has been repatriated recently by Chinese newcomers to our side of the Pacific rim. Gazpacho, as I've also said, crisscrossed the Atlantic, too, ending up as a thoroughly Californized dish. Or will it re-hispanicize itself in the future?

The evolution of American cuisine continues, and we can see the typical mechanism of creative change—substitution of one ingredient for another—going on before us every day. These recent developments reflect their time. They involve mostly non-European immigrants and exotic ingredients now making a home for themselves in the United States. Mexicans, Caribbean islanders, and South Americans have brought with them a new larder, one especially rich in root vegetables and in recipes with an African heritage tempered for centuries in the Americas. In some cases food technology has put an American stamp on "foreign" foods—the olive, the pistachio, the date, and the cherimoya. Marketing has brought us the kiwi and radicchio. I've gathered a selection of these new wrinkles into a second section. They belong together as a family of twentieth-century newcomers variously affected by the forces of our time. Also, in their greater exoticism, they fit together with the intellectual changes uniting the world's kitchens in the cosmopolitan atmosphere of the nouvelle cuisine discussed in the next chapter, where our story ends for now.

U.S. COLONIAL
SURVIVALS

W H E N I F I R S T began thinking about food in public in 1971, I knew of nobody spending serious time on food history. There were collectors of old cookbooks, and there were a few earnest souls reprinting them. Williamsburg had its publication; so did Maryland. But the bulk of the effort of preserving and serving traditional American foods was a catch-as-catch-can business occurring in the odd showplace restaurant or at special holiday celebrations or chamber of commerce events celebrating local history once a year or once every centennial. Most of the "traditional" restaurants owed almost nothing to the past. But even though they frequently distorted culinary history, these regional restaurants were frequently the only places where an outsider—or in many cases a local person—could experience even an unreasonable facsimile of regional food.

Today a fever for these hoary dishes and rustic ingredients possesses the land. The tradition-obsessed, rare-ingredient-mad American nouvelle cuisine purveyors have battened on ye olde American cuisine with a vengeance. I have chosen a few of these distinctive ingredients and frontier dishes in order to give a flavor of an unreconstructed America, an America that improvised these dishes because it had to. This is not in any sense a complete survey of the historic foods and recipes of the United States. It is a highly selective look at almost a dozen foods and recipes, and what has happened to them now that the world suddenly cares about them once again. Some of them. Wild mushrooms are now routinely available in supermarkets, but native persimmons are still not raised for market outside southern Indiana. Why have some regional foods been swept into the nouvelle maelstrom and others left behind? That is part of the evolutionary tale. Let's begin with a success story.

CHAPTER I

OLYMPIA OYSTERS

THE OLYMPIA OYSTER is unquestionably the emblematic creature of Puget Sound. The whole region around Olympia, Washington, once based an important part of its economy around the harvest of these minute bivalves. In the San Francisco of the Gold Rush, rowdy millionaire prospectors and madams from the Tenderloin ate Olys by the hundreds. By the time I arrived in Olympia in the mid-seventies there was only one restaurant and one oyster company where you could reliably find the region's characteristic food. The restaurant served them deep-fried in a thick breading that masked any natural oyster taste not destroyed by the cooking. The enterprising person with all morning to spend at it could locate the oyster company on a back road behind piles of thumbnail-size shells where some teenagers were shucking Olys. So it was possible back then for the determined person to get a taste of Olys. It was much more possible, however, to be served an oyster cocktail of giant and tasteless Pacific oysters and have them passed off as Olympias because they had grown in nearby waters. Not many people seemed to care.

All that has changed. In the seventeen years I've been the food columnist of *Natural History,* American cuisine has captured the popular imagination. Chefs have built careers with resurrected antique recipes. Suppliers have made young fortunes shipping Olys and other regional specialties to distant urban centers. And jaded gourmets from Berkeley, California, to Houston, Texas, and points east have learned to love those fanciful adaptations of traditional American dishes that comprise American nouvelle cuisine.

Part of the reason for this, a good part of the reason, is the public's far greater fund of information about what American food is supposed to be. As more and more Americans have traveled in Europe and come to expect regional specialties on the menus of serious restaurants, they have demanded the same thing at home.

Restaurateurs and food writers were quick to respond. The writers researched the history of the foods and found the sources for them. The restaurateurs stepped in and provided a steady market for Olys and for a whole menu of items that once would have been unobtainable outside their traditional local center, if there. Wild rice is probably the most phenomenal case of all, for it was transformed almost overnight from a true wild crop harvested in the age-old manner from canoes on Minnesota lakes to a cultivated crop with significant production in California.

CHAPTER 11

WILD RICE

T H E O N L Y native North American grain, wild rice grows naturally and without human intervention in the lakes and rivers of Minnesota, upper Michigan, Wisconsin, and adjoining parts of Canada. Wild rice is an aquatic grass, appropriately labeled *Zizania aquatica* in scientific nomenclature. At least the second half of the scientific name is appropriate; *Zizania* was picked as the genus name for no obvious reason. It comes from a Greek word for a weed, probably the darnel, that grows among wheat. The vernacular name is even more misleading since wild rice is not an uncultivated type of domesticated rice, *Oryza,* but closer in nature to wheat. The early French explorers added to the confusion. They called it *folle avoine,* crazy oat.

The important point here is that when European settlers confronted wild rice, they learned to harvest and process it from Indians. Even today local enthusiasts preserve the primordial method of reaping wild rice as described, for example, in a memoir written in 1820: "It is now gathered by two of the women passing around in a canoe, one sitting in the stern and pushing it along, while the other, with two small pointed sticks about three feet long, collects it in by running one of the sticks into the rice and bending it into the canoe, while with the other she threshes out the grain. This she does on both sides of the canoe alternately, and while it is moving."

Eventually, the canoe fills up with rice and goes to shore, where the Ojibway Indians then cured it to prevent spoilage and to make it possible to remove the hull. Before colonization, Indians dried wild rice in the sun or over smoky fires. Settlers showed them how to toast the grain in caldrons, stirring with canoe paddles. At this point the process becomes men's work. They dig a shallow hole in the ground, line it with skin, and pour in cured rice. Wearing moccasins and leather gaiters to keep rice from working its way inside the moccasins, they literally dance on the rice to loosen the hulls, leaning on poles planted outside the hole for balance and leverage while jigging.

I was able to witness Indian wild rice jigging in the late seventies. It was a staged demonstration in a park, but there were still connoisseurs who would only approve jigged wild rice and who turned up their noses at industrially processed grain. Canoe harvesting was also very much a part of the wild rice cuisine for such aficionados. They viewed with alarm and distaste the onset of cultivated wild rice planted in man-made paddies and harvested by special combines. This was obviously where the commercial future of the grain lay. Today it is the main source of wild rice for nonhobbyists outside Minnesota.

Wild rice ceased to be wild or, rather, became a cultivated grain during the late seventies and early eighties when growers developed a strain of the plant with two crucial characteristics that allowed it to be harvested economically: Its seeds did not shatter at maturity and fall on the ground, and all the seeds matured at the same time. When the combine passes through a wild rice paddy, trundling along on half tracks, all the grain is still on the plant and stays attached during harvesting; none of the grain is immature. Wild wild rice shattered; that's what made the Indian method possible—the threshing stick gave the seeds the last nudge they needed and sent them shattering into the canoe. And the Indian method left the plants intact so that the immature seeds could continue to ripen and be harvested later.

Does wild wild rice, hand-toasted and jigged, taste better or even different from cultivated wild rice processed in a modern factory? I once went to some effort to find traditionally gathered and processed wild rice and then did a comparative tasting. Yes, there was a palpable difference. The old-style Indian rice was paradoxically much tamer than the store-bought rice. The jigging had taken off nearly all of the hull, leaving a softer, milder grain. Indians and other local enthusiasts considered the more refined rice superior. Commercial rice, they said, started out as harder seeds that had to be cured longer and ended up darker. But this is exactly the "wild" texture and flavor that I associated with wild rice. It was wilder, crunchier, more appealing to someone who was not eating wild rice as his staple grain.

Our mission here, however, is not to decide this aesthetic dispute but to observe that the post-Columbian history of wild rice is an ideal model for explaining the evolution of American cuisine. Step 1: Settlers discover this native foodstuff and learn the native methods of preparing it. Step 2: They adapt it to their own foodways. First, they add European technology to the processing (caldrons for toasting seeds; machinery for automatic jigging). Second, they incorporate it into the cuisine they brought with them, creating recipes for wild rice muffins and other whole-grain dishes and substituting it for plain rice in European dishes, especially game dishes, on the theory that wild goes well with wild.

There the matter stood for two centuries until the demand for scarce wild rice—a demand whose growth coincided with the rise of interest in American regional foods—gave economic encouragement to the development of cultivatable wild rice that could be produced in large quantities.

CHAPTER III

APPLES

A MORE important and complex case of this process of adaptation and development is the apple.

The apple pie contest I once witnessed at the Buchanan County Fair in Independence, Iowa, was a worthy successor to the apple-centered pioneer life described by Crèvecoeur, the French writer who lived in Ulster County, New York, after the Revolution. Dried apples were a staple for him, and he wrote, "My wife's and my supper half of the year consists of apple pie and milk." Ulster County, where I now spend weekends, is still an apple center, but neither the trees I see nor the ones Crèvecoeur depended on could be called native plants. The apple is, in a sense, the mirror image of wild rice. Before Columbus there were no apples in the Americas. Settlers brought seeds and grafts, hoping to re-create their old way of life. They found that seedlings did much better than pure European strains brought in as scions. Seedlings, like human children, are all unique products of sexual reproduction. Each one is, technically speaking, a new variety. And so, almost immediately, farmers were in possession of new apple varieties sprung from New World soil under New World conditions. The ones that prospered were fastened on by acute orchardists and stabilized into commercial types unique to this continent. By 1741, American apples were exported on a regular basis to the West Indies. And in 1758 the industry really came of age with the first transatlantic shipment. It was highly symbolic, a package of Newtown pippins (a variety developed near the Huguenot settlement of Flushing, New York) delivered to Benjamin Franklin in London. Franklin brought the fruit to a friend's attention. The friend placed an order with a Philadelphia supplier, and a brisk trade began.

With apples, then, the frontier moment pitted an Old World plant against New World conditions and brought something new into existence, literally thousands of varieties of apples, most of which have all but vanished in our day, overwhelmed by the mass market for fruit that demands redness and uniformity before all else. Anyone interested in getting a sense, if not an actual taste, of what the apple became on our soil should go to the library and page through S. A. Beach's *The Apples of New York,* a splendidly illustrated survey put together by a noted horticulturist at the New York Department of Agriculture's Geneva Experimental Station just before World War I.

The apple trees in the orchard that surrounds us in the mid-Hudson Valley are efficient successors to their ancestors in Beach. They are bare as I write this, but soon they will be blooming and our Eden will be given back to us. The trees are small, hybridized to be that way for efficient picking, and the fruit they produce is redder than it is delicious, but I am happy with the scene nonetheless. I would be happier if it were sprayed less (one summer the wind blew up suddenly, and I was literally sprayed), but this is "paradise enow." Besides, the main alternative to it seems to be paradise lost: real estate development. So I am ready to fight to keep that orchard there, but you can't blame me for feeling wistful when I page through Beach's record of real paradise.

Apples is the greatest of a series of fruit handbooks published by the New York Department of Agriculture Experimental Station in Geneva, way upstate. These handsome yet businesslike tomes catalogue in practical terms grounded in serious horticultural science all the varieties of fruit current in the state. Beach describes some seven hundred named varieties of apples, many of which are displayed in tantalizingly beautiful color plates.

I use the word tantalizingly in its root sense, coming from the name of the ancient malefactor Tantalus, the first foodie martyr. As you will recall, this Lydian king stole ambrosia and nectar, the food and drink of the gods. The divine meal made him immortal, so his punishment was everlasting. The best description of it is Homer's. When Odysseus visits the underworld, he sees Tantalus immersed in water up to his beard, but when the poor man bends his neck to drink, the "daemon makes it vanish, swallowed up, leaving behind black earth." There are also trees near Tantalus "pouring fruit from their leafy crowns, pears and pomegranates and bright-fruited apples, sweet figs and flourishing olives. And each time the old man stood up to grab at them, the wind blew them away to the shadowy clouds."

So when I see the bright-fruited color plates of apples in Beach, I am properly tantalized because most of the varieties depicted are not available to me except in special farmstands.

Take, for example, the Winter Banana. It sounds dazzling in Beach's description: "Fruit large, clear pale yellow with beautifully contrasting pinkish red blush, attractive in appearance, characteristically aromatic, of good desert quality . . ."

I've never tasted a Winter Banana. Perhaps it isn't worth the trouble. Undoubtedly many of the hundreds of abandoned apple varieties this country produced from the seventeenth century on were not worth growing. Beach deliberately included varieties he didn't like or approve, to provide a useful contrast to the fruit he deemed successful. Today, his successors at the Geneva station still have hundreds of varieties to compare and contrast, but the commercial market has become much more uniform. People who buy apples only in supermarkets are normally limited to three or four insipid varieties selected for their redness, size, and sweetness. Today's commercial standards are brutally narrow.

To an apple marketer, the Winter Banana would doubtless seem to have only disadvantages, apart from its size. It is, for one thing, not red, and it is not even brightly colored but pale yellow. Its flavor is delicate. It shows bruises, and it is not regular in shape. That it comes into season late hardly recommends it to a system dependent on intense spurts of picking by migrant laborers in mid-fall but not later. And the Winter Banana's good keeping qualities are largely irrelevant in a world that has discovered a way to store any apple in an anaerobic atmosphere of nitrogen. Obviously no sane mass marketer would risk his fought-over, scarce shelf space on this nonstarter and wouldn't gamble that the consumer would venture beyond surface impressions, sink his teeth into a Winter Banana, and discover a flesh "whitish tinged with pale yellow, moderately firm, a little coarse, somewhat crisp, tender, juicy, mild subacid, distinctly aromatic, good to very good."

That all-but-vanished taste is a relic of one of the richest, most inventive and abundant traditions in the history of horticulture. And for someone who sits, as I do, in a Huguenot homestead in the midst of flourishing apple production, the apple situation in the Hudson Valley and elsewhere in the country is poignant. But our American apple traditions have not totally vanished, not yet. Not at places like Breezy Hill Orchard.

Breezy Hill is a working apple farm on a pretty road that runs north from Poughkeepsie in western Dutchess County. It's not fancy and it's not big, just thirty-five acres that slope up sharply. But those thirty-five acres produce thirty-five different varieties of apples, apples that find their way to the 14th Street Greenmarket in Manhattan. The young woman who owns and operates the orchard is one of several small producers in the Hudson Valley who are determined to preserve and restore the diversity of apples common in our grandparents' day in this country.

Elizabeth Seton Ryan is not a radical zealot. She is a pomologist from Cornell who bought her place in the mid-eighties from people who loved their trees and wouldn't sell to a real estate developer for top dollar. They wanted to retire with an easy conscience. They were looking for serious, competent farmers who would continue bringing apples to the greenmarket. Ryan and her husband, a linguist who has learned to do close-quarter mowing in the orchard, filled the bill. On the strength of her Cornell degree, Ryan was able to get credit from a grudging lender who really didn't think agriculture was a viable activity within two hours of New York City. She runs her orchard without herbicides, something she can manage with a husband willing to maneuver a tractor armed with a sickle bar mower in and out of closely planted trees and an orchard small enough for him to cover.

On the sociological front, she works during winters on the Hudson Valley Fruit Growers History Project, gathering old photographs, printed material, and equipment, videotaping interviews, and working with a photographer to record and preserve documents and memories of the local apple industry.

For an outsider, however, the most evocative and potent piece of historical material that Ryan has to show is a renewable resource called the Golden Russet apple. This is an old-fashioned strain that was formerly produced in sufficient quantities to be listed in U.S. Department of Agriculture apple statistics, but it had several innate problems. It does not conform to the standards of appearance that mass marketers have come to demand in apples in recent years: It is not red but yellow, and—kiss of death—its skin is russeted, marked with rough brownish dots.

As a late-maturing apple, it once filled a niche in the market succession of different seasonal varieties. Today, this is no advantage at all. The economy of large-scale picking makes late varieties unprofitable, while modern storage methods make the Golden Russet's excellent keeping qualities irrelevant. Today's popular varieties—Delicious, Golden Delicious, and Cortlands—can be stored all winter in anaerobic "controlled atmosphere" coolers filled with nitrogen.

Beach saw all this in 1904. He wrote:

Among the russets which are grown in central and western New York, the Golden Russet ranks second only to Roxbury in commercial importance. . . . In recent years the season of good red winter apples has been extended by means of cold storage, with the result that long-keeping russet apples are less profitable than they were formerly. . . . The fruit hangs well to the tree till loosened by frost. It is borne on the ends of the branches, making it hard to pick. This habit and the smallness of the fruit make the picking and packing comparatively expensive.

The eating, however, is worth the trouble and cost—or it ought to be. Ryan gave me some of her Golden Russets to taste. They were surely plain to look at and their texture was not melting, but the flavor was as complex as a well-made wine. The basic taste was tart but not severely so. I suppose that this is what Beach meant by "subacid," an unfortunate term. The tartness of the Golden Russet is a subtle sort of bite, a love bite you might say. And it arrives on the tongue coated in perfume.

As with good wines, you don't have to be Alexis Lichine to get the point of Golden Russet's appeal. The connoisseurship would come in distinguishing while blindfolded between a Golden Russet and a close cousin such as the Roxbury, if we could ever find both varieties to try a comparative tasting along the lines of a standard wine tasting. Just getting hold of Golden Russets themselves requires vigilance. Ryan sells hers for a dollar a pound in the greenmarket and says she has to limit customers to five pounds a day. "They'd buy forty pounds of them if I didn't," she says.

This sounds like good business, and it is. "Ten years ago the break-even point for apples was said to be nine dollars a bushel," Ryan said. That works out to about twenty-three cents a pound, but the mass market's demand for perfect-looking, ever-redder apples forces nonqualifying apples into underground elite channels such as greenmarkets and local farmstands. But these alternative marketing outlets can't handle the glut of apples that aren't red enough.

"Redder sports are coming on the market all the time," Ryan says. "Double reds. Triple reds. Today you can't even give Romes away. You wouldn't believe what we can buy for a nickel a pound to make cider. And the only reason is they're not red enough."

Ryan and other small, specialty apple growers can buck this trend with modest success because they can market their old-fashioned apples directly to consumers who want them. The smallness of their operations is itself an advantage, allowing them to pick each variety when it is ready, instead of being forced to pick one large tract of, say, McIntoshes too early because they can see their "Cortlands will be right on top of them."

Ryan also says that her kind of small orchard makes better use of its coolers. There aren't truckloads of apples coming in all day, so the cooler doors are almost always closed and the inside temperature stays at an optimal 35 degrees. Constant traffic at big coolers forces farmers to keep the cooler doors open for extended periods, and temperatures can often rise to 50 degrees on a busy day, she asserts.

Not everyone in the apple business agrees with Ryan. She herself readily concedes that big producers do a remarkable job on a remarkable scale. She is essentially in a different business from them. One Hudson Valley apple expert told her she's marketing nostalgia, "selling to people who remember having a Baldwin when they were kids." The same man, an apple scientist, dismisses her antique varieties as garbage apples. This is not so much the voice of a paid tool of the mass apple system, I think, as the sincere opinion of somebody whose taste has been formed by the aboveground, narrow definition of what an apple is. I gave one of Ryan's Golden Russets to a good friend without making much of it before he tasted it. "It's green," he said, "isn't it?" He couldn't relate the subacidity of the Golden Russet to anything else in his experience except the few really green apples he'd picked from trees himself.

Corruption of taste and narrowing of thresholds of acceptability—these are the real evils that megamarketing of apples brings us. But there are healthy examples of a countertrend even in supermarket bins. The Granny Smith apple came to us from Australia recently and caught on in a big way. It is an interesting apple by anybody's standards. So is the Ida Red my neighbors in Gardiner produce. They arrived from Idaho after the war, and they offer big growers a quality alternative to the Delicious. Ida Reds satisfy all of the mindless requirements for big-time success: They are big and very red, but they also have a noticeable taste. Pass the word, but don't tell anyone about Golden Russets until I get mine.

CHAPTER IV

NATIVE PERSIMMONS

I F   Y O U are really attracted by the idea of tasting a recherché relic from frontier days, go foraging in the fall for native persimmons. This fabulous fruit never went into commercial production, it just remained a folkloric curiosity best known in southern Indiana. Around places like Gnaw Bone you can find people making persimmon fudge and persimmon pudding. These dishes were invented during Indiana's log cabin period, that brief time of pioneering in the nineteenth century. Settlers inevitably noticed that in the fall big hardwood trees of the ebony family put out small, walnut-size red-orange fruit. They were extremely astringent until fully ripe. This happened so late in the season that Hoosiers came to believe the astringency was somehow quenched by frost and the good fruit was to be found only on the ground, not still attached to the tree. This is false. Native persimmons will ripen very well if picked hard and allowed to sit. Horticulturists recognized this and began to release commercial varieties around the turn of the century. But before city folk had a chance to get to know the truly fabulous fruit of *Diospyros virginiana*, the Japanese began sending over their giant persimmons, the product of centuries of cultivation and hybridization. They marketed them skillfully, and today you can find them nearly everywhere, produced locally, just as Japanese cars are assembled in our midst. But the superior little native persimmon is waiting to be rediscovered.

Frankly, I doubt this will happen. Even the Japanese persimmon is a specialty fruit, and like all fruits that can't be eaten out of hand almost immediately after purchase (gooseberries, medlars), they are bought only by the most alert segment of the food public. They are as astringent as native persimmons and have to be kept around the house until they almost collapse from ripeness. Then they provide a slithery, mouth-filling taste experience that most people find weird rather than comforting.

We are not living in log cabins in nineteenth-century Indiana in a marginal frontier economy where fallen persimmons were a godsend at harvest time. Back then, Hoosier housewives gladly pulped the fruit and bent it to their will in fudges and puddings. But the era of scarcity passed, and even traditionalists around Gnaw Bone mostly switched to supermarket Delicious apples.

CHAPTER V

KEY LIMES

THE SO-CALLED key lime is another superior fruit with a lustrous frontier past that has been eclipsed by a more practical import. In case you thought this was a native plant found only in the Florida Keys, welcome to the mad, mad, mad world of lime marketing. What you and I grew up calling limes are really an anomalous hybrid lemon that arose spontaneously in this country, as well as anyone can tell. It is marketed green in order to distinguish it from lemons. This so-called lime is more accurately referred to as the Tahiti or Bears lime, but it is really not a true lime. The so-called key lime is in fact the true lime, *Citrus aurantifolia,* the fruit the rest of the world calls a lime. It is not a rare fruit in Mexico or in other hot places. In this country it was marginal even in the tip of south Florida and on the Keys. Today there are very few trees left. The largest stand, on Islamorada Key, is nothing more than a backyard grove. A hurricane took most of the others, and that was the end of the key lime in most of our lives. The other lime has been a survivor, however, and its juice is similar to the juice of the real but all-but-vanished key lime. So folks interested in serving you a tasty regional dish developed during the brief heyday of key limes in the Keys, go ahead and make key lime pie with Tahiti lime juice. The result isn't as tart, but almost nobody notices. For our purposes it almost doesn't matter. What does count is the history behind this travesty.

The key lime pie could only have arisen in the Keys when they were first settled. Trees were established as early as 1839. Gail Borden invented condensed milk in 1853 to give people in pioneer conditions, especially on wagon trains, safe milk that would keep longer than fresh whole milk. Some creative genius in the Keys combined sweetened condensed milk with key lime juice and eggs, and discovered that the mixture would turn to a smooth custard and was delicious in a new way. You can imagine the exhilaration in that kitchen on that day when the inventor saw what he had done. The discovery could not have occurred before 1853, and it would probably not have happened too much later than that, after south Florida ceased to be so remote that it depended on condensed milk. It certainly couldn't have happened after the hurricane of 1926 knocked out the key lime groves. They were never replanted. It made more sense by then to build vacation homes on the same land.

CHAPTER VI

CORN

P E R H A P S the key lime strikes you as a marginal item. Ditto the American persimmon. So let's look at a really central example. Let's think about corn.

I think most people who have thought about these questions have all agreed that corn is the most important New World food plant. In North America its culinary potential was first tapped in Amerindian corn dishes such as hominy and succotash. But there was more to come. Early settlers in North America took maize to their bosoms from the local Indians and, so to speak, ran with it, creating dishes that merged Old World techniques and ingredients with corn and corn products (Indian pudding: corn and molasses; corn pone). We could also talk about the immensely innovative role of West African cooks in early plantation cookings, leaving us, for example, the Afro-American casserole that mixes corn, okra, and tomato, and we could use corn fritters as a wedge in the door of that spacious subject, southern frying.

To see more clearly how the genius of our American culinary impulse worked itself out in corn, we can look at the most primitive colonial form of corn bread, which is known variously as hoecake, ahcake, spidercake, and johnnycake. My most vivid contact with these cornmeal pancakes that are fried in open hearths occurred through the unlikely instrumentality of an irregularly published newsletter called *Dwarf Conifer Notes*. As many of you already know or have guessed, this publication is devoted to dwarf conifers, but its editor has a far-ranging mind and does not always limit himself to tiny trees. Some time back, for instance, he delivered himself of a disquisition on the Rhode Island johnnycake.

This is not a narrow subject. Judging from the intense barrage of mail I received from readers of a column of mine that vulgarized the pure serenity of the johnnycake doctrine espoused by *Dwarf Conifer*

Notes, matters such as the exact strain of corn and the precise mill, which side of which Rhode Island River, and so forth, make all the difference between a real Rhode Island johnnycake and pretenders to the title. For someone not resident in Rhode Island these claims are impossible to test, but I do not doubt that they are based on more than microchauvinism.

One need only reflect on the multifarious changes rung on the parallel recipe that transforms wheat flour and water into bread to see why one man's johnnycake may not be another's. But still it is possible to consider the fundamental dish as a single food idea despite significant culinary differences from one place to another.

The proliferation of names suggests that the same wood fire fry bread was invented over and over again. *Johnnycake* itself is ambiguous and may come from *journey cake* or, more probably, *Shawnee cake,* to show its Indian origins. *Pone* comes from an Indian word, *apone,* but the other names imply an adaptation to European utensils: the hoe used as a long-handled skillet, or the spider, a skillet with feet placed in the fire. Indians most likely used green wood, as Thoreau did. In *Walden* he says he made Indian hoecakes "before my fire out of doors on a shingle or the end of a stick of timber sawed off in building my house: but it was wont to get smoked and to have a piny flavor."

Every single one of these corn breads, including those baked in cake tins and muffin tins, are attempts to solve the problem faced by consumers of cornmeal from Rhode Island to Oaxaca: how to make bread with a grain that does not have wheat's glutinous elasticity, a grain that won't rise optimally even when combined with yeast. The solutions worked out all over the Americas are worth a treatise.

In this country the highest form of corn bread is a cryptosoufflé, an airy pudding puffed up with eggs and called spoon bread. It is remarkably delicate, but the most remarkable thing about it and its humbler hoecake-type cousins is their rapid-fire creation and then their equally decisive relegation to regional peculiarities. Only standard corn bread escaped the fate of being a museum piece.

Well, yes and no. I think that even corn bread, for most of us, has an aura of southern or old-time America. The proof of this may be that in the new American nouvelle cuisine restaurants springing up in the Southwest and West, plain corn bread is being presented in sophisticated forms as a postmodern token of American tradition.

CHAPTER VII

UTAH SCONES

THESE FRIED BREADS emerged somewhat mysteriously out of the frontier contact between Mormon missionaries, Mexicans, and Indians. Now they are available around Salt Lake in fast-food chains. Few people buying them have any sense of their origins among Indians, on the one hand, or back in England, on the other.

Like me, most of you probably grew up thinking of scones as rich muffins. My mother used to bake small circular ones when I was growing up in Detroit. Later, when I lived in England, I ran into similar buns at teahouses.

In Utah, however, by the evidence both of local cookbooks and three local restaurants, the scone starts out as a yeast-raised sweet dough that is cut into two-by-two-inch squares (or other shapes of similar surface area) and deep-fried. The most popular method of service is with butter and honey. That is how I ate a midmorning scone at Johanna's Kitchen in a mall at Jordan, Utah. They didn't bother to bring honey at the Pepper Tree in Salt Lake City, but they did advertise a free scone with each breakfast "entree" on the sign out front.

Clearly, the Utah scone is not a vanishing bread, certainly not at the two-restaurant chain in Salt Lake called Sconecutter. At these twenty-four-hour drive-ins, the Utah scone rises to challenge the doughnut and the hamburger bun as a fast-food staple. Cooked on the spot from yeast dough, the scones come out crisp, puffy, and rectangular. The dough inside is airy and pleasantly chewy. But these aren't scones in the traditional, back East, English mode. So what are they? Where did they come from? How did they arise in Mormon Zion?

Traditional English scones are too diverse to classify easily, as Elizabeth David warns us, but they do generally qualify as muffinish quick breads, and mostly they are baked. According to the *Oxford*

English Dictionary, scones (derived from middle low German *schonbrot,* fine bread) are baked, cooked on a griddle stone, or even fried, but not deep-fried. Yeast does crop up sometimes in English scones, for example in the recipe Jane Grigson gives for Northumbrian whole-meal scones in *English Food.* But no traditional English scone I have ever eaten or read about comes close to resembling the Utah scone.

When I asked her about it, Donna Lou Morgan, food editor of the *Salt Lake Tribune,* guessed that pioneer Utah cooks, who were inveterate bread bakers, had taken to frying some of the yeast dough they often had on hand. She remembered her own mother pinching off pieces of bread dough and frying them, but Morgan's own recipe for scones in *What's Cooking in Utah* is not based on a conventional bread dough. It is richer and sweeter and has chemical raising agents in it, undoubtedly to boost the puffing of the scone as it fries.

The first time I ate a Utah scone I was not reminded of bread or traditional muffin scones. I thought instantly of two other puffy fried breads popular in the American West: Navajo fry bread and New Mexico *sopaipillas.* The taste of both of these regional breads is very close to the taste of Utah scones. Yes, the shapes and textures vary a little, but with the *sopaipilla* there is an extra link. Like Utah scones, *sopaipillas* are served with honey.

Until some researcher makes a lucky strike in a Mormon woman's diary or pioneer cookbook, we are never going to know for sure how it is that Navajos, Chicanos, and Mormons ended up eating similar fried breads. It could all be coincidence, but in the absence of hard facts it is tempting to construct an explanatory scenario that will connect all the fried breads so popular in the mountain time zone from Bountiful, Utah, to Hatch, New Mexico.

Let us suppose, then, that both the Navajo fry bread and the *sopaipilla* predate the Utah scone. They are simpler to make, and history is on their side. Both Navajos and hispanicized New Mexicans were in their present regions long before the Mormons emigrated to Utah. Navajo and Chicano fry breads are almost identical, and so it makes sense to look for an archetypal southwestern fry bread from which both descend. Since most culinary ideas in the U.S. Southwest moved there from the South when Mexico controlled the whole area, there ought to be a Mexican ancestor for the *sopaipilla* and for Navajo fry bread.

In fact, as Diana Kennedy tells us, there are *sopaipillas* in the Mexican state of Chihuahua, which adjoins New Mexico. But the Chihuahuan *sopaipillas* contain neither yeast nor a chemical raising agent. This greater simplicity argues in favor of Chihuahua as the birthplace of American fry bread.

It may be that the Chihuahuan *sopaipilla* is a later simplification of a New Mexican original, but I doubt it. Common sense tells me that the baking soda now used by Navajos and Chicanos came to them at a relatively late date, through contact with colonizing Anglos. The unleavened fry bread now still occasionally found in Chihuahua was probably once available throughout the entire region north to Utah and now survives only in remote, isolated Chihuahua.

Most probably, then, when Mormons first came into contact with southwestern Indians, they found them eating a flat fried bread that puffed up a bit in hot oil. Inevitably they tasted it and liked it. Mormon women then tried to duplicate the recipe and to improve on it by adding a whole battery of raising agents they knew about as Anglo cooks. They also put in buttermilk because they had to, to give the dough the necessary acidity required to activate old-fashioned tartrate (single-acting) baking soda. Following what they knew as bakers of sweet breads (not sweetbreads!), they added eggs and sugar and ended up with a delicious and original bread, related in kind to the deep-fried *beignets* of France but really a thing unto itself. Lacking a name, they came up with scone, quick, sweet breads from back home that were also cut into individual serving pieces before cooking. The result lends itself to rapid, mass preparation and mixes nicely with ground meat and other conventional fast-food preparations stuffed into hamburger and hot dog buns in other parts of the country. Those regions don't really need another fast-food gimmick, but England, where scones began, would be a fine place to test market these Utah specialties. Perhaps it would be a good idea to change the name, though. The British think they know everything there is to know about scones.

TURKEY

THE TURKEY is a native American fowl that everyone con-
nects with our oldest food tradition, Thanksgiving dinner. That goes
without saying. The Thanksgiving turkey is supposed to be an exotic
New World bird eaten for the first time at a New World feast in a white
Anglo-Saxon setting of bravery and exploration. But the turkey we eat
is not a descendant of the elusive North American wild turkey. And
turkey history does not begin at Plymouth. Its first apotheosis came,
as far as we know, among the Aztecs, who braised it and ate it on
special occasions in a hot sauce containing chocolate. The dish survives in modern Mexico as *mole poblano de guajolote.* The authentic
turkey recipe, then, belongs to the heritage of speakers of Nahuatl, not
English.

The Daughters of the American Revolution cannot even fall back
to claiming that the turkeys they now eat descend from wild fowl
domesticated by their foremothers on American soil. The first domesticated North American turkeys were, in fact, imported from Europe.
The Black Norfolk and White Holland varieties came to the British
colonies from England where they had first been bred. The first truly
American hybrid, the Mammoth Bronze, was bred later from birds
with a European heritage, at Point Judith, Rhode Island.

Worse yet, most Europeans in the colonial period had no idea
that they owed turkeys to the New World. They confused them with
guinea fowl, whence the generic name, *Meleagris,* which means just
that. The Linnaean species name, *gallopavo,* also betrays confusion; it
means chicken-peacock. But all this is only learned error. Our collo-
quial name, turkey, arose from a parallel conflation of avian identities.
The guinea fowl was imported to Europe via Turkey. One thing led
to another, you see, it being so hard to keep all those strange foreign
places straight. (Think also of guinea pigs, which really came from the
Andes.) Why, in France they thought turkeys came from India

(d'Inde). Eventually the apostrophe dropped out, leaving the modern French word for turkey, *dinde.* (French guinea pigs also are supposed to have come from India; they are *cochons d'Inde*.)

Domestication followed close on the heels of those first misnamed turkeys imported to Europe in the early sixteenth century. At a wedding in 1560 in Arnstadt, Germany, 150 birds were slaughtered. Flocks were thriving on the lower Rhine by 1571. In France, Charles IX feasted on turkeys at a special dinner in 1570. And the English custom of the Christmas turkey was established in 1585, thirty-five years before the first Thanksgiving.

So the Thanksgiving myth should be rewritten to take into account the historic reality of turkeys and to show how neatly they fit into our frontier cuisine. The earliest settlers ate wild turkeys, but once they were truly settled, they brought better turkeys in from Europe, improved on them further, and adapted them to the Thanksgiving meal. It is the menu of turkey combined with local foods (cranberries, sweet potatoes, pumpkin pie) that makes it special, not turkey alone. Children should be taught that the ensemble bespeaks New England and the Pilgrims, but the turkey carries a larger message, about a century of previous European contacts with the bird in Mexico and a long tradition of commercial breeding in Europe that gave us back our American bird much improved by its grand tour.

CHAPTER IX

FILÉ

P R O B A B L Y few if any of the Pilgrims had the gastronomic perspective on their turkey feast to see it as a continuation of Aztec turkey feasting well launched in Europe. Perhaps it is asking too much of beleaguered settlers, even if they had the knowledge, to require that they should indulge in such impractical reflections. Certainly I did not find United States Customs ready to banter about our gastronomic heritage when I arrived at Kennedy Airport in 1972, returning from a trip to New Orleans and the French islands with a bottle of green powder in my luggage. The agent smiled, it is true, but he smiled as only a Customs agent can smile when he is sure he has caught someone smuggling marijuana.

"What might this be?" he asked with a twinkle.

"Filé," I said pointing to the label.

"Oh, is that what they call it in French?"

"Yes, it means ropy because it turns viscous and ropy when you cook with it. I bought it in New Orleans where they use it in gumbos when they're not using okra for the same purpose."

The man took the bottle and went away to an office. Perhaps he gave it to a specially trained, marijuana-detecting bloodhound to sniff. I devoutly hope he tried to smoke some. Whatever method of analysis he used, it convinced him I was not trying to import a potent drug. He returned with the bottle and waved me back into the country.

Ironically it was as a drug that filé first came to prominence in the world. Filé is prepared from the leaves of the sassafras tree, *Sassafras albidum*, whose aromatic bark, leaves, and roots were highly sought after in the early days of exploration for their supposed medicinal properties. *Gerard's Herbal* (1597) asserted that "the roote of sassafras hath power to comfort the liver, and to dissolve oppilations, to comfort the weake and feeble stomacke, to cause a good appetite, to consume windiness, the chiefest cause of cruditie and indigestion, stay vomiting, and make sweete a stinking breath."

Gerard had much more to say about the beneficial qualities of this native American tree, which explorers found growing from southern Maine to Florida and west to the Mississippi. There seemed to be almost no human ill it would not cure, from plague to syphilis. Prices for this newfound panacea skyrocketed, and it rapidly became one of the chief early-American exports to Europe. Annals of late-sixteenth-century exploration are full of excited accounts of discoveries of stands of sassafras. Walter Raleigh did his best to claim a monopoly on East Coast sassafras trade; in 1602 he confiscated a cargo brought back to England by an independent expedition from Cape Cod.

Indians had helped the men on that voyage harvest sassafras on Cuttyhunk Island off what is now New Bedford. They were already convinced of the curative powers of sassafras tea, and their British visitors were given concrete proof of its benefits when one of them took it to relieve a bellyache brought on "by eating the bellies of Dogfish, a very delicious meate."

Eventually, as Thoreau wrote, sassafras "lost its reputation." That is, it was no longer prescribed for infectious diseases, and the bottom fell out of the market. But even today sassafras tea is sold in health-food stores. I recently brewed some and found it mild, appealingly red in color, and unremarkable in flavor. On the other hand, sassafras trees are quite remarkable. They reach a height of ninety feet in the Great Smoky Mountains and may live for a thousand years. They produce three kinds of leaves, some lance-shaped and entire, some three-lobed, and some that are mittenlike with an oblique lobe on either side. Old trees have deeply furrowed, reddish brown bark, tinged with ash gray. The wood itself is reddish. Branches spread almost at right angles from the trunk and support smaller vertical branches.

Not only did the Indians teach the settlers to use the various parts of these magnificent trees for teas and gumbo thickening, but the settlers quickly began adapting sassafras to a recipe they had brought with them from Europe. With the bark, they brewed beer.

In colonial days, sassafras beer was only one of several "root" beers decocted from things growing in the woods. Birch beer, spruce beer, and sarsaparilla beer were all common early-American beverages produced with roughly the same simple techniques European farmers used to make beer from barley. But these tree-derived drinks had a negligible alcohol content, and they were thought to have medicinal, or tonic, properties. This is why even today in New England carbonated drinks are called tonics.

Modern manufacturers make their soft drinks fizz by forcing

carbon dioxide into them under pressure, and the soft drinks we buy are truly soft because they are not fermented. Traditional root beer and the other sylvan beers were genuine beers in the sense that their bubbles arose naturally as a by-product of yeast fermentation.

A typical colonial recipe for root beer began with the making of a syrup. People boiled molasses and water, say one and a half gallons of molasses to five gallons of water, and then let the syrup cool for three hours. Into the syrup went a quarter pound each of sarsaparilla root, bruised sassafras bark, and birch bark, which added a winter-green flavor. Finally, our forefathers stirred in a cup of yeast and enough water to top off the vat at sixteen gallons. The mixture was then allowed to ferment for twelve hours. Finally, when drawn off and strained, the root beer went into kegs or other sealed containers and continued to build up its fizz through secondary fermentation.

Usually the alcohol content of such old-time root beers remained below 2 percent, too low to be intoxicating. Some intrepid root brewers prolonged the initial fermentation so that the alcohol level rose as high as 10 percent, enough to make them feel silly. But under normal circumstances root beer and the other forest beverages were low in alcohol and were classified as small beers. During Prohibition, root beer substituted for illegal malt-and-hops beer and was sold out of kegs in bars. Some commercial breweries switched over to making root beer.

By then it was no longer necessary to decoct flavorings from roots and barks as part of the actual brewing process. Chemists had learned to extract the essential oils of sassafras and wintergreen in the early nineteenth century. Later they discovered methyl salicylate, a chemical also known as artificial oil of wintergreen.

Modern root beer manufacturers also dispense with molasses and resort to caramel coloring, which is sometimes souped up with soybean protein to make something known as foaming-type caramel. This is only one of several agents employed to give root beer a foamy head. Manufacturers also mix in a small amount of citric acid as a preservative that attacks bacteria responsible for cloudiness, syrupyness, and ropyness.

If all this organic chemistry makes you never want to drink root beer again, you can, without much trouble, hunt down a bottle of root beer extract at your local country store and brew your own. If that isn't natural enough, you could start from scratch, locating a sassafras log and stripping the bark. For an even more authentic and sophisticated flavor, extirpate a sarsaparilla shrub (*Smilax glauca*), dry the bitter roots, and throw them into the caldron along with stems and leaves of the wintergreen *(Gaultheria procumbens)* or the young bark of the sweet birch *(Betula lenta)*.

These other plants are not only traditional but entirely safe. Natural sassafras, however, is something you will probably want to avoid. Modern experiments have showed that the major constituent of oil of sassafras, a chemical called safrole, caused liver damage in dogs and cancer in rats and mice. The Food and Drug Administration banned safrole, which forced root beer manufacturers to forgo the use of oil of sassafras altogether. One soft drink executive told me that the flavorings he now uses, such as oil of sweet birch, are not nearly as tasty as sassafras.

More recently, sassafras bark was banned for sale as sassafras tea unless it has been processed to make it safrole-free. Federal labeling requirements do not oblige manufacturers to state whether sassafras tea has been purified of safrole, but in any case it seems pointless to buy the stuff. Either it is dangerous or it has had its principal flavoring element removed.

Filé remains available in its traditional form, apparently because it is a completely natural product, nothing but pulverized sassafras leaves, and isn't sold specifically for human consumption. Is it harmful? One thing is sure: Sassafras trees themselves are harmless as long as you don't chew them. Myself, when I need a panacea to ward off civilization's discontents, I sidle up to an S. *albidum* in the woods, break off a sprig, and inhale the aroma, following the example of the Onondaga Indians who called sassafras twigs "smelling sticks."

CHAPTER X

MULBERRY

A N O T H E R neglected tree with an international past is the mulberry. If Walter Raleigh lusted for sassafras, a much better poet extolled the mulberry. In *Venus and Adonis*, Shakespeare wrote:

> *When he beheld his shadow in the brook,*
> *The fishes spread on it their golden gills;*
> *When he was by, the birds such pleasure took,*
> *That some would sing, some other in their bills*
> *Would bring him mulberries . . .*

Lacking the physiognomic dazzle of Adonis, I have never been brought mulberries by any bird or even any person. And until recently I had never knowingly seen, not to mention tasted, the fruit of *Morus nigra* or *alba* or *rubra*. Had you asked me about it, I wouldn't have been sure the mulberry was edible. For me it was just one of those old-time fruits like the medlar or the bullace that crop up in English literature but not in American markets.

Enter Nicholas King, savant Manhattanite, keen urban observer, who led me, folding kitchen ladder in hand, to two fruiting white mulberry trees behind a low fence next to P. S. 6 at the very edge of Madison Avenue. King bent the branches down; I plundered the soft, pale white berries. This was a sight that jarred even jaded East Siders: two men, one of them distinguished looking (King), picking strange fruit.

"Are they some kind of raspberry?" a woman inquired. It was a good question. The mulberry looks a bit like a raspberry, but the raspberry (along with the other brambles, members of the genus *Rubus*, such as the blackberry) is an aggregate fruit generated by a single, if complex, flower. The mulberry is a so-called collective fruit, the product of many flowers originally attached to a single catkin. The fig, another example of a collective fruit, is a member of the mulberry family, the *Moraceae,* as is the banyan, the breadfruit, the hop, and the osage orange.

We botanical sophisticates can easily see how taxonomists linked these plants, but pre-Linnaean folk looked at black mulberries and blackberries and saw mostly similarities. This is why the common French word for mulberry, *mûre,* which is descended from the Latin *morus,* is also the French word for blackberry. When they want to distinguish the two fruits, the French call blackberries *mûres sauvages* (wild mulberries), *mûres de ronce* (thorny mulberries), or *mûres de haie* (hedge mulberries).

I doubt, however, that anyone would confuse blackberries and mulberries in a blind tasting. Like all the bramble fruits, blackberries are each a collection of small, individual fruits with palpable internal seeds (they're drupelets, to be technical about it, miniature versions of drupes such as peaches and plums). Mulberries are softer and juicier, and you don't notice the seeds. Mulberries are so delicate, in fact, that they don't ship well at all and therefore have never had a career in commerce as whole fruit. Most people who know about mulberries today are aware of the black variety and regard it as a nuisance of early summer, a soft fruit that falls, goes smash, and stains cars.

Washington, D.C., is annually deluged by messy black mulberries. Articles appear in the *Washington Post* about coping with mulberries—apparently few people in Washington are clever enough to spread sheets under the trees (a traditional harvest method) to collect fruit for pies, jam, sauce, or eating out of hand.

In medieval times people turned the staining powers of black mulberry to account. They used the juice as a dye and as a food coloring in a sauce called *murrey.* *Murrey* was so widespread that several recipes for it appear in the fourteenth-century manuscripts collected in 1985 as *Curye on Inglysch.* There were even mock *murreys* containing other colorants but no mulberry.

But even in those days there was no need for mulberry orchards: Mulberries are easy to grow from seed or hardwood cuttings, and the most practical scheme was to plant a backyard tree that would provide a convenient supply of fruit in late June or early July and attractive shade with its large leaves for the rest of the summer. This still holds for modern Americans who can freeze the excess fruit, which needs no sugar or special treatment or parcooking. It goes into the freezer and comes out later unharmed, just like blueberries. But if you are going to plant a mulberry, taste the fruit of the tree you plan to take a cutting from. There is wide variation, and you might as well propagate good genes.

Once you start looking you will have no trouble finding mulberries in this country. *M. rubra* is native, but its dark purple fruits are not deemed choice. The black and white European varieties, however, were imported in quantity starting in the eighteenth century. Earlier attempts at mulberry culture had failed here, just as James I had failed to establish an English mulberry/silk industry.

One Jared Eliot introduced the white mulberry to the New World in the early 1700s. He knew that its leaves provided silkworms with optimal fodder from which to metabolize the fine threads for their cocoons, but those cocoons had to be toilsomely unwound and processed. High labor costs torpedoed the infant silk industry in Connecticut and Pennsylvania; in Georgia, however, American silk flourished briefly. Experienced Italian silk growers accompanied James Oglethorpe's original colonists, and Georgia silk was presented to the queen in 1735. Yet the industry soon succumbed to competition from rice and cotton.

This did not deter George Washington from grafting English mulberries on native stock, nor did it discourage Thomas Jefferson from planting a "mulberry row" or from ordering trees in 1789 from France, "the best for silkworm."

The dream of an American silkworm industry died hard. American interest in mulberries for silk accelerated around 1825. The sober author of *A History of Agriculture in the State of New York* (1933), Ulysses Prentiss Hedrick, called it a craze.

It all started in 1824 when a new mulberry was imported from the Philippines to France. *Morus multicaulis* sprouted at its base and provided silkworms with a fabulous abundance of huge leaves. This tree was vaunted as the traditional feeding ground for Chinese silkworms. If Westerners grew it, they could then compete with the age-old Chinese silk industry. Hedrick writes: "In 1826, William Prince and Son, proprietors of the Linnaean Gardens and Nurseries, Flushing, Long Island, imported *Morus multicaulis* and began its propagation. It grew like a weed and its fame spread like wildfire."

Congress had already taken a stand in favor of mulberry cultivation and silkworm breeding. The secretary of the treasury published a 220-page manual in 1828. State legislatures got on the bandwagon, and over the next twenty years, four specialty magazines were published, including *Flushing Farmer, Silk Culturist,* and *Flushing Silk Jour-*

nal. Nurserymen in New York State virtually abandoned the propagation of other trees and devoted themselves to the mulberry. "A tree was worth more than a pound of silk," writes Hedrick. "Nurserymen made fortunes in a single season. It was said one nurseryman grew 30,000 trees on a single acre which he sold at a profit of $30,000." Hedrick quotes a contemporary account of the mulberry frenzy:

> They met in solemn conclaves over bundles of *Morus multicaulis* twigs, discussing seriously the glorious time when, in the not distant future, every farm would be a nursery for the young trees, every house have its cocooneries attached. . . . The farmers' wives and daughters, when not engaged in feeding the worms, were to reel the silk, and perhaps to spin and twist it, till silk should become as cheap as cotton, and every matron and maid rejoice in the possession of at least a dozen silk dresses. It does not clearly appear where and on what occasions they were to wear these dresses, while their whole time was to be occupied with the care of the silk-worms and cocoons.

The boom collapsed by the fall of 1839. Disease and winter cold finished off the *multicaulis* groves. All that remained were the hardier standard species, and they still remain, sometimes reaching a height of eighty feet and a girth of more than sixteen. The mature mulberry is no bush, you see, and it can produce a monster amount of fruit. And then there are the curiously diverse leaves, sometimes notched, sometimes lobed, sometimes of multiple shapes on the same tree, always big. They may remind you of the leaves of their kin, the fig. (By legend a late Byzantine emperor saw a resemblance between the shape of a mulberry leaf and of southern Greece, which he named Morea.)

When you do locate a mulberry tree near you, watch for the first leaves to sprout in the spring. They are latecomers, and folk wisdom says that the appearance of mulberry leaves signals the end of frost danger. Perhaps so, but they definitely do make a fine noise in the wind. The Bible invests this natural phenomenon with drama and divinity. It is written (I Chronicles 14:14–15):

> Therefore, David inquired again of God; and God said unto him, Go not up after them. Turn away from them, and come upon them over against the mulberry trees. And it shall be, when thou shalt hear a sound of marching in the tops of the

mulberry trees, that then thou shalt go out to battle; for God is gone forth before thee to smite the host of the Philistines.

With this in mind, I feel tough and exultant when the tempest howls through the non-native mulberry in my yard. But this descendant of European botanic tradition, this link with the roots of the Judeo-Christian tradition in the Holy Land, is also an example of a fundamental mystery. Why should quite similar versions of the same plant have developed independently in North America and in the Old World? The mulberry is only one of many examples. Take English walnuts and pecans or native and Old World gooseberries. Did Nature repeat herself, or almost? Or was there some much earlier and unrecorded vector of transmission from some unique point of origin? Did, for example, migratory birds carry seeds with them across the ocean? We can't say for sure, any more than we can explain the mystery of how New England's most traditional soup got a French name.

CHAPTER XI

CHOWDER

O U R C H O W D E R descends from a fish soup of France's Atlantic coast. In name, at least. Long ago it must have happened that French fishermen crossed the Atlantic and took their favorite fish soup with them. Then, in the mouths of neighboring English speakers, *chaudrée* turned into chowder. (It is also possible that the word chowder descends from *chaudière*, a French term for pot that is also applied to a Breton fish stew.) And in their hands the former fish stew turned into a milk-based clam soup with bits of rendered salt pork and potato cubes.

This account of the origin of New England clam chowder leaves out a great deal. It does not explain why or when a quite original soup was created. As with most traditional recipes, no one knows how it began. It is not hard to locate recipes for traditional French soups that mix cream and seafood. The Breton *cotriade* calls for a mixture of fish and a modest amount of *crème fraîche* added to the broth. Even closer is the Norman *soupe aux coques,* which brings together the little bivalve of the Norman shore known in English as cockle (*Cerastoderma edule*) with *crème fraîche.* But I have yet to find a really close analogue to our clam chowder in a French cookbook, and I doubt I will find one because the plainness of our New England chowder is its hallmark and its genius.

Somehow, then, the term *chaudrée* (or *chaudière*) got anglicized and attached to a soup built on the cheapest, most universal ingredients along the North Atlantic coast of the New World. Was the birthplace of chowder in Newfoundland where French and English colonists mixed? Nobody knows. And the exact moment of inspiration that mixed milk and bivalve, pork and potato is lost in the mists of the early days of colonial America. But the dish caught on and survived.

By the late eighteenth century the word *chowder* had appeared in print, and by the mid-nineteenth century it received its literary apotheosis in *Moby Dick*. Melville devotes an entire chapter to Ishmael's chowder supper with Queequeg at the Try Pots in Nantucket. "Oh, sweet friends! hearken to me," he wrote. "It was made of small juicy clams, scarcely bigger than hazel nuts, mixed with pounded ship biscuit, and salted pork cut up into little flakes; the whole enriched with butter, and plentifully seasoned with pepper and salt."

This is rich stuff, but you could not use it as a recipe. It doesn't mention milk. It does not give a precise description of the salt pork, which should be chopped and crisply rendered. Purists will shudder at the presence of cracker crumbs (the pounded ship biscuit), and they will also shake their heads at the idea of tiny clams instead of quahogs.

The purists are right, of course. Melville's chowder is not the dish that survived the test of time and got enshrined as a classic of New England cookery. The classic way is also the more delicious way to make the soup—and the simplest, most basic method. It is the epitome of early New England.

NEW(ER) WRINKLES IN NORTH
AND SOUTH AMERICA

IN NORTH AMERICA we are living through a historic flood of immigration, mostly from the South. Inevitably these new arrivals have brought their food with them, in particular an amazing array of root vegetables but also much else, from special chilies to tropical fruits. Los Angeles's Grand Central Market is the place to see these exotic edibles all in one place. But the alert person in almost any big U.S. city will have noticed what is going on. And little by little the new foods and recipes infiltrate the rest of the society. Mass-market cassava chips recently appeared on the shelves of a supermarket in the heart of the posh World Financial Center in lower Manhattan.

No doubt South American and island cookery will not completely swamp our foodways, but the exotic food bins in the Grand Central Market and elsewhere symbolize the new cuisines and foods emerging all over the country in a second wave of food colonization—colonization from below. This is occurring at the same time that people living at the top of the economy have become remarkably open to new and exotic food experiences.

There are many strands to this situation of novelty and experimentation. In the discussion that follows I will be looking at a disparate set of foods, some with long histories just arriving here from south of the border, others deliberately naturalized by the food industry and subjected to the homogenizing force of technology and mass production (olives, dates, and pistachios), and still others emblematic of the carefully marketed world of gastronomes in search of a new taste thrill (cherimoyas and radicchio).

Anyone trying to make a clear trend out of these unrelated

developments would be a fool. But out of the turmoil of immigration, food science, and high-priced exotic novelties for the epicure, the future is surely emerging as the latest phase in the role of the Americas in the development of global foodways. Perhaps the most convenient place to get an introduction to what is happening is Los Angeles's wonderful covered market.

CHAPTER I

LOS ANGELES'S
GRAND CENTRAL MARKET

T H I S   I S the L.A. version of the Lexington Market in Baltimore or the Municipal Market in Atlanta—a big indoor market in an old inner-city location where poor people shop at dozens of competitive retail stalls that specialize in everything from fruit to nuts to meat and even wigs. The Los Angeles Grand Central Market is the most exciting example of this vanishing, old-fashioned form of food merchandising that I know. More than that, as even my screenwriter friend David on a whirlwind foray out of Filmland could not fail to notice, this shabby-looking food circus reflects the noncinematic realities of today's polyethnic California in a wonderfully vivid way. Down there on Broadway where Hollywood directors like to shoot movies set in the "forgotten" California of the thirties and forties, directly across the street from the historic and incessantly photographed Bradbury Building, the market reveals various truths about the Golden State that one would hardly divine at the movies, on a tour of the homes of Hollywood stars, or window-shopping among the chic boutiques of Rodeo Drive in Beverly Hills.

Aquí se habla español. They speak Spanish here, without even waiting to try English first. Oh, if you really can't manage, the shopkeepers will switch to serviceable English, but the basic idiom of the Central market is Chicano: confident, relaxed, sure that this is Hispanic turf.

But that's not all. California's Oriental population, rooted here since railroading's dawn in the previous century, runs restaurants unconverted to the new gospel of torrid Sichuan regionalism. This is America, and they serve Chinese-American specialties in the birthplace of chop suey. Orientals also run the biggest health-food counter you are ever likely to see, complete with an on-duty acupuncturist and a section for taking a customer's blood pressure. At a tropical-juice bar across the aisle, aficionados can order a five-vegetable "potassium" cocktail or mixtures of apple, alfalfa, grape, mango, tomato, papaya, boysenberry, grapefruit, pomegranate, pineapple, coconut, carrot, orange, celery, spinach, parsley, watercress, cabbage, passionfruit, beet, prune, garlic, or guava juice.

I bought a glass of papaya-banana-guava and felt much better about life, standing there by a portal open to the legendary California sun. Outside is a city street, but inside, a whole block deep, are festoons of fabulous produce just trucked in from the state's Central Valley, the most productive farmland on earth. From lettuce to kiwi fruit, the bountiful greengrocers' and fruiterers' stands spill over with bright colors.

We expect good produce in California, and David can find as good near his house at the justifiably famous Farmer's Market. Connoisseurs will insist, correctly, that California kiwis may be bigger but not better than the New Zealand imports and that the giant Mexican papayas at the Central market do not compare favorably with Hawaiian varieties flown in at great cost to New York.

But you will travel far before you find retail butchers with the variety of cuts routinely displayed at the Central market. In addition to all the usual pig parts familiar to anyone who shops in markets catering to those with a small budget and a southern background, here they also butcher the whole steer.

Dodging a cart full of beef hindquarters, I goggled at the whole beef heads complete with tongue (there were calves' and lambs' heads as well), and I was taken aback to see three of the four kinds of beef tripe. When they sell tripe at all, U.S. markets normally offer only the honeycomb tripe from the second stomach of the animal. Cattle, as true ruminants, have four stomachs: the rumen (or paunch), the reticulum (or honeycomb), the manyplies (or psalterium or omasum), and the abomasum (or read). All four, canonically, go into the classic French tripe stew, *tripe à la mode de Caen.* I knew from reading that they have different textures, smooth or leafy, but never having been able to buy tripe from more than the first two stomachs, I was out of my depth and couldn't tell which one was missing in this market. I also lacked the twelve hours of stove time necessary to cook *tripe à la mode de Caen.* But I urge readers in southern California to energize the butchers and encourage them to supply the missing fourth type of tripe so that a great Norman recipe can be prepared, perhaps for the first time, in a completely authentic manner in this country. It would certainly be a rare gastronomic occasion.

So, too, for most of us, would be the chance to cook the beef testicles, big as mangoes, nonchalantly on sale next to more quotidian cuts. And for the truly experimental there are beef hearts, feet, cheeks, and lips split open and bristling with white nodes resembling wheat grains. Presumably all these oddments find purchasers who know what to do with them, perhaps clever Chicanos who haven't yet forgotten what they learned in their home villages in Mexico.

Some of the grocers sell nothing but dried foods. These specialists purvey an encyclopedic stock of chilies. There are big, black-red, wide *anchos*; wizened, brownish *mulatos* for the Aztec turkey extravaganza *mole poblano de quajolote* (famous because the sauce contains some chocolate); smoky *chipotles*; long, thin, pointy *guajillos,* also called *traviesos,* or naughty, because of their sting, and sometimes called *cascabel,* or rattle; and the holy grail of chilies, the true *cascabel.* This small, spherical chili, which sounds like a rattle when shaken, is smooth, brownish red, and tastes nutty and relatively mild when toasted for the sauce that the intrepid cookbook author Diana Kennedy first encountered in the forests of the Yucatán and recommends for tacos. Finding the *cascabel* is usually hard but a cinch at the Grand Central Market.

Once you have the *cascabeles,* the same man will sell you Mexican dried shrimp, which have the skin and tail still on. This makes them hard to clean, but they are tastier than the dried shrimp sold in Oriental markets. Mexican whole dried shrimp are usually unavailable in this country. Once you have them and the *cascabeles,* nothing can stop you from duplicating the dried shrimp consommé that Diana Kennedy learned to make in Guadalajara from Clara Zabalza de García. This is the same Señora García who pickled chilies every year in pineapple vinegar.

I did not locate any pineapple vinegar in Los Angeles, but the Grand Central Market did tempt me with *nopales,* fresh, green, edible cactus "paddles," as well as bags of precut cactus *nopalitos.*

The real connoisseur will next make a beeline for the dairy counter, where they sell two varieties of cultured butter, slightly tangy and whipped in great mounds, and the *crème fraîche* snob will want to try a blind tasting of the three styles of Hispanic sour cream: Mexican, Guatemalan, and Salvadoran. The differences among them are slight but provocative. All three are more delicate than commercial sour cream.

This is obviously a great place to shop if you want to prepare the classics of Mexican cuisine. But if you are only passing through Los

Angeles, as I was, and have no time or kitchen for serious cooking, you can still get a tantalizing taste of what might have been by lining up at one of the Mexican food counters that operate in the market.

These are not fancy places, but they do turn out some of the most delicious and authentic Mexican food to be found north of the border. Off in a corner, not too far from the tropical-juice bar, is an extremely unassuming taco stand. You can buy two fresh tortillas rolled around a nondescript filling of chopped meat and lettuce. There is a mildly hot red sauce with chunks of tomatoes still visible in it, guaranteeing that it was made on the spot. And you can also munch the fresh little yellow chilies that sit on the counter as a sort of condiment. Nothing could be simpler. What makes it work are the tortillas. They are fresh, pliable, and taste strongly, you might even say aggressively, of corn.

This is not the sugary flavor of fresh corn on the cob but the musty, vaguely sour taste of hominy, which is dry corn from which the hull and germ have been leached with wood ash or quicklime. This prehistoric process was common to the agricultural Indian peoples of the Americas. They knew that the lye present in wood ash would separate the hulls from the nutritionally useful interior of the corn kernel. When ground, the resultant cornmeal, or *masa harina* in Spanish, was compact and stored well. Furthermore, it had a complex taste.

This taste pervades the cuisine that descended to modern Mexico from the Aztecs. It is a flavor impressed on the taste memories of millions of people whose basic bread is the flat, circular masa pancake called tortilla. Non-Hispanic Americans also eat tortillas by the million in pseudo-Mexican restaurants, but these mass-produced tortillas have only a formal resemblance to the genuine article, pressed out by hand and cooked on a griddle over a wood or charcoal fire in the traditional manner.

The heaviest dose of transplanted Mexican authenticity in the Grand Central Market is available at Ana Maria's, a centrally positioned counter restaurant. There, a young woman in a pink dress reaches into a white plastic tub and pulls out some tortilla dough. With the precision of gesture the French call a *tour de main* (we might say "knack"), she pats the dough into thick disks, much thicker than regular tortillas. She plunks a set of them on a big griddle and cooks the batch slowly and carefully. These are called *gorditas*, "fat little cakes." When you order one, she splits it and fills it with various meats and vegetables.

Ana Maria's also runs a taco operation of serious refinement. The all-important tortillas are kept warm and moist in an electric warmer, and the customer selects the filling for his taco from a bracingly chilified selection that includes blood sausage, brains, the roasted bits of pork called *carnitas,* and the stew of mixed meats called *birria.* This apparently mundane carry-out restaurant is careful about the origins of what it serves. The *carnitas* are denominated *estilo Tepatitlán,* in the style of Tepatitlán; the *birria* is *birria estilo Jalisco.*

Of course even these delicacies are only humble representatives of the full magnificence of Mexican cookery with its two thousand recipes and its utterly original approach to the edible biosphere. Ana Maria's prepares what it prepares with real flair, but its offerings are limited to the informal foods Mexicans call *antojitos,* or "eye-pleasers." But this restaurant is a symbol for a momentous change occurring in our midst. Millions of immigrants, official and unofficial, most of them speaking Spanish, are bringing us their food and adapting it to American conditions. In California this means that Mexican food is pervading the whole food life of the state in ever greater intensity. It also means Vietnamese and Thai food. Meanwhile, in the East, Puerto Ricans, Dominicans, Colombians, Peruvians, Ecuadorians are putting down roots, transforming themselves into Americans and us into Hispanics, a bit, sometimes without our knowing it. This came home to me recently at Thanksgiving time when I went looking for sweet potatoes.

CHAPTER 11

TUBERS

E V E N   I N the most lily-white suburban markets there is deep confusion about sweet potatoes and yams. Even without all the other hairy, scaly tubers and rhizomes now appearing in urban markets with a Hispanic clientele, the sweet potato/yam dilemma causes enough trouble by itself. Sweets and yams look alike, but yams were said to be moister and tastier than normal sweets. The truth is that the yams and sweet potatoes that Anglo America debates about—the moist, the dry, the yellow, the orange, the Georgia jet, and the vineless Vardaman—belong to one species, *Ipomoea batatas*. What's more, no *Ipomoea* is really a yam, and there are lots of appealing *Ipomoeas* now competing for space in U.S. vegetable bins (along with real yams, which I'll get to in a minute).

The genus *Ipomoea* was named by Linnaeus and means "resembling the convolvulus." Indeed, its five hundred mainly tropical species are in the *Convolvulaceae* family. The morning glory is an *Ipomoea*, but the most important congener is *I. batatas*. Originally found in tropical America, it now flourishes throughout the warm parts of the world. Even when limited to the edible species *(I. batatas)*, a thorough investigation of the genus *Ipomoea* would range from China to Africa. In Mexico and Hispanic America, a sweet potato puree is a sought-after dessert. In her encyclopedic *Classic Indian Vegetarian and Grain Cooking* (Morrow), Julie Sahni writes about a *poori*, a puffed bread whose dough contains pureed sweet potato. Brazilian cuisine includes sweet potato soup, candy, puffs, and dinner rolls.

Hispanic America, the original home of *I. batatas*, seems to be the richest source of sweet potato dishes, and Elisabeth Lambert Ortiz's standard, *The Complete Book of Caribbean Cookery*, catalogues two sweet potato breads, one with coconut mixed in, as well as cakes from Haiti, Martinique, and Cuba; sweet potato chips; a sweet potato crust for chicken pie; a dessert paste; a pone; and a tart. The most tantalizing fact about this repertory is that the sweet potato most prized for many of these recipes—the variety most admired in the region where sweet potatoes are most used—is neither our yam nor our "true" sweet potato.

The *boniato* (or *batata* or *batata dulce*) is an almost spherical, small tuber with a single point. Its skin is brown or pink; its flesh, white. And its flavor, while less sweet and sultry than our local varieties, is far more aromatic. Islanders prefer it. So will you.

Boniatos are not hard to find. Now that I know what to look for, I see them everywhere—in the vegetable bins of little Hispanic bodegas and even in New York supermarkets. Usually they are labeled *batatas,* if they are labeled at all. The assumption of the grocers selling them seems to be that people who are likely to buy them will already know what they are. You and I, after all, don't need a sign to tell us that conical orange vegetables with lacy green tops are carrots.

So the *boniato* lurks within the hermetic world of *productos tropicales,* anonymously for sale in every big city in this country but almost completely ignored by Anglo cooks, even those with a passion for the exotic. And in those same bins, beside the *boniatos,* lie various hairy, wrinkled root vegetables known by a host of imprecise or confusingly multiple dialectal names. Some of them are taros (*malanga, tannia)*; others are cassava *(yuca).* Still others are true yams (*ñames, mapueys).*

The true yams look nothing at all like sweet potatoes, nor are they related. The roughly six hundred species of true yams spread throughout the world's warm countries are all members of the genus *Dioscorea,* which is named after the ancient naturalist Dioscorides. The Central American *D. composita* is a natural source of cortisone. *D. elephantipes,* or Hottentot bread, grows to a humongous 700 pounds in the deserts of South Africa. *D. alata,* the winged or water yam, is distributed worldwide and may extend six feet in length and weigh 150 pounds. As far as I can tell, the much smaller, cylindrical, brown-skinned, white-fleshed yam normally sold in my Manhattan neighborhood is either *D. alata* of modest size (two feet long, 4 to 5 pounds) or *D. trifida,* six to eight inches long and very similar in taste quality. The vernacular name yam derives from a West African word that came into Spanish as *ñame,* French as *igname,* and Portuguese as *inhame.* One imagines that slaves brought the word to these shores and applied it to sweet potatoes because they were also root vegetables.

Apart from its size and the confusion that surrounds it in American life, the yam is not a vegetable likely to interest people who already

have access to the potato and who can easily latch on to the *boniato.*
The true yam has a neutral, starchy flavor. The yam seems to have
originated in Asia and was eaten in China from earliest times. West
Africans depend on it although its protein content is small. Perhaps
the best thing that can be said about it is that it really is a yam.

I much prefer the sweet potato and couldn't be happier that my
Hispanic neighbors have brought in an interesting new variety as well
as canned sweetened dessert purees. These are a vestige of the tastes
of the Spanish conquistadors who preferred sweeter varieties of *I.
batatas* to the starchier varieties then normally cultivated by local
farmers in tropical America. Their preference helped to reduce the
genetic variety of sweet potatoes in cultivation, with "sweet" sweet
potatoes favored. *Boniatos* are a surviving example of the starchier
kind of sweet potato.

Over the centuries ever more consolidated agriculture and markets reflecting stratified national tastes have put continuing pressure
on sweet potato diversity. As high-yielding varieties took over production even in third-world fields and as more sophisticated and powerful
systems of marketing made it possible to pinpoint consumer taste, the
number of varieties was further reduced.

So in order to help preserve genetic varieties, the International
Potato Center (CIP) in Lima began collecting donations of sweet
potato genetic materials in 1985, and within three years was maintain-
ing over five thousand types of germ plasm from all over the world.
When I heard about this new program, I nodded politely, thinking
that sweet potatoes were surely of minor importance in the planetary
scheme of things. But this is definitely a first-world reaction.

I was pulled up short when the CIP researcher, Zosimo Huamán,
told me that the sweet potato ranks second in the world, after the
potato, among root and tuber crops. More surprising still is its importance in China.

I was dimly aware that the Chinese eat sweet potatoes. A *Natural
History* reader in Peking once wrote me to protest that I hadn't mentioned China in a column I once did that purported to survey sweet
potato cookery around the world. A street vendor, he said, was selling
roasted sweet potatoes outside his office.

Even still, I had no idea that China is by far the world's largest
producer of *I. batatas.* China now produces 80 percent of all the sweet
potatoes in the world. Other Asian countries account for another 6
percent. Africa produces 5 percent, and Latin America, 2 percent. In
other words, the third world produces 98 percent of the world's sweet
potatoes, and virtually all the sweet potatoes on earth are eaten by

people in subsistence economies whose ancestral larder did not include this versatile plant.

In absolute quantity, too, the consumption is staggering, especially from the first-world perspective, because the consumption of root crops in the developed countries has lately been in decline. But in developing countries, root crop production has been rising. The potato is by far the leader, almost everywhere. But the sweet potato is still immensely important. As of 1984 the average world per-capita consumption of root crops was estimated at seventy kilograms, of which thirty-two were potatoes and nineteen were sweet potatoes (cassava accounted for sixteen kilograms and other crops rounded out the other four kilograms).

What accounts for the sweet potato's emergence as a world crop? Why is it now grown in more developing countries than any other root crop? A CIP publication says it best:

> Sweet potato's high concentration of carbohydrates and vitamin A and its relatively low water content make it an excellent food source. It grows well under a wide range of farming conditions and has a comparative advantage over many crops in warm areas subject to drought, numerous pests, and poor or waterlogged soils. Furthermore, it is inexpensive to produce, easy to cultivate, has a short growing period, and gives generally high yields.

Even so, the sweet potato was slow to take hold in China. According to Chinese authority Yu Youtai in *Feeding a Billion: Frontiers of Chinese Agriculture* (Michigan State, 1987), the sweet potato made its way to China in the sixteenth century, either through India and Burma to Yunnan Province or to Fujian Province by way of the Philippines. It spread over the Yangtze and Yellow river valleys over the next century and eventually throughout the country.

The Mandarin word for sweet potato, *fanshu,* is one reason to put the plant's arrival in China back before 1600. *Fan,* meaning foreign country, was prefixed to the names of plants introduced to China after the tenth century; the tomato is *fangie;* the pomegranate, *fanshiliu.* In earlier times, foreign plants were prefixed with *hai,* meaning sea: *haitung* for crabapple, *haizao* for date palm. After the seventeenth century the prefix became *yang* because all foreign countries were then called *yang.* Hence, *yangchong* means onion, *yangjiang* means Jerusalem artichoke.

The sweet potato has many vernacular, local names in China:

mountain taro, golden potato, red potato, white potato, and ground melon. Ninety to 100 million tons are produced annually. The actual area planted in sweet potatoes has declined, but yields have increased steadily at roughly 3 percent a year. Chinese acreage devoted to sweet potatoes ranks behind only that planted in rice, wheat, and corn.

Traditionally, the sweet potato has filled an important niche in Chinese agriculture, writes Youtai, as a crop that

> has saved millions from starvation when wheat and rice crops failed. . . . Today, in the streets and lanes of both small and large Chinese cities, street vendors sell freshly baked sweet potatoes—a favorite with children and adults. The baked sweet potato ("*kaobaishu*" in Chinese) of Beijing is especially well known. Dried sweet potato slices can be easily stored for year-round use. Many Chinese eat sweet potato slices as they would fruit. Noodles made from sweet potato starch are one of the most popular processed foods. Moreover, sweet potato starch is an important raw material for many light industries, for food processing, and for the pharmaceutical industries. In China, sweet potatoes are used in the manufacture of liquor, vinegar, gourmet powder, glucose, alcohol, plastics, synthetic rubber, artificial fiber, color film, citric acid, and erythromycin. Roots, stems, leaves, and starch residues from the sweet potato plant are good feedstuffs for livestock. Sweet potato stems and leaves are used for silage and are as nutritious as alfalfa when fed to cattle. It is said that fanshu is a treasure trove "from head to toe."

The sweet potato will probably never be so crucial in the U.S. kitchen as it has become in China, but American consumers now have ready access to greater *Ipomoea* diversity than ever before, right at their doorsteps, not to mention the other exotic roots, the taros and the real yams. It would be a crime against gastronomic good sense if we ignored this new cornucopia with the same philistinism we turned on the olive not so long ago.

CHAPTER III

OLIVES

E V E N N O W, with modest exceptions among urban gastronomes, we as a nation continue to support a domestic olive industry in which thousands of years of experience in Europe have been distorted by a perverse homegrown method of olive curing. The balance could so easily have tipped the other way.

High above Santa Barbara, in a hill garden that stands between rising slopes and a Pacific vista spreading out to the Channel Islands at the shimmering horizon far below, is a big gnarled olive tree. It is home to a bevy of topknotted California quail, and it still bears olives, apparently for its own amusement. They fall on the ground and have to be cleared away by the owner of the land and of the house across the lawn. These are real black-ripe California olives from a tree said to have been planted in the previous century, an abortive offshoot of Spanish civilization brought here by missionaries.

Olives were first brought to the New World in the fifteenth century, but the North American industry did not begin in earnest until Mexican cuttings from trees established in the seventeenth and eighteenth centuries were brought to the San Diego mission in 1769. Franciscans kept on planting new trees as they established missions farther north along the California coast. By 1825, fifty-six hundred trees were in the ground at the twenty-one missions between San Diego and Sonoma. By 1884 olive trees planted on one thousand acres were producing 21 tons of fruit. Between then and now, the industry grew to cover thirty to forty times that acreage and has produced as much as 146,000 tons of table olives (in the bumper year of 1982), mostly in groves in the Sacramento and San Joaquin valleys with their long hot growing seasons and cool but not lethally cold winters.

In this country, California is virtually the only state that grows olives at all. Arizona makes a statistically unmeaningful contribution.

But even California is a minor factor in world olive production. Ninety-eight percent of world olive acreage is in Mediterranean countries. Among them, Spain, Italy, and Greece produce more than half of the planet's olive tonnage, almost all of it in the form of oil. But these countries, as well as France, North Africa, the Levant, and even Chile, do sell roughly a tenth of their olive crops as table olives, ranging from tiny shriveled salt-cured blacks to mushy salty reds to fermented greens.

Within this specialized world of traditionally cured table olives, California does not compete at all except in one subspecialty where it reigns supreme. I am talking about the so-called black-ripe olive. We have all eaten them—big, meaty, shiny, black olives with gray-green flesh, tender but not mushy. Admirers refer to the taste of the black-ripe olive as mild, but other words come to mind. One thing is certain: The black-ripe olive is neither naturally ripe nor black, and it tastes as little like an olive as technology can make it.

The process is Californian, usually said to have been invented by one Freda Ehmann at the turn of the century while she was experimenting with olive canning methods on her back porch in Oroville. Mrs. Ehmann (or possibly C. M. Gifford of San Diego or Emily Roberson of Auburn) first contrived to process green olives so that they would turn black and could be canned for long storage. Industry sources today hail this achievement as "the key to successful, large-scale olive production."

I quote from a pamphlet handed out to visitors by the Lindsay Ripe Olive Company, a growers cooperative established in 1916 and now an industry giant with an enormous thirty-acre processing facility at the edge of the small Central Valley town of Lindsay. I toured the Lindsay plant at the tail end of the olive harvest last November. In front, immaculate men and women were pruning a grove of beautiful old olive trees. Out back, dozens and dozens of redwood and fiberglass tanks were holding tons of handpicked green olives in a mild brine until they could be processed.

This outdoor scene had a certain ageless charm, especially the lines of weathered redwood tanks dating back as far as 1916. Inside was a scene out of *Modern Times*: gleaming tanks, elevated metal catwalks, and forests of pipes through which olives could be "flumed" (pumped along in water from place to place) on their way to being canned.

These outward trappings are not what is wrong with black-ripe olives. Not primarily, at any rate. The flaw goes back to Mrs. Ehmann who discovered that you could turn a green olive black while you cured it in lye. Then you could cook the olive and can it in mild brine.

The secret to blackening is air; air bubbled through the curing tank oxidizes and blackens the olive. According to the Lindsay pamphlet, oxidization also gives the black-ripe olive its "distinctive flavor." This is a hard point to discuss if you think that the black-ripe olive is almost without flavor, compared to all other table olives in the known world. But since I have lately been able to taste unoxidized, lye-cured, canned "green-ripe" olives and noticed only a visual difference with the black-ripes, I feel fairly confident in saying that the oxidation changes nothing but the outer color of the fruit, from a beige-green to a very dark brown that looks black. The black color is definitely more attractive than the canned green, and I presume that truly ripe black olives would be far less convenient to can since they would already be soft before they were pressure-cooked in an industrial retort.

In the processing plant, California-style olive canning works basically like this: Whole green olives go into tanks containing a mild caustic solution—water and lye (sodium hydroxide). Lye is a strong chemical. It will burn the skin on contact, remove paint, and eat its way through clogged drains, sometimes burning a hole in the pipe on the way through. Perhaps it was because she knew these things about lye that a New York food reporter told me she thought it was the lye bath per se that deflavorized California black olives. In fact, lye-curing of olives goes back to the Romans and is the fundamental method used in Spain.

Lye efficiently leaches out a natural chemical constituent of olives, the bitter glucoside called oleuropein. But Spanish green olives, which are cured in lye, are not traditionally held in it long enough to allow the chemical reaction to reach all the way to the pit. Some natural bitterness is left in, which is a plus for any of us who want to taste the oliveness of olives.

At the Lindsay plant I tasted a "raw" (uncured) olive and found it excessively bitter but not much more bitter than some excellent Mediterranean olives cured only in salt or brine. Evidently this taste was what once held back mass sales of olives to the U.S. public, it and the color green. Many people evidently liked the idea of a black (ergo ripe, ergo not unripe) olive, but didn't like the, to them, aggressive olivey taste of traditionally cured, tree-ripened olives picked black or blackened in the open air during curing.

Enter Mrs. Ehmann's modern epigones. They cure the green

olive in three different lye baths over seven days, and all the while they are blowing air through the tanks. The lye goes all the way to the pit, and the air turns the fruit a beautiful black, which is stabilized with a small amount of ferrous gluconate, also found in iron pills.

Now it is time to size and pit the olives, stages that exemplify the American industrial approach even more than the curing. California olive sizes are something of a joke because they are so blatantly boastful. Currently there are seven sizes, with four being larger than "large." For the record, the seven sizes (reduced to that from a once much longer and more fanciful list) are small, medium, large, extra large, jumbo, colossal, and super colossal. A small olive weighs from 3.2 to 3.3 grams. A super colossal weighs from 14.2 to 16.2 grams, according to data provided by the California Olive Industry, a trade organization in Fresno.

A machine does the sorting (olives roll along pairs of tightly stretched cables that start out close together and spread farther apart along the way; small olives fall between them early on, and larger ones last until the end, before falling into hoppers below). Most olives next go to an automatic pitter that can pit one thousand olives per minute. Experience shows that Americans like the convenience of pitted olives. Pitting also improves olive shelf life slightly. Lindsay operates a battery of pitters that, according to a Lindsay publication, can pit 14 million olives in an eight-hour shift. The pits themselves are burnt to provide heat for cooking canned olives in a pressure cooker at 260 degrees for fourteen minutes (another Lindsay source specifies 269 degrees for twelve minutes). This is a necessity for canning black-ripe olives, which are known technically as low-acid fruit.

As any home canner knows, low-acid fruit has to be meticulously heated after canning because the airless medium in the can is a perfect environment for anaerobic bacteria. A rash of deaths from botulism in the early days of olive canning in California made packers properly cautious. (Green Spanish-style olives undergo a lactic acid fermentation, which preserves them and also protects them from anaerobic bacterial contamination so they can be packed without being cooked.)

Not all California olives are processed as black-ripes. There is a burgeoning quality-oil industry that is striving to compete with European extra-virgin, cold-pressed oils. And small specialty producers are working with tree-ripened olives or with green olives lye-cured in moderation. In other words, the same kinds of developments are occurring at the high end of the U.S. olive industry that have occurred in the domestic wine and cheese industries: European-style quality is at last being nurtured despite an overwhelming domestic tilt toward the production of bland, physically perfect, super-jumbo-colossal olives attractively packaged and priced, with shelf lives of more than a year.

At the moment the boutique olive producers have not progressed as far as their wine and cheesemaking cousins. Too often U.S. specialty olives are just mass-produced green olives bottled with aggressive spice mixtures or stuffed with jalapeño peppers and then marketed as gourmet olives. No doubt there are important exceptions to this rule, but for the moment the key to olive quality seems to be the open vat. Anything in a bottle or a can seems always to be inferior to olives sold from open bulk containers, whether in supermarket deli departments or in the kind of amazing display of international diversity available at sophisticated retailers such as Sahadi of Atlantic Avenue, Brooklyn. The whole of the olivaceous Mediterranean is there, from chewy little bitter black orbs of the Maghreb to nutty Spanish Sevillian greens, and the legacy of the conquistadors mixes together with Greek methods in that Arab-American emporium to bring us squishy red Royal Victorias from Chile. Meanwhile, the black-ripe California olive is bravely making its way in the world. The Lindsay company is selling them in Japan, and I saw a can in the fancy-food department of the main Madrid branch of the Spanish Bloomingdale's, El Corte Inglés.

CHAPTER IV

DATES

A T A B O U T the same time that Freda Ehmann was perfecting the process that made this plague possible, other hopeful fruit growers in California were hard at work trying to naturalize another Old World plant, the date palm. The first date palms were brought to the United States in tubs on shipboard from Egypt in 1890 and transplanted successfully at Salt River Valley, Arizona. Date palms travel well. It takes only a few years for a tree to grow from seed or sucker to maturity. Eventually a mature plant may stretch up, nearly straight, a hundred feet, and it may easily produce more than one hundred pounds of the one- to three-inch-long berries with grooved seeds that we call dates. Since palms bear dates for as much as a century, it may still be possible to eat dates grown on the original American trees.

Date cultivation was just as practical in the desert climate of southern California around Indio near Palm Springs, the eventual capital of the U.S. date industry, as it had been for millennia in the deserts of the Near East.

Tall palms heavy with bunches of dates gave an exotic tone to the desert. Indio's souvenir shops invited tourists to stock up on the "Arabian" berry with the grooved seed that put Indio on the map. In the spotless town itself, the fairgrounds looks like the set for the casbah in a silent-era Hollywood backlot epic, evoking more innocent times before the word Arabian was dated and when the Middle East was still a harmless, picturesque place famous mainly for Sheherazade, Sinbad, and T. E. Lawrence.

In Indio, eating date ice cream, surrounded by trees that were planted several decades ago at the dawn of the U.S. date industry, one momentarily manages to forget the tensions of the Arab world. If time has not exactly stood still in Indio, this is nevertheless a place devoted to a fading moment in our history when California was still a pioneer state full of boundless optimism. The chief wonder of this sunny

paradise was its unplumbed but obviously fabulous agricultural potential.

I am talking about the early years of this century, the springtime
of the modern era in southern California, before serious in-migration
turned the area into a megalopolis. A woman I knew, who was born
in Covina in Los Angeles County just before World War I, used to
boast that her birth certificate had a number with only three digits
because so few people had been born there even by that relatively late
date.

At about the same time, a band of farseeing horticulturists and
high-risk speculators decided to introduce useful plants from tropical
countries to the almost embarrassingly hospitable soil of California
(and other warm American states such as Florida).

Today dates are a specialty crop. As a nation we consume only
a few thousand tons a year. Americans have never developed much
of a taste for them. I found that I could barely give away dates to most
of the people at my hotel in Palm Springs. And these were not just
any old dates; they were jumbo, unsulfured royal medjool dates
straight from the grove.

Rebuffed, I felt a rush of sympathy for the Indio date growers who
must fight such philistine indifference every day. Back in the beginning of the Indio date gardens, evangelizing on behalf of their dates
must have been a positive pleasure for the growers, but decades later
their mission has largely failed to make the date an American staple.
To visit the gardens and endure the sales pitch concocted in a simpler,
more optimistic era is a chastening experience. For the full treatment,
the peripatetic fruit historian stops at Shields Date Garden, an Indio
landmark since 1924 when E. Floyd Shields and his wife Bess first
took possession of a few trees imported from Algeria. By 1977 they
had expanded their garden to some twelve hundred trees and had also
developed a variety of schemes for packaging, shipping, promoting,
and dramatizing their luscious fruit.

Shields Garden has not only trees and a retail store but also a
date theater, with 108 seats and a continuous audiovisual presentation. The big sign outside proclaims: SEE IT NOW. ROMANCE AND SEX
LIFE OF THE DATE. IN SOUND AND COLOR. IRRESISTIBLE.

I bought a date milkshake, intense with date flavor because it was
made from date crystals (coarsely ground dried dates), and went into
the darkened auditorium.

It is easy to make the Shields show sound ridiculous. In the richly
overmodulated tones of an announcer from the golden age of radio,

the voice of the recorded narrator propounds the case for dates with all the sloganeering and cuteness of a commercial created at the dawn of broadcast advertising. With the modesty of a used-car salesman he talks up the unique virtues of the hybrid Shields Black Beauty date, twenty-three years in development, so precious that each customer may purchase only one. These "blackest of black dates" are "red when they're green."

Sophisticated viewers may laugh at pictures of the late E. F. Shields wearing a pith helmet and holding fluffy bunches of female and male date blossoms. But behind all the self-promotion and the preposterous joking about date sexuality is a remarkably detailed exposition of the facts of date horticulture. Even the most jaded visitor cannot fail to learn something about the strenuous symbiosis between human effort and date biology that eventually produces the moist, rich dates on sale at the counter outside the theater.

Each tree sends out either male or female blooms. Shields employees bring the male pollen to the female flower. Climbing up the trees on fixed ladders, they "visit" each female tree twice a week during February, March, and April searching for open blooms, which must be pollinated in the first three to four days after opening or they will dry up and mature inadequately.

Before pollination, the spathe, or outer covering of the bloom, is removed and the end of the bloom is pruned away. As the dates start to grow, the bunches have to be thinned and tied up to keep the stem from breaking under the weight of the fruit. Such careful management allows a tree to produce fruit of good quality year after year without depleting its energies.

Even without manual pollination there would be enough pollen carried from tree to tree by the wind to ensure the survival of the species. This is nature's way, but it isn't thorough enough to produce a serious bunch of dates on every tree. In southern California growers also have to irrigate their date gardens with water brought in by the All-American Canal from the Colorado River 209 miles away. As a brochure on sale at the Shields Garden explains, "Date Palms get thirsty about every week or ten days." They use as much water as a willow, and gardens have to be flooded periodically. Maturing fruit must also be covered with waterproof bagging to protect dates from rain damage in August and later in the year.

The picking season starts in September and runs through Christmas. Afterward the trees are cleaned up, old fruit stems cut off, and thorns removed from new leaves so that workers won't get pricked when they come to pollinate the blooms.

Dates will grow from seed, but this is not a good way to reproduce choice, productive strains. Vegetative propagation from the offshoots that each tree sends out is the preferred method even though it takes several years before an offshoot can be cut away and rooted on its own, and then it will not come into fruit production for another eight to fifteen years.

Obviously the entire arduous process of date farming is a costly and difficult business. Not everyone who plunged into it zealously before World War II has bothered to continue. According to the Shields brochure, "many of the date growers are digging out their beautiful date gardens in spite of the fact that the palms are right in their prime because they are not receiving enough for their dates to pay the cost of production."

When I was in Indio in October 1981, at the height of the season, jumbo medjools were selling for just over four dollars a pound at the Shields store, which seemed reasonable for such superb fruit. An even greater variety of dates, at a somewhat lower price, was available at Albert's Ranch Market in Banning, on the way back to Los Angeles. Not only medjools but also deglet noors, halawys, soft honey dates, zahidis, and my favorite, barhi honeyballs, literally dripping with sweetness.

You will have no trouble locating Albert's. It is a big red barn just off the freeway with a large statue of a hen in the parking lot and a sign advertising CACKLE FRESH EGGS FROM OUR HENS. Inside they are selling the bounty of the earth, and posted by a water fountain is one of the country's great signs: OUT OF COURTESY TO OTHER PATRONS. DRINKING FOUNTAIN ONLY. DO NOT WASH FALSE TEETH, HANDS, OR FRUIT HERE. THANKS, MGMT.

CHAPTER V

PISTACHIOS

I F T H E California date world has a musty, failed aura, hope and optimism pervade the state's newest exotic fruit industries. The major new wrinkle is pistachio production on a huge, mechanized industrial scale. Events of the last decade as widely scattered as the fall of the shah of Iran and the installation of an aqueduct in California have turned the pistachio into a booming American crop, perfected botanically, harvested by the latest techniques, and launched by a tax loophole.

The pistachio began as a wild tree, probably in Asia Minor where Neolithic peoples latched on to its grapelike clusters of red-hulled fruit and learned to like the meat they found inside the hard ivory kernels. Carbonized nuts from Stone Age settlements excavated in Jordan and Turkey have been dated to about 7000 B.C. Between that time and the 1970s, people spread *Pistacia vera,* a smallish, twenty-five- to thirty-foot deciduous tree, around the Mediterranean. Iran became the world's pistachio leader, with production centered in the Kerman region, also known for its rugs.

For the pistachio, botany was destiny. Like the peach, the pistachio is a drupe; its hull surrounds a hard-shelled kernel with a crunchy, oily green or yellow "nut" inside. In fact, the pistachio is a member of the same family, Anacardiaceae, as are two other drupes of great economic importance, the mango and the cashew. To see the relationship between them graphically, cut open the stone of a mango and note the cashewlike nut hidden there. Pistachios do not look anything like cashews, but certain varieties have a turpentine flavor also common to some strains of mango and to all unripe mangoes. Indeed, *Pistacia terebinthus,* a cousin of the pistachio of commerce, is the original source of turpentine.

In most parts of the world the nuts of *P. vera* are still harvested and processed by hand. The red clusters are left to dry in the sun and then, at a later, more convenient time, soaked in water to facilitate hand hulling. The defect of this method, even in countries like Iran where labor is cheap, is that it allows the pigment of the hull to stain and mottle the shells. If pistachios were sold as naked, shelled nutmeats, this would make no difference, but they are almost always roasted and salted in the shell because, ideally and usually, they emerge from the hull "smiling," with their shells split at one end, easy for the eater to shell on his own. Since they are small as nuts go, the producer derives an enormous advantage from selling them unshelled. You could say, moreover, that the pistachio nut is a naturally packaged convenience food, protected from harm by its shell but relatively easy to open. (This is not always true. A certain percentage of the nuts do not split and are a boon to dentists with pistachio fanciers in their practice. One of the main aims of modern pistachio culture is to develop cultivars that grow fewer or no unsmiling, closed nuts.)

To mask the mottling left from dilatory, old-fashioned processing, traditional pistachio merchants dyed their nuts red. Unblemished nuts were sold in their natural state, but most Americans came to know the pistachio as a red nut sold in vending machines. Most of these nuts used to come from Iran where a tree said to be seven hundred years old still stands as a symbol of the world's most important pistachio crop.

But in this country the Islamic fundamentalist regime ruling Iran has undermined Iran's American pistachio sales. Albert Zaloom, of the pioneering American pistachio distributors Zaloom Bros. in Secaucus, New Jersey, points out that this coincided with huge expansion in production of pistachios in California. He remembers the days when America grew only 1.5 million pounds, but now he anticipates that trees planted in the seventies in the San Joaquin and Sacramento valleys, which grew 40 to 50 million pounds of nuts in the early eighties, will surpass 100 million pounds when they come into full maturity in the 1990s.

The California pistachio boom got a major push when the Internal Revenue Service allowed Americans to invest in tax-sheltered pistachio orchards. Building on this "seed money," growers applied advanced plant science and mechanical harvesting to their new trees. In California, *P. vera* is typically grafted onto hardier rootstocks from other members of the pistachio genus. Systematic pruning and strategic placement of the pollinating male "Peters" variety (one for each eight to ten female "Kermans") have helped establish flourishing, efficient groves.

Conventional soft-fruit-type harvesting equipment collects nuts from two trees per minute, shaking the nuts loose, cleaning them, removing leaves and twigs. Two men can harvest an acre in an hour.

The most dramatic improvement mechanization brought to pistachio processing is the ability to dry and hull the nuts within twenty-four hours of collection, which greatly reduces mottling of the shells. Most nuts are now hulled by the friction of rubberized belts running parallel to each other and at different speeds. This pinching conveyor spews the hulled nuts into a water bath that washes them. Empty nuts float; filled ones sink and are sent on to a forced-air drier for a ten-hour treatment. An electric eye then sorts out any blemished nuts.

California pistachios are not only prettier than Iranian ones, they are also bigger. Iranians range from eighteen to forty nuts per ounce. Californians run as big as fourteen to the ounce. And many more unsplit Iranian nuts reach market.

But do the Californian nuts taste as good?

"Considerable controversy exists in the United States concerning the relative merits of homegrown, as opposed to imported, pistachios," writes Frederic Rosengarten, Jr., in *The Book of Edible Nuts.* "The American importers of Iranian and Turkish pistachios describe the California counterparts as beautiful but tasteless. The California producers, on the other hand, claim their pistachios taste about the same as the imported nuts but are larger, fresher, and easier to open."

Mr. Rosengarten, an associate in economic botany at Harvard's Botanical Museum, does not take a stand on this dispute. Mr. Zaloom says, "The American consumer prefers the California nuts. The California pistachio is an attractive nut, and the consumer is not that discriminating about subtle distinctions in taste. The California nut does tend to seem drier. The drying process is harsher than sun drying, but it's a very subtle difference."

To see for myself, I bought two different brands of California pistachios, labeled as such, in a supermarket. Unable to locate Iranian pistachios at any Manhattan gourmet food shop, I went to Atlantic Avenue in Brooklyn, the national center for direct food imports from the Near East. At Sahadi's market I obtained two kinds of Iranian nuts, one unlabeled, the other Zenobia's Shah variety. All four kinds of nuts I tasted were unblemished and undyed. There were virtually no unsplit nuts in the two vacuum-packed jars from California. There was a small but noticeable number of unsplit nuts from Iran. The Californias were slightly larger. As to taste, the Zenobia Shahs stood out. They were faintly aromatic, more complex. The other three were all perfectly good nuts, however, and I ate them all, leaving a large pile of tan shells on my desk.

This was a highly informal test, of course, and it did not include Albert Zaloom's favorite kind of pistachio, the tough little nuts grown in Sicily and rarely exported. (Nor did it include Turkish nuts, which by 1990 were the only Near Eastern nuts that Sahadi was selling. They were also superior in taste to California nuts, in my view.) I emerged from my pistachio feast feeling largely content with the first fruits of the California boom, glad that the price of pistachios is dropping rapidly, and completely unsated in my appetite for this delectable drupe.

CHAPTER VI

CHERIMOYAS

I FEEL even better about the California production of an even better and more exotic fruit, *Annona cherimola,* the cherimoya.

This giant pearl of the Andes has the most exquisitely refined climatic requirements, but in the end what has prevented U.S. growers from producing cherimoyas in commercial quantities is the extremely chaste and all but inviolable shape of this tree's female genitalia. I would not be titillating you with such arcana if the cherimoya were not at last available—at a price, but available nevertheless—to fruit lovers across the United States. Total acreage in North America is measured in the hundreds, so we are not on the verge of a cherimoya bonanza—and we probably never will be. But fancy fruiterers carry them in sufficient quantity to satisfy the curiosity if not the appetite of the pomologically alert.

That we have a commercial cherimoya crop at all is due to the efforts of a few determined growers, mostly in California. I visited the largest of these cherimoya operations in the hills near Santa Barbara. California Tropics had all of twenty-five acres of cherimoya trees in cultivation. The proprietor, Peter Nichols, grew up in the fruit business, but when the family avocado ranch was hit by devastating root rot, he turned to new crops. There were already half a dozen cherimoya trees on the property, and Nichols, inspired by their success, took the plunge and committed himself seriously to cherimoliculture. "We really rolled our sleeves up eight years ago," he told me. And that was an understatement.

The cherimoya is a subtropical, semideciduous tree that is viable along the California coast from Santa Barbara south to Mexico. It originated in Ecuador and Peru, but cultivars have survived in California for at least a century. The moderating sea air soothes these plants, which will not set fruit in temperatures exceeding 85 degrees Fahrenheit. The comparative dryness of the southern California coast helps too, but December rains sometimes make the big green fruits crack open.

This is a minor danger, however. Nichols asserts that the cherimoya's precarious situation in California improves its taste. "It's the same with apples," he says. "They have to struggle a bit."

Nichols knows the meaning of the word struggle since he has to fight the cherimoya's biggest battle for it. He and his laborers must pollinate the trees by hand. Airborne pollination will not deliver a dependable crop. Nichols tried getting bees to carry the pollen from male to female flowers. He set up eighty hives and waited, but the tiny, three-petaled white cherimoya flowers were too small and narrow. Bees couldn't penetrate them. If you are wondering how in the world *A. cherimola* managed to reproduce itself efficiently in its natural range, the answer is that in South America tiny nocturnal insects do the job, but nothing like them exists in California.

So in midsummer Nichols and other California growers go out in the late afternoon and do the job themselves, armed with water-color brushes that have their bristles cut down. They collect the pollen and later apply it to the female flowers, which are receptive for only twenty-four hours—and not all on the same day in the same tree. Ergo, each tree must be visited eight to ten times. To facilitate this process somewhat, the trees are pruned low. "We pollinate only what we can reach," Nichols says. The same is true for the cherimoya harvest, which is all done by hand. The fruit bruises very easily, and it does not mature all at once. Pickers must be adept at judging when the fruit is ready; they pass through each tree several times, noting slight changes in the color of the rind.

I saw the Nichols trees in spring at the end of the growing season. At first I thought the season was over because I didn't see any fruit at all, just the big green velvety leaves. You have to walk "inside" the tree, under the canopy, then you see plenty of fruit dangling down like green hand grenades all covered with indentations that are technically known as carpels. They start as nodules and flatten out when the fruit matures. Experienced pickers can detect a slight yellowing of the thin leathery exterior of the cherimoya. The trick is to collect the fruit a week before it is fully ripe.

At least in this respect the cherimoya makes life easy on the grower. It gives him the margin of a few days to get his fruit to the consumer in optimum shape. Cherimoyas picked a tad before they are perfectly ripe really do develop off the tree without loss of quality, but time is still of the essence. It is possible to ship a cherimoya to New

York from California and have it ripe and ready, but the job is not simple. Long delays are deleterious to the fruit, so is rough treatment, and so is cold. Just as you must not refrigerate your cherimoya until it is ripe (soft to the touch but not mushy), so the cherimoya shipper must try to protect his still-green fruit from the winter outside the truck. Cold dehydrates the fruit. Over-the-hill or frozen fruit will be dark all over or splotchy. Frozen fruit will not ripen properly. Growers are acutely aware of this, and because they are in business on a small scale and work through specialty distributors and retailers, their cherimoyas do tend to make it to market in fine fettle. You will pay for the privilege of eating a cherimoya (several dollars a pound) but it is worth it, and compared with the twenty-dollar price tag that the fruit-worshiping Japanese have been paying, the American price tag is a bargain.

Here is what to do after you bring your cherimoya home: Let it sit on a counter in the kitchen just as you would an avocado. When it feels a bit soft, chill it. This improves the taste. Take the chilled fruit from the refrigerator, slice it in half, give one half to someone you like, and keep the other for yourself. Now take a spoon and eat the pure white flesh, discarding the black seeds as you go. The taste of the cherimoya flesh has been compared to the taste of almost all other high-class fruits. The California Tropics flier says the cherimoya has a custardlike texture and a flavor "like a subtle, mouth-watering blend of papaya, pineapple, and banana." You will come up with your own description.

As you may have gathered, I think this fruit is the nuts. I particularly like its texture, which is indeed like a custard. But it is not completely like baby food either. In her book, *Uncommon Fruits and Vegetables* (Harper & Row), Elizabeth Schneider calls attention to a delicate granularity of the sort found in a ripe pear. This is a subtle feature, one you probably will not notice in the first rush of excitement after tasting a cherimoya. Served ice cold, it should seem like sherbet.

Then you should think of this: Peter Nichols's trees are only in their teens. In South America they say a tree is not at its peak until it's fifty.

CHAPTER VII

RADICCHIO

U N T I L those bumper crops start rolling in, the cherimoya is doomed to be a fabulous novelty, but the really big new success in the U.S. grocery, the glamour vegetable of the eighties, and still counting, is radicchio.

I first encountered this dark-red salad "green" with an attractively bitter taste in Vienna in 1978 just before Christmas. Moving southward into Italy, I kept seeing heads of this red "lettuce" everywhere. Upon returning to New York I began seeing it in supermarkets, where it sold for a small fortune.

The process by which this distinctively colored and flavored traditional winter green of the Venice region achieved its current status as the very signpost of chic dining in advanced American restaurants is not recorded. But it happened very rapidly, as part of the general hunger for dramatically exotic foods inspired by the nouvelle cuisine. A computer search of the *New York Times* shows how quickly radicchio ceased to be a mysterious oddity and was turned into just another familiar feature of gastronomic chic.

On April 19, 1981, a reader's query to the garden page asking for a source for radicchio seeds drew a blank from "Garden News," but by May 3 the newspaper of record had recouped. Alert readers had supplied two sources for "the hard-to-find seed of Italian red chicory, radicchio," which was also identified in the same paragraph as *red verone.*

This clarification led to more confusion. Red verone was a half-baked version of the French name for radicchio, emanating from the French seed company, J. A. Demonchaux, of Topeka, Kansas, which was one of the two suppliers mentioned in the article. Then there was the business of calling radicchio *chicory.*

Perhaps gardeners were not confused by this identification. Well-grounded Linnaeans would have known that true chicory, *Cichorium intybus,* is what U.S. supermarkets and most of the rest of us call *endive* (also *Belgian endive,* or *witloof*). This expensive blanched product is usually produced in Belgium. The white, boat-shaped leaves, called *chicons,* grow on parsniplike roots that are marginally edible but most commonly employed as an admixture to coffee. In the mid-nineteenth century someone noticed that chicory root left in the dark produces white leaves. The head horticulturist at the Brussels Botanical Gardens, a certain M. Brezier, perfected the new vegetable. The first box was sent to the United States in 1911.

Weed-conscious Americans also know true chicory in a wild form that produces appealing blue flowers alongside roads. We have had these weeds since the last century, but I don't recommend trying to grow Belgian endive from their seed. You certainly shouldn't try to use their seeds to grow true endive, *Cichorium endivia,* which may belong to the same genus as chicory but is quite different. American markets sell its green leaves as chicory and escarole. The scientific names for these two species of *Cichorium* are confusing in themselves, since *intybus* and *endivia* are actually both reflexes of a Greek word meaning, you guessed it, *endive* or *chicory.* And since the art of plant description in ancient days was primitive, it is impossible to tell if the ancestor words for chicory and endive were meant to refer to different plants in a consistent way or were used redundantly.

Today, even with binomial names and a relatively stable horticultural situation, confusion is the word on the *Cichorium* front. Endive is a chicory, chicory is an endive, and radicchio . . . well, according to the *New York Times* food advice column of April 27, 1983, radicchio is a "wild form of chicory most commonly associated with the Veneto region of Italy."

There is some truth in the above, far more than in the contradictory and incomplete information the newspaper had earlier printed on radicchio culture. Radicchio is a true chicory (the same species as Belgian endive), but it certainly isn't wild. Only careful treatment will encourage the roots to produce those red leaves that have made the plant an international superstar. This is not the place nor am I the fellow to advise you specifically about the appropriate methodology for growing one's own radicchio in, say, the New York metropolitan area. A great deal seems to depend on climate, but the classic method generally begins with a midsummer planting. Before winter, radicchio grows a first crop of mild green leaves suitable for salad. After these are cut back, if the roots are kept warm—but not so warm and humid that they rot—cold weather will promote the appearance of a second crop, this time of red leaves.

The radicchio we tend to see in our markets comes in tightly "hearted" heads. This is the traditional radicchio variety of Castelfranco, a town in the Veneto region where the great Renaissance painter Giorgione was born. In nearby Treviso there is a different variety that does not heart but produces long, straight leaves, somewhat like Romaine lettuce, with white, celerylike stalks and white-veined ruby red leaves.

Sometimes the two varieties are mixed to make a so-called Treviso salad, but if we are to believe the late food historian Waverley Root, the two are never mixed in Treviso. Trevisan radicchio is so prized in Treviso that, before Christmas, it has its own market in the loggia of the Palazzo dei Trecento. And the plant has its own folk jingle:

> *Se lo guardi, egli è un sorriso*
> *Se lo mangi è un paradiso*
> *Il radicchio di Treviso.*

> *(To look at, it's quite nice*
> *To eat, it's paradise*
> *The radicchio of Treviso.)*

All in all, this is a good description of an extremely attractive leaf vegetable. For the gardener, radicchio will provide a test of skill at controlling a winter environment somewhere between outdoor reality and the centrally heated indoors. Treviso obviously has a milder climate than most northeastern winters. The only reliable-seeming account of radicchio culture outside Italy that I have seen is in Joy Larcom's *The Salad Garden* (London: Windward). She is the only writer on the subject who actually seems to have grown the plant, and she recommends high polyethylene tunnels. But I would embark on this only in an experimental spirit under American conditions.

As a cook, however, I feel more confident about tackling radicchio. If you serve it raw, it adapts well to new companions and goes into salads of almost any mix. If you want to enact a sort of Linnaean pun, you could serve it with the true endive we call chicory. Or you could do what the Market Dining Room in Manhattan's World Trade Center does and mix it, shredded, with its species mate, the true chicory we call endive.

Radicchio can also be cooked. I first experienced radicchio grilled in olive oil one New Year's Eve in the early eighties. Subsequently the same elegantly bitter mixture of radicchio and olive oil flavors showed up as a garnish for a concoction of salmon mousse and crayfish at the Depuy Canal House in High Falls, New York.

This was a relatively restrained use of radicchio during the high tide of its fame and glamour. The *Times* data search turned up dozens of references to radicchio extravaganzas in restaurant reviews. *Times* critics were not given pause by such edible gewgaws as a "duck salad consisting of leaf lettuce and radicchio leaves tossed with slivers of duck in a raspberry-accented vinaigrette" or on the West Coast the Mexican nouvelle cuisine menu that included radicchio and smoked chicken tacos with red chili mayonnaise.

This instant naturalization procedure is typical of the heady period we are living through. The sudden availability of fresh exotic ingredients from almost everywhere, brought together with that cosmopolitan, adventuresome attitude toward new food combinations called nouvelle cuisine, has set in motion the most radical process of larder refurbishing since the sixteenth century.

PART VI

REVOLUTION NOW

I HAVE BEEN arguing here for the primacy of flux. The evidence of documents and of common sense shows that culinary tradition in the civilized world took a radical turn after 1492 and was transformed from top to bottom. The process moved at different speeds in different places, but it affected all the cultures whose cooking matters to other cultures. Eventually in each society the Columbian food revolution did settle down and coalesce into a national or ethnic cuisine. There is no pinning these things down to a certain date, but by some time in the nineteenth century it made perfect sense to talk about national food styles and traditions in Europe and the Americas. Indeed, it is these established cuisines that persisted well into the sixties and looked immutable to a young person at the time. Normal processes of change had been suspended by two world wars, an intervening depression, and a protracted period of postwar recovery.

There were, logically speaking, two possible positions toward these so-called traditional cuisines for gastronomically serious people circa 1960. There was the radical position, which surfaced insidiously as the nouvelle cuisine when the world least expected it, and there was the much more widespread conservative position, which was meant to defend the authentic cuisines of the world against adulteration.

THE CULT OF AUTHENTICITY

For the entire time I have paid attention to food, the cry of almost every serious person in the field has been "authenticity." Surrounded by bogus adaptations and substitutions for classic and traditional foods, two generations of writers and chefs have battled for the real thing.

They have battled against ersatz ingredients and distorting processes in industrial products. They have campaigned, often in violent
language, against recipes and restaurants that falsified our culinary
heritage. The best of them spent their lives promoting authentic food
ideas by publishing authentic recipes and insisting on authentic ingredients. Although I have been mounting an argument in this book
against the more exaggerated claims made for authenticity in cuisine,
I have been taking the long view. In a more confined perspective—say,
looking backward no more than a century—it obviously does make
sense to talk about tradition and authenticity. The people who have
done so, myself included, have been defending something real—mature national and regional styles of cooking that evolved over many
generations in relatively stable agricultural and social environments.
These cuisines assimilated the radical inputs of New World ingredients and nation-state ethnicity; they emerged from this crucible al-
loyed into something clearly identifiable as, say, Italian cooking. Without doubt these cuisines were worth defending against the malign
forces working to dilute and distort them for ignoble ends.

No one writing in the English language has fought harder and
more intelligently for gastronomic authenticity than Elizabeth David.
For forty years David has been leading a crusade with her pen, in
cookbooks that brought the real food of France and Italy as well as
her native Britain within the reach of everyone. Since the early fifties
she has also pursued this mission as a journalist in various British
publications. Her articles range widely across many areas, from the
arcana of sardine preservation to a vivid account of the white truffle
market at Alba in the Italian Piedmont. These still-important essays
achieve an unacknowledged unity as an investigation of authenticity
in the kitchen.

I think I may be making David sound something of a tedious
caterwauler, but a brief glimpse of her method as she lets fly at bogus
mayonnaise should remove any impression of shrill pedantry.

In "The True Emulsion," which appeared in the *Spectator* during
the summer of 1962, she begins: "With the mayonnaise season in full
blast, once more the familiar complaints about bottled mayonnaise
and salad creams are heard in the land." Now if you have missed the
buried allusion here to the cooing of turtle doves in the Song of Songs,
it should still be obvious that the lady is mocking food purists at the
same time that she joins them in deploring bottled mayo. For David
it is not enough to repeat an old grumble; she examines it and finds
legal, historical, and social causes for the abomination.

False mayonnaise predominates on English tables not because people are too lazy to make the real thing but because they actively prefer the fake. Why should this be? David shows how food experts were misleading the public as far back as Mrs. Beeton in 1865, but the coup de grâce came in 1906 when the renowned chef and author Herman Senn revised Beeton and substituted two recipes, each wrong-headed in its own way. The first, although basically correct, called for more than two cups of olive oil, a disconcertingly huge amount, especially considering "the national English fear and dislike of olive oil." This, David argues, encouraged cooks to choose the preposterous second recipe, a sort of custard including plenty of milk. She writes,

> By the thirties there was already a vast public brought up in the belief that mayonnaise was a sauce which could only be produced in a factory, which contained no olive oil—and tasted mainly of acetic acid. And that is what the great majority of people have come to expect when they see mayonnaise announced on a menu. It is not unnatural that they should be suspicious and indignant when confronted with the authentic sauce.

So, if you are Mrs. David, you speak out to combat the historical corruption of public taste; you decry a flawed system of labeling laws; and you wring your hands over ingrained English indifference to the actual ingredients of foreign dishes whose exotic names are blithely attached to anything that the chef or the manufacturer pleases. It would appear that we have settled the matter of authenticity. Unfortunately, authenticity is as slippery a notion as happiness. Everyone (or almost everyone) is for it, but it is hard to get people to agree on what it is. Perhaps you are thinking that an authentic dish (or recipe) is one honored by long tradition in a settled cultural milieu. This implies that an authentic recipe is the one preferred by most people in its country of origin, and yet this test of popularity (in the dish's native region) is not at all what food experts or folk of refined taste would probably say was decisive in establishing a recipe for, say, chili.

Texan chiliheads abhor beans; New Mexicans routinely put them in their version of chili. Similarly, each village along the French Mediterranean coast has its own "authentic" mixture of fish for its own "authentic" bouillabaisse. Aren't these really distinct regional variations, each authentic for its town or state? If so, to what size must we whittle down our definition of region without allowing free rein to dozens of equally authentic, neighboring recipes for dishes all bearing the same name?

There is, in fact, no limit to this. In my family, people disagree about the authentic way to make dishes handed down from the same older relative, and I myself waver frequently between the versions, which must mean that even an individual is too large a cultural unit for determining authenticity.

So what should the inquiring gastroethnographer think when an informant, perhaps his aunt Betty, tells him how she makes apple pie? How can he be sure that the old gal is not passing off some flapdoodle on him just for laughs—or because she doesn't know any better?

If this fieldwork were taking place as part of the first contact with a hitherto isolated people (call them the Mem!tomos), the ethnographer would want to ask around the village a bit and see how the informant's pie matched up with others. If they were all the same, he would clearly have found out what an authentic pie was. But if they were only similar—some had top crusts, some had cream added to the apple mixture, some had only butter in the crust, others only margarine, but all of them had a circular crust baked with apple slices on top—then he would have to decide which features were fundamental and which were variations or extra fillips. Otherwise it would be impossible to publish just one recipe and assert that it was the authentic apple pie of the Mem!tomos. The careful ethnographer might want to poll all the cooks and ask them what they thought was the essential pieness of their pie.

This process of taking an average or platonizing an ideal recipe from the raw data of individual cooks' testimony is not, however, what has typically occurred in even the most scrupulous studies of regional or ethnic foods. In every case I know of, from true anthropological work with preliterate people to the reportage conducted in France by Curnonsky, only one or, at most, a very small number of practitioners were consulted. Their recipes were then written down and acquired the prestige we attach to the "authentic" practices of the naive.

Publication leads to codification. From many Homers, each singing the traditional epic-formulaic material in his own way, the Greeks passed on only one. Once the *Iliad* and the *Odyssey* had been transcribed, they became official texts, memorized and studied to the point of stultification by the time of Theocritus.

Something like that has been happening in the 150 years or so since the great early nineteenth-century chef Carême codified his magisterial practice. The grand dishes of the nobility were frozen, given standard form. In other words, haute cuisine acquired criteria of authenticity that were modified—mostly simplified—but that remained essentially unaltered until twenty-five years ago. In this century the process of codification—one almost wants to say licensing—was extended to the regional cooking of France and, gradually, to ever more remote localities and foods: the Mekong Delta and its fish, India and its desserts.

Writing down these exotic food ideas has been and continues to be an important and laudable activity. Without it, whole cuisines would vanish as the world inexorably homogenizes. But authentication is a procrustean bed; it lops off the messy edges of cooking. Cookbooks not only preserve, they overdefine and delimit cooking when they set forth a single version of a dish and, explicitly or implicitly, suggest that other versions are spurious.

Mrs. David, for instance, ever the evangelist for the foods of the Mediterranean where she formed her basic tastes, assumes without discussion that the authentic mayonnaise will use olive oil. But there is a perfectly respectable tradition in northern France and elsewhere that employs peanut and other neutrally flavored oils; its proponents are as committed to their practice as those who insist that truly ideal mayonnaise will avoid vinegar altogether in favor of lemon juice.

To be fair to her, David is not a purist, pure and simple, and often presents the case for many versions of the same basic dish. She goes out of her way to praise culinary mavericks like Edouard de Pomiane, whose original contributions to French food provoked a furor from traditionalists. Indeed, she holds him up as a precursor of nouvelle cuisine:

> I wonder how many of the younger of today's professional chefs realize that some of their most publicized inventions were not theirs at all but were derived, however indirectly, from the Polish and Jewish recipes published or described by Pomiane in his books and radio talks of the 1930s. Michel Guérard's *confiture d'oignons*, for instance, surely derived from Pomiane's dish of sweet-sour onions in which the sweetening elements were sultanas and *pain d'épices*, the spiced honey cake of central Europe, and which Pomiane had in turn borrowed from the Jewish cookery of his native Poland.

Without directly saying so, David is acutely aware of the tension in all cooking between the traditional and the new. Anthropologists might call this same opposition a conflict between the synchronic and the diachronic point of view. In plain language we can regard mayonnaise as a given, a static artifact existing outside history whose authentic nature is as unchanging as a primordial totem. Or we can suppose that mayonnaise had and continues to have a history, that its authentic nature is redefined each time you or I whip some up.

Both points of view are always valid, I think, in cooking as in the rest of life. The synchronic strand is always there, making sense of the diachronic. Our notion of authentic mayonnaise underlies our certainty that an egg and oil emulsion aggressively flavored with chipotle chilies from Mexico is still a mayonnaise.

REDEFINING TRADITION

This interplay between the previously defined—the authentic—and the newly evolved makes judgment and taste possible. If we know what mayonnaise has been, we have a baseline for discriminations about the mayonnaise that a chef has just created. These discriminations are difficult; they rest on the elusive idea of authenticity. But without some rough sense of where we have been (the authentic), we cannot reasonably embrace the new or reject the bogus. It is from this position that the current revolution in food begins. The nouvelle cuisine is reordering the world that emerged in the world's kitchens after Columbus, but these changes rest solidly on the modern tradition of national cuisines that exploit both New and Old World ingredients. This revolution began undramatically, and its most committed leaders misproclaimed its significance.

In 1972, before Paul Bocuse was a household word or *nouvelle* had entered our language as a culinary buzzword, I visited Bocuse's restaurant in the village of Collonges-au-Mont d'Or in almost perfect innocence of the worldwide revolution in taste that was fermenting there on the peaceful banks of the Saône. Much had been written in France, in murky prose, about what was taking place chez Bocuse and at a few other luxury establishments owned by young chefs who had studied with Fernand Point at Vienne and then fanned out across the countryside. Dedicated to a new, minimalist style of cooking, they shunned the stuffiness of the haute cuisine codified by Escoffier in the early years of the century.

WHAT EXACTLY IS NOUVELLE CUISINE?

At that time—before nouvelle cuisine had spread around the world, turning up even on menus in French restaurants as improbable as the one I recently visited in a shopping center in suburban Sarasota; before the term *nouvelle cuisine* had surfaced as a signpost of the new glamour in fine dining—it was especially difficult to say in concrete terms what was up.

On the technical level, all the chefs in the Young Turk movement agreed that flour-thickened sauces were an abomination, but their preference for sauces built around heavily reduced stocks or stocks thickened with cream or egg yolks or hollandaise sauce did not amount to a revolution. Neither did the new emphasis on fresh ingredients, al dente vegetables, and raw fish and meat. It was this side of early nouvelle cuisine that understandably misled people into thinking that Bocuse et al. were a bunch of stylish health-food enthusiasts. Bocuse encouraged this confusion when he said his innovations were aimed at the new gourmet, a theoretical diner consumed with a passion for great food but preoccupied as well with staying trim.

This was undoubtedly a shrewd insight into the upscale client of three-star restaurants, but even a cursory glance at the ingredients actually served up by the Young Turks should have convinced us all that the dietary claims blandly served up in interviews by Bocuse and Alain Senderens of Archestrate in Paris were a soufflé of rationalization.

Michel Guérard, in my view the real genius of contemporary French gastronomy, contributed to the confusion still further with an authentically low-cal menu he concocted at his Lucullan spa at Eugénie-les-Bains in the southwest of France. *Cuisine minceur,* as he dubbed the recipes he worked out for diet-conscious guests, was an ingenious, fat-free program that attracted large dollops of publicity. Guérard published a successful book. His svelte wife told reporters: "We will not grow fat together." And for a time in the seventies, *nouvelle cuisine* was widely misunderstood to be just another name for *cuisine minceur,* which was really no more than one facet of one inspired chef's practice. Guérard later published a much more important book of unhealthful but truly innovative foie-gras and butter-laden recipes called *Cuisine Gourmande.*

Hidden behind this screen of contradictions and opportunistic rhetoric, nouvelle cuisine was actually something radically new that had sprung right out of the social fabric of postwar France. Young chefs had eliminated the formally garnished banquet platters of Escoffier (which were themselves simplifications of the grandly sculptural cuisine inherited from Carême and other classical nineteenth-century practitioners, who had labored primarily for noble houses with crowded tables or for bourgeois restaurant patrons in love with pomp and circumstance). In this cleansing of the repertory, these chefs were following not only the relatively inconspicuous and mild reforms of Escoffier but also the more trenchant and simplifying example of their mentor, Fernand Point. They were, in fact, picking up a thread first spun in the period between the wars when the influential gastronomic writer Curnonsky had directed the attention of chefs like Point to the treasures of regional cooking. Curnonsky not only recorded these local dishes but also insisted that they should reflect their ingredients, should not disguise the taste of the things from which they were cooked. Today this may seem like an obvious principle, but the extremely complex recipes of nineteenth-century haute cuisine did deliberately concoct edible fantasies remote from the raw materials of the larder.

And so, when Paul Bocuse prided himself on his *cuisine du marché* (market cooking) and took reporters with him to the market in Lyon to hunt for the best raw materials available on a particular day, he was showing his commitment to ingredients, to their intrinsic taste and quality, and to the resources of his own region. But by the time Bocuse and the other Young Turks had achieved national and international fame, they had gone further than Point.

DESIGN FOR EATING

The best way to see this is to compare the pictures in Point's posthumous *Ma Gastronomie* (1969) with the pictures in Guérard's *Cuisine Gourmande* (1978) or with those in *Cuisiniers à Roanne* (1977) by Jean and Pierre Troisgros. Point's food is simple enough, compared with the plates of more classic food in the *Larousse Gastronomique*, with their garnishes of turned vegetables and stuffed artichoke bottoms, but with Point we are still in the world of the banquet, the world of the platter on which a suckling pig or a whole tart is presented to a tableful of people or a large family assembled for a dramatic occasion.

The younger chefs selected photographs of individual plates, with the food on them arranged meticulously to make a visual effect on its own. In their book the brothers Troisgros credit their father as the source of the "custom of both presentation and service on each guest's individual plate—very large plates, which we were the first to use."

By now we have all encountered the nouvelle cuisine plate and its studied placement of sliced vegetables, arranged in circular or other geometric patterns. While it would be wrong to dispute that this new mode of decoration arose in France and quite naturally from trends in force over decades, it is also the case that the full efflorescence of nouvelle cuisine was, to an important extent, an exotic bloom fertilized by new ideas, aesthetic and culinary, that traveled to France from abroad, in particular from Japan, and found receptive soil in traditionally xenophobic France.

In the postwar era, exotic ingredients—the avocado, the mango and, before all others, the kiwi—arrived in France by jet. Meanwhile, French people traveled outside the mother country in unprecedented numbers. Bocuse himself traveled so often to Japan that diners complained the master was abandoning his own stove. Senderens studied Japanese cuisine.

The flow of ideas from Japan to France brought a highly developed food aesthetic—one based on delicate visual effects and achieved most often on individual plates—to young French chefs already predisposed to paint with food on the circular field of a plate. Nouvelle cuisine rapidly evolved into a feast for the eyes, *à la japonaise.* It also incorporated some of the culinary feathers of Japanese food, notably a predilection for raw ingredients, which fulfilled Curnonsky's dictum to perfection. A slice of raw scallop tasted, by definition, of nothing but the scallop itself.

The success of this new mode of cooking is a fact of contemporary life. Nouvelle cuisine triumphed in France and then radiated outward throughout Europe, to the United States, and back to Japan. In its full cosmopolitan form, nouvelle cuisine has now inspired Japanese-French restaurants in New York. It is to this global yet regional school of cookery that we in America now owe the so-called new American cuisine, which combines French principles of food preparation, Japanese plate decoration, and regional, folkloric American ingredients.

On wings of chic, the new gospel has soared over oceans and continents. Japanese chefs trained in France reign supreme in Manhattan. Homegrown cooks have also learned the lessons of the day and now present sophisticated diners from coast to coast with morels

foraged in Michigan woods and hitherto neglected sea urchin ovaries
from Pacific waters. Aided by food processors, modish restaurants
offer julienned vegetables of every hue with each floridly designed
entree. Following the lead of their French mentors, they are open to
ideas from cooking traditions around the world, mixing all the great
ethnic and national dishes in a mishmash of eclecticism that is every
bit as intricate in its way as were the now-abandoned platters of
yesteryear.

DECODING THE MENU

Even this superficial analysis of nouvelle cuisine would have surprised
most of its happiest consumers, but there was more to this global
movement in the kitchen than unfamiliar ingredients and painterly
plates. Considered historically, nouvelle cuisine had deep roots in
European gastrolinguistic tradition and was the logical conclusion of
centuries of change in the way food was brought to the table and
served to individual diners.

I thought about these matters first during a visit to New Haven,
Connecticut, in 1985. I spent some time then in a small church
meditating about deconstruction. Have no fear—the episode was brief
and did not recur. I was early for a friend's wedding and had a few
moments of repose during which I reflected with some amusement on
the contrast between the exceedingly old-fashioned appearance of
Yale and its recent conversion to the modish vanguard of French
thought. Yale is the American capital of deconstruction, a method of
literary criticism difficult to perform and more difficult to explain.

I propose to give only a practical and nonliterary demonstration
of the method, leaving it to the learned gentlemen and gentlewomen
of the Yale English Department to expound the central dogma of
deconstruction and its intricacies as a tool for peeling away the arti-
fices of authors and unmasking the meanings for which their tropes
and symbols are cleverly misleading signposts.

So there I was in the Yale chapel, flanked by wife and colleagues,
bathed, you might say, in the sauce of nuptial bliss, and still my mind
turned momentarily from the happy scene to a riveting idea that
amounts to a deconstruction of the nouvelle cuisine.

Almost all of the original claims made about and for the cuisine
now look more like public relations than theory, but everyone who
has experienced the thing itself knows that it can be recognized on

sight. It is a style, but it is a sly style, one whose true nature has barely ever been discussed by its practitioners. They are not shy, but the language they use is almost an ideal text for deconstruction because it is so purely metaphorical. I am using language here in a broad sense to include chef's words—their menu language and their recipes—as well as their dishes. The world of nouvelle cuisine, as I am about to show, is a forest of symbols and allusions that the knowledgeable diner can "read" and decode much as a literary deconstruction might decode the figurative code of a poem.

Classic cuisine was also a code, literally, that included the language of menus and cookbooks. Dishes were identified with terms such as Montmorency and Paloise, words that in ordinary speech refer to people and places but that in the world of traditional haute cuisine denoted, respectively, a roast duck sauced with cherries and a béarnaise sauce made with mint instead of tarragon. In most cases these chef's terms were a pure code without even a tangential connection to their name's everyday referent. Espagnole sauce was in no way Spanish. The old culinary language simply gave names to dishes that honored people and places and rarely gave the uninitiated any direct information about the dish they were going to get. A thorough deconstruction of this code would undoubtedly reveal symbolic patterns of high interest (even though the historic documentation would necessarily be spotty), but for the moment we must limit ourselves to noticing that the nouvelle cuisine chefs were all trained in a system of cookery that they had learned to describe in a special code. They all knew exactly what garnishes and sauce went with *sole à la normande.* The sole, poached in fish and mushroom stock, was surrounded by poached mussels and shrimp with a line of four poached oysters and four fluted mushroom caps alternating down its center. All of this was coated with *sauce normande,* an elaborate concoction of fish stock, mushroom and mussel cooking liquids, egg yolks, and cream, and then additionally garnished with six truffle slices and six croutons cut in lozenges alternating around the perimeter of the sole. Four gudgeons, the freshwater fish *Gobio gobio,* fried at the last minute and themselves decorated with manchons (paper sleeves?) were arranged on the platter with four medium "trussed" crayfish. All the elements were compulsory; not until 1912 did Escoffier finally concede in parentheses that the truffles were optional.

The names of haute cuisine dishes were primarily useful as shorthand devices. They not only dressed up a menu, they performed a real service for people who did not want to take time to rattle off the four canonical garnishes associated with *rôti de veau Maubeuge.* Haute cuisine lingo saved everyone the bother we now endure from waiters who do not benefit from a convenient code and have to tell you that tonight's special is moose haunch with wild rice balls, broiled shiitake mushrooms, and a partridge in a pear mousse. Wouldn't it be easier if that particular collection of foods were always identified as *moose Mamaroneck?* It would be simple, but the culinary world we live in is an unsettled place. You can almost count on not getting moose with the same accompanying side dishes on another night. But in the world set down in Escoffier's *Guide Culinaire* they did repeat garnish combinations. Over the 150 years that stretched from the time of Carême in the early nineteenth century until the dawn of nouvelle cuisine, French chefs refined a closed system of dishes whose basic unit was a serving platter filled with a main food item, say a roast, tricked out with its prescribed garnishes. Nouvelle cuisine not only subverted the old culinary code, it also abandoned platter service and substituted for it an equally intricate method of service based on individual plates arranged in the kitchen.

These attacks on the structure and meaning of the old style of dining are the truly revolutionary part of nouvelle cuisine, but the threat to the old order was masked in many ways. Nouvelle cuisine was marketed as the cuisine of modern slim people who valued fresh food or food presented with streamlined simplicity and provocative ingredients. All those elements were present and important, but they fronted for the real revolution that transformed the old code by using it as material for a most elaborate system of culinary parody, punning, and metaphor. Nouvelle cuisine looks at Escoffier through the wrong end of the telescope. It puts ironic quotation marks around Carême and sets the old code in italics so that the old words all mean something else, are metaphors for new ideas for which no names previously existed.

Nouvelle cuisine itself is a kind of metaphor. It does not actually mean a new cuisine. When the adjective precedes the noun in French, it takes on a figurative sense. So nouvelle cuisine is new in a figurative—and problematic—sense, like New York or New Orleans (Nouvelle Orleans). Just as these cities of the New World (*nouveau monde,* not *monde nouveau)* are reflections of York and Orleans, not re-creations or renovations of them, so nouvelle cuisine refers back to classic French haute cuisine, neither as a copy nor as a radical reform. It is instead a parody or perhaps a pun based on the old culinary code of Carême and Escoffier.

In the dawn of what we may, with appropriate irony, call the new era, gastronomic pilgrims trekked to dismal Roanne near Lyon to eat chez Troisgros, where they were served the great prix fixe menu of the postwar period: a deceptively dull-looking black-gray thrush pâté with juniper berries, scallops of salmon in sorrel sauce, Charolais beef in an intense but transparently clear brown sauce, and a tray of many, many desserts.

I ate this meal in 1969, long before the term *nouvelle cuisine* had been coined by the French food journalists Henri Gault and Christian Millau. But the experience already embodied the key elements of the mature movement. The salmon dish, especially, was a sign of things to come. The sauce was pulled together quickly, without flour for thickening, from a highly reduced fish stock, *crème fraîche,* and sorrel. The taste was extraordinary, as was that of the salmon, almost Japanese in its near rawness. And what might be called the design of the dish emphasized lightness with its unnaturally thin pieces of fish.

These were the things that caught my eye in 1969 in that poky little dining room across from the Roanne rail station. But the most important feature of the dish was the name on the menu. If the salmon had been cooked until it flaked and if the sauce had been thick and conventional, this dish would still have been a symbol of revolt because it justified its witty name: *escalopes de saumon.* The Troisgros brothers were serving salmon scaloppine. They had transferred (metaphorized) a classic food idea onto a surprising and provocative new ingredient. The sharp-eyed diner would notice that the chef had cut the salmon into thin flat slices or scallops and then had pounded them thinner, just as he would have pounded veal scallops, except that he would have pounded the veal because he wanted to make it tender as well as attractively thin. Pounding salmon will change its texture in a minor way, but the main gain is conceptual. The thin salmon pieces are mock scaloppine. They are delicious, but they are also witty. They turn the old world on its head, but it is important to remember that salmon-as-veal is not just a stunt. This metaphorical notion is the inspiration for a brilliant dish whose magic has many facets, but the original imaginary metamorphosis organizes the others and gives them point.

If you look at nouvelle cuisine cookbooks and menus with this in mind, you will find abundant examples of this metaphorical principle at work. Paging through *The Nouvelle Cuisine of Jean and Pierre Troisgros,* I noticed a vegetable terrine that was a playful nonmeat copy of the traditional meat terrine and a recipe for oysters with periwinkles—that is, shellfish topped with shellfish. Obviously not every nouvelle cuisine dish is a straightforward culinary pun or figure of culinary speech, but almost invariably the memorable recipes start from a witty reinterpretation of a standard dish. It is this "literary" aspect that saves nouvelle cuisine from being merely a collection of outrageous novelties. The nouvelle cuisine's greatest failures always have been the entirely new dishes, concocted with no reference to the past. Its greatest triumphs have sprung from tradition seen through a glass brightly.

SERVICE INCLUDED

The other crucial feature of nouvelle cuisine—its studied and original arrangements of food on individual plates—is also a clever reaction to French tradition in the kitchen and at the dining table. If the cuisine's menu is a witty revolt against the sclerotic culinary code that French chefs inherited from the nineteenth century, the nouvelle method of food arrangement and presentation is a pseudo-Japanese innovation that is the third major form of getting dinner on the table since the Middle Ages—plate-centered service.

The cuisine of our grandparents' time called for edible designs to be executed on serving platters that were brought out from the kitchen, proudly displayed to a table of diners, and then professionally carved or otherwise parceled out to individual diners. But by the time the plate got to the table, the logic of the dish had been somewhat lost. This method of getting food to the table was called Russian service. Was it really Russian? I have no idea. It emerged as a radical dining reform in the nineteenth century, triumphed, and held sway in luxury establishments right into the 1970s.

Russian service depended very heavily on the labor of waiters. In establishments that practiced this method to the fullest, meals were served on a platter, banquet style, even if the diner was eating alone and had ordered something that could just as easily have been put intact on a plate in the kitchen and brought right to the table. Instead, sole meunière would be presented in a serving dish, then transferred to the plate at a buffet or rolling table near the dining table. The waiter might bone the fish and then add the sauces. Often, waiters performed crucial finishing stages of actual cooking at tableside.

Despite all this elaborate to-and-froing, Russian service was originally considered a radical simplification of the form of service it replaced: French service. French service evolved out of the smorgas-bordish anarchy of medieval dining—a table-oriented, self-service meal with a bewildering number of dishes. Onto this basic structure was grafted an exceedingly complex order of, and service within, courses. Each stage had its own French name, and these names, slightly altered in meaning, came into English toward the end of the eighteenth century.

Roughly speaking, French service began as seven courses, which were eventually collapsed for convenience into three that still included the separate categories of food from the original seven. The first course came in two stages: Soup was set down in tureens at the corners of the table with hors d'oeuvres or side dishes next to them; when the soup was finished, it was removed and replaced with fish and entrees, which were lighter dishes that served as the entry to the next, main course. The dishes after the soup came to be called relevés because the soup was "removed" by them.

The second French-service course contained, at a minimum, the *rôts*, or roasts, sometimes called *grosses pièces* or *pièces de résistance* (because you had to wait for them). There followed *entremets* (literally, between foods), other lighter concoctions that prepared for the third course, what we would call dessert. Dessert is derived from the verb *desservir* (to clear the table) and is the food you eat after the plates from the rest of the meal have been taken away. Over time these categories shifted in meaning, and two of the terms came to be applied to the courses or types of food they had originally introduced. *Entrées* became main courses instead of their preludes, and *entremets*, similarly, became dessert.

It appears that French service confused even those who had grown up with it, and even in great houses with many attendants, meals with dozens of separate dishes were prone to mismanagement. As Abraham Hayward wrote in the 1830s:

> Servants, meaning to be very polite, dodge about to offer each entree to ladies in the first instance; confusion arises, and whilst the same dishes are offered two or three times over to some guests, the same unhappy wights have no option of others. . . . Where there are more than four side dishes besides flanks and removes, the entrees ought to be in duplicates at opposite corners. The true principle is few entrees but well-filled dishes; for if the entrees are first-rate, the presumption is that each guest will eat of each. The

[newer] service *à la russe* divides the opinion of the best
judges; but once we saw it most pleasingly and originally put
in practice . . .

It took most of the rest of the century for Russian service to sweep
away French service. With French service perished the simultaneous
profusion of dishes, the architectural table decoration, and the sculptural set pieces that had marked the grandiose age of the first and
greatest modern chef, Carême. Russian service, championed in the
1860s by the influential chef Felix Urbain Dubois, allowed people to
eat one dish per course.

As a result chefs turned to perfecting each individual dish instead
of concentrating on an array of dishes. This led to multiple garnishes
and platters bristling with ancillary foods that were minidishes in
themselves. In less than a century, dissatisfaction with these overdone
platters led to a further reduction in the scale of food presentation.
The nouvelle cuisine restricted itself to the individual plate.

One stage builds on the next. There is no discontinuity, no
revolution that obliterates the past. Nothing arises from nothing.
Every so often the chefs clean house in the name of simplification and
then find new ways to complicate their task.

KIWIS WITH GRITS: POSTMODERN
AMERICAN CUISINE

By the late 1980s the news about nouvelle cuisine had spread across
the Atlantic with a vengeance. I recall a hot night in June when a
thousand people in formal dress trooped down to New York's Rockefeller Plaza to eat the splashiest buffet dinner in local gourmet memory. Each diner paid a minimum of $250 for the privilege of tasting
food prepared by a dozen innovative chefs from around the country.
The contributions, every last cent of them, went to Citymeals-on-
Wheels, a program sponsored by the New York City Department for
the Aging that brings hot food to the house-bound elderly. All in all
it made a dignified and appropriate wake for James Beard.

Beard had died at age eighty-two a few months before this memo-
rial celebration, after years of intermittent illness and many decades
as the uncrowned king of the American culinary world. This portly,
sensual buddha of food had thrown his great influence behind City-

meals-on-Wheels with the same generosity that had launched and fostered the careers of scores of people in the food field. Indeed, several of his more recent protégés had come to Rockefeller Plaza from their own newly famous restaurants to serve their specialties.

This food, much of it squarely in the center of what has been called American nouvelle cuisine, made a fitting tribute to Beard's crucial role in guiding and refining the nation's growing culinary sophistication. No one had done more to preserve traditional American food ideas, but no one had ever supported the creativity of young chefs with greater energy and intelligence than Beard.

The menu that night ran the gamut from the solidly old to the tremulously new. Larry Forgione of Manhattan's An American Place prepared a well-known Beard recipe for strawberry shortcake. Bradley Ogden of San Francisco's Campton Place Hotel struck the eclectic note of today with blue corncake with caviar. Paul Prudhomme, the bearded and Beard-size New Orleans restaurateur, overwhelmed Rockefeller Center's ventilation system with the smoke from his Cajun blackened redfish. At other buffets, representing other restaurants, there was orthodox Spanish roast suckling pig and unorthodox grilled shrimp-and-scallop brochette with peanut chili butter.

Had Beard been present for this ambulatory feast, he would surely have been struck by two things: the emphasis on regional or ethnic specialties and the readiness to combine ideas and ingredients that had never been mixed before. If cooking had ever had a "modern" period, it would be appropriate to call this new menu postmodern. Certainly it shares with postmodern architecture an unabashed zest for slapping together classic motifs and elements of the past in unexpected and ostentatious ways. None of this would have escaped Beard, who had so lovingly wallowed in classic American cookery and watched it begin to move beyond those colonial traditions.

What is afoot in our land is not the birth of a vernacular cuisine in the traditional sense. That would be impossible. With the exception of Native American recipes (including Aztec dishes that may have been eaten here before geopolitics converted them into Mexican food), nothing we consume has evolved in the autochthonous, slow manner that produced the cuisines of traditional cultures. We lack, furthermore, the standard focuses of cuisine formation; we have no court and no peasants. It was in the American analogues of royal and peasant kitchens, in fact, that our regional dishes did develop—in the briefly creative moments of princely wealth in colonial cities and southern plantations and when pioneers adapted European cuisines to the natural world of the frontier. But these short periods of culinary invention did not survive the homogenizing forces of settlement. Regional dishes survived as relics, endangered items on a menu trotted out mostly for visitors.

A typical example of this kind of showcase regionalism flourishes near the Denver rail yards. The Buckhorn Exchange bills itself as a "historic museum, restaurant, and saloon." The two-storey Victorian building is chock-full of game trophies and frontier art. The menu features Rocky Mountain oysters (sheep testicles: oblate, chewy, and insipid), buffalo, and elk.

In the real world outside, a monstrously efficient agribusiness network, linking farming regions by truck with big-city supermarket chains, has long since undermined true gastronomic regionalism almost completely. As a creative proposition, regionalism dried up when polyglot immigration swamped the eastern cities' pristine colonial cultures and when mechanization sent farm families packing to find jobs in town.

But the regional foods did not completely perish, and knowledge about them persisted and spread, especially after 1980. By then a generation of Americans had lived through the so-called culinary revolution. They had been to Europe and had learned firsthand what traditional cuisines were and how to cook them. They had also observed how the most famous French and Italian restaurants prided themselves on keeping regional foods and food ideas alive on their tables. By 1980 a new freedom had also swept through previously conservative and culture-bound French restaurant kitchens. Nouvelle cuisine reveled in exotic ingredients and bizarre food combinations presented with a Japanese flair.

By 1980, French nouvelle cuisine restaurants had opened in this country on both coasts, but at the same time Americans well grounded in French ideas combined the new European grammar with an American vocabulary. Especially in California this meant mixing ingredients with ahistorical abandon and putting special emphasis on ingredients of a markedly local and recherché sort—wild mushrooms, native chestnuts, fiddlehead ferns.

At Rockefeller Plaza one of the practitioners of this new eclecticism, Jeremiah Tower, passed out menus from his San Francisco restaurant, Stars. Among the daily specials listed were mint aïoli, rillettes of smoked fish, and oysters with spicy lamb sausages.

It was not necessary even then to leave home to sink your teeth into this nouvelle mishmash. Books came out with recipes from the chefs at the Beard dinner and other practitioners of their ilk. The deep-fried catfish in Japanese sauce made from sake, rice vinegar, and soy sauce that Wolfgang Puck provided diners at Chinois on Main in Santa Monica appeared in Diane and Paul von Welanetz's *L.A. Cuisine: The New Culinary Spirit* (Tarcher). The same primer published John Sedlar's Franco–Santa Fean recipe for green *chile relleno,* stuffed with *mushrooms duxelles* and served with *garlic chèvre sauce,* as Sedlar prepared it at Saint Estèphe in Manhattan Beach, California.

There was more of the same in Linda West Eckhardt's *The New West Coast Cuisine* from *saffron challah* to *jalapeño hollandaise.* Eckhardt expounded a new cuisine she saw pullulating from Vancouver to San Diego. Her recipes stressed local products, the Pacific coast ethnic mix, and the health food "tradition." I am not convinced that her *cranberry salsa* or any of the other concoctions in her book will survive into the next century, but even if they don't, it is the approach that matters.

The von Welanetzes were definitely on to something when they talked about the new culinary spirit. The Californians' willingness to experiment, in this case at least, was not just an unbridled adventure. Most of the new-wave cooks were building on solid knowledge of several vernacular traditions and mixing them up with a good sense of what would work and what wouldn't. To spike the classic French emulsified sauces with chili is not barbaric; it follows logically from age-old Provençal practice—spicy aïoli, a garlic mayonnaise, points toward "hot" hollandaise. With the fiercer American newcomer, something is lost perhaps, but something is gained.

The main interest of postmodern American cuisine, at this early stage, is its free but informed attitude toward the rich world of possibilities open to American cooks. Perhaps a vocabulary of new "American" dishes will ultimately shake out from all the fervid experimentation. But for now it is the process that counts. The manipulation of local ingredients with culinary ideas inherited from many national pasts is a sensible extension of the notion of the melting pot—and an intrinsically American way to go.

This current rage for the cross-cultural manipulation of traditional food ideas reminds me of my visit twenty-five years ago to the laboratory of Claude Lévi-Strauss at the Collège de France. It was all quite unexpected and intimidating. I had never read a word of the great structural anthropologist's work—something I had certainly intended to do before I met him—and had to ask the questions cabled to me by the *Newsweek* science editor. (*The Savage Mind* had just been published in the United States, and my magazine hoped to dress up its account of the book with a few quotes from the author.)

That day I had merely meant to make an appointment with the professor's secretary; I stopped off in person at the college because the phone there was out of order. But Lévi-Strauss was in his office, nattily attired and dictating a letter accepting the offer of an honorary degree from the University of Chicago. He would see me right then and there.

Fortunately, I had brought along the cable from New York. I took it out and translated the questions into French. They were naive. Also, my retranslation of *The Savage Mind* back into French did not duplicate the original, which is *La Pensée Sauvage.* My improvisation— *La Mentalité Sauvage*—was not totally witless, but it wasn't the real title, as Lévi-Strauss gently explained.

He disposed of the two questions in the cable quickly. In what school of anthropology did he put himself? His own. What practical applications did he think his work brought to the lives of ordinary people? None.

I sat there in acute embarrassment, unable to think of anything else to say but unwilling to admit it. Perhaps the ridiculous situation reminded him of his fieldwork in the Amazon, where he had faced tribal informants as totally unable to communicate with him on his level as I was. He chose, at any rate, to switch from the nominally intellectual arena to that of the physical. He led me into his lab and showed me his most treasured possession, a bank of files containing abstracts of ethnographic research from hundreds of thousands of expeditions to every corner of the world. This symbolic *tour du monde* brought the encounter to a graceful close.

Some time later, after I had read through much of the man's mazy synthesis of myths from the Americas, it occurred to me that the giant file must have played a crucial role in the development of his thought. With such easy access to so many myths from so many scattered peoples all in one place, he had naturally tended to see them as all emanating from one collective brain, from a single savage mentality.

I was reminded of all this the other day as I reshelved my collection of cookbooks. Here was my own gastronomic equivalent of Lévi-Strauss's file. I have the food of the world's peoples at my fingertips, in the abstract and comfortingly definite form of recipes. Without much real effort I can range through this database of the edible, comparing how Tibetan and Irish cooks have treated lamb, scanning all that people have thought to do over the centuries with rice or eggplant.

This freedom is a new development in human life. The production of reliable cookbooks about the cuisines of the world did not begin in earnest until twenty years ago. Since then, essentially oral or, at best, local traditions of food preparation have been transcribed and translated so anyone with a will to do so can acquire easily accessible records of virtually the full range of human food practices and store them in one relatively compact place.

For most people in the world this is of no direct importance, but to food-mad novelty seekers in the industrial nations, the recipe database supplied by modern cookbooks is a creative prod that encourages them to think of the previously anarchic diversity of human cuisines as a unitary phenomenon—multifaceted, yes, but all of a piece. Just as one great file lumping together all the cultures of the world encouraged Lévi-Strauss to shuffle the myths of the planet as if they were cards in one vast deck, so our library of cookbooks makes it natural for cooks and restaurateurs to combine methods and dishes from hitherto discrete cuisines as part of a single grandiose repertory.

This hypermenu, if you will, is normally referred to as nouvelle cuisine since the essence of the new cookery is its openness to unprecedented combinations of food known to no traditional cuisine. The process is still in its infancy and has so far largely involved adding exotic ingredients, particularly folkloric American or Asian ingredients, to classic European recipes.

Elizabeth Andoh took this process a step further. She is an American with years of experience in Japan. Her first book, *At Home with Japanese Cooking,* is the best book in English on traditional Japanese cuisine. In *An American Taste of Japan* she embarked on an exercise in "cross-cultural cooking" that sought to "integrate Japanese ingredients, kitchen techniques, and culinary philosophy with American foodstuffs, kitchen appliances, and eating habits."

Andoh is as saturated with traditional Japanese food and culture as an American is ever likely to be. Beginning as a student in Japan more than twenty years ago, living soon after in the bosom of a Japanese family, she now teaches Japanese cooking in New York, so when she branched out into cross-cultural improvisation, it was no impromptu affair. Indeed, much of what she put in her book records actual cross-cultural dishes already entrenched here and in Japan—or she improved on them. For example, take *aka dashi,* dark bean soup with bean curd and okra. Japanese have embraced the okra introduced to them by Americans. They even like the ropy texture it acquires when fully cooked. But Andoh knew that many Americans detest gluey okra, so she blanched it before adding it to the soup, revamping it for American taste.

Conversely, in *mirugai no omi-otsuke,* mussel and leek chowder, she invented a Japanese soup, with a *dashi* broth (kelp and bonito) and bean paste, to exploit two non-Japanese ingredients (mussels and leeks) popular with Japanese living abroad. And she developed a clear recipe for the most established American-Japanese neologism, the California roll: a sushi filled with avocado and crabmeat.

Many of the recipes were ingenious applications of Japanese methods to the American larder and to American dining practices. Tosa-style grilled beef took a technique originally meant for fresh bonito and adapted it to a meat-centered diet. This dish was the inspiration of Andoh's Japanese sister-in-law, a New Jersey suburbanite for many years.

Much of Andoh's provocative book showed us ourselves through Japanese eyes. On every page I felt the sensibilities of émigrés evolving a workable new way of eating on our shores. Menu plans were almost completely Americanized, and a chopstick-based cuisine was made to accommodate larger pieces of food more appropriate in a land where knives and forks are universal.

Is this a crime against authenticity? I don't think so. I think it is the beginning of the next phase. And even if today's cross-cultural cooking is a form of culinary sacrilege, it is also the latest phase of a Darwinian process that has been shaking up the kitchens of the world since the beginning of human appetite.

PART VII

SAVORY

A T V E R Y traditional dinners in England, after the dessert (always called the "pudding" in such settings), sometimes you get a supererogatory dish to go with the port. These extra little trifles are always salty, which is why they are called savory (the old-fashioned British antonym of sweet). There is a minicuisine of savories, and Escoffier paid it the compliment of including it in his books, but they are quaint dishes with quaint names like angels on horseback (oysters wrapped in bacon). With the exception of Welsh rarebit, none of them has traveled except as part of the food repertory of truly unreconstructed sons of empire. Even in Britain today they tend to be offered as hors d'oeuvres or as lunch fare.

Despite the rampant internationalism and appropriation of other people's food traditions rife just about everywhere now, there are some foods, like savories, that just don't have legs and that will never show up on menus in foreign restaurants except as a stunt. Certainly they will never influence the culinary future either abroad or at home.

It would be amusing to make a list of these comestible dead ends. Some of these stay-at-homes would just taste too odd except to folks brought up on them (Norwegian *lutefisk*). Others would depend on ingredients too bizarre to attract a wide following outside their natural "habitat" (sheep eyeballs from the Middle East or chicken entrails from the Philippines). Then there would be nontransferable food ideas or customs that didn't fit into life in other places—picking up food in banana leaves or chapatis instead of with knife and fork or chopsticks.

The savory course is an excellent example of such a cultural isolate. Only in the post-Victorian aristocratic British context, where gentlemen gather after the meal and take postprandial port and are accustomed to top off their meal with a nonsweet food that will set them up for a long night of drinking in comfortable chairs, does the savory course make sense. But in another way, at least, the idea of savory does symbolize the future of eating.

Where dessert puts an end to a meal, savory is intrinsically forward-looking. It signals a fresh start, and there will surely be one. After all the obvious distillations and reshufflings of nouvelle cuisine have been done and done to death; and after the inevitable conservative backlash has made a vogue of the old and hoarily local, of roasts and chops in England, of onion soup and *canard a l'orange* in France and *risotto* in Italy; something new is bound to come along. There will be new frontiers, new pioneer situations, new opportunities for culinary bricolage, for brilliant making do in the kitchen. Even with no new worlds for new Columbuses to discover, the human imagination is always hungry for the new and eager to concoct it.

INDEX

ABOUT THE AUTHOR

RAYMOND SOKOLOV is the food columnist for *Natural History* magazine and editor of *The Wall Street Journal*'s Leisure & Arts page. He lives in New York City.